Despite the "warmly persuasive" and utopian quality that the word "community" possesses, with its suggestion of a locality defined by common concern, reciprocity, unity, shared beliefs and values, and so on, it cannot be assumed that the conditions of domination alone [a]re sufficient to create a sense of common values, trust, or collective identification [amongst those of us suffering from the events of colonization and slavery and their legacies]. The commonality constituted in practice depends less on presence or sameness than upon desired change — the abolition of bondage [and the decolonization of peoples and places]. Thus, [for those of us making common cause at the confluences of the movements for abolition and decolonization,] contrary to identity providing the ground of community, identity is figured as the desired negation of the very set of constraints that create commonality — that is, [our] yearning to be liberated from the condition[s] of enslavement [and colonization] facilitates [our] networks of affiliation and identification.

— Saidiya V. Hartman from Scenes of Subjection

The War on Terra
& The New Underground Railroad

Muindi Fanuel Muindi

SFPML

www.solutionsforpostmodernliving.org

First Printing, 2022

ISBN 979-8-218-02872-5

For my community.

TABLE
OF
CONTENTS

PREFACE

It is one thing to think outside of the box, it is another thing to break out of the box, and it is something else to live outside of the box.

- To think outside of the box is to ask and answer the question, "How might life differ if I didn't find myself trapped in a box?"

- To break out of the box is to ask and answer the question, "How might I free myself from the box in which I currently find myself trapped?"

- To live outside of the box is to ask and answer the question, "How can I survive and thrive without being trapped in a box?"

Whereas my previous four books invited readers to think outside of the box in rather general terms, the present book invites readers to break free from the specific boxes in which they presently find themselves trapped and, further, to live outside of the box. Thus, unlike my previous books, this book names and attends to the prevailing power formations that are presently putting each of us "in our place", either in boxes accustomed to us or in boxes we are liable to become accustomed to.

Put more forcefully, this book, unlike my previous books, names and attends to the competing ethnocidal and ecocidal power formations that are prevailing over and decimating Mother Earth and her peoples at the time of this book's writing: imperialist white-supremacist capitalist patriarchy and its would-be successors.

If I hesitated to name and attend to presently prevailing power formations in my previous books, it was out of a concern that naming and attending to them in their specificity would enhance their power over me and over my readers. I have learned from my encounters with my readers, however, that this concern has no basis in reality. My hesitancy to name and attend to presently prevailing power formations has, in reality, only given these formations greater power over me and my readers. Avoiding presently prevailing power formations in their specificity only serves to ascribe an undue significance to thinking outside of the box and to diminish the significance of breaking out and living outside of the box. The reality is, however, that our thinking outside of the box is only ever significant in relation to our attempts to break out and live outside of the box.

FOUR
ESSAYS
ON
REPARA-
TIONS

THE WAR ON TERRA & THE NEW UNDERGROUND RAILROAD

Essay One

The Sublime Art of Making Reparations

Kintsugi, Psychoanalysis, and the Sublimation of Disturbing Realities

In the last period of his work, Freud [...] noticed something new, the strange phenomenon he called the splitting of the ego. In this phenomenon, the ego, when faced with a disturbing reality, neither represses it nor denies it. Rather it simultaneously accepts and rejects it, thereby splitting itself into mutually incompatible states. The "side" of the ego that rejects the disturbing reality replaces it with a wish fulfilling fantasy. Here, we see the basic operation of primary process – wish fulfillment and defense working in tandem to get rid of a disturbance. But the new angle on this process is that the ego clearly would not undertake such a complex defensive manoeuvre if it did not in some way know exactly what it appears not to know. [...] [W]hat the ego knows, but defends against, is on the "side" of increased tension, the pain of life. The "side" of the ego that rejects the disturbing reality is self-destructively using wish fulfillment and defense to maintain inertia, the reflexive withdrawal from certain kinds of pain. In other words, the ego attacks its own knowledge of precisely what it needs."

— Alan Bass from "The Work of Psychoanalysis: Play"

13

The more that I consider my facticity — my thrownness in space, time, nature, and culture; my being a black man living in the United States of America four-hundred some years after the docking of the White Lion, not a descendant of Black Atlantic slaves but of peoples who survived the Belgian genocide in the Congo and the depredations of German and British imperialism in East Africa — that is to say, in other words, the more that I wonder at the world that I call home, for better or for worse, the more and more compelled I am to articulate my position on the matter of reparations.

I do not imagine that my position on reparations is of great significance to my world: I am a black man lacking in stature and authority, who can only speak for himself. Yet I feel compelled to speak on the matter of reparations precisely because few care if I speak, precisely because of my lack of stature and authority, precisely because I am only able to speak for myself and for no one else. It is not that I would gain stature and authority by speaking, nor that I would have the ability to speak for others. To the contrary, above all else, it is because I can only speak for myself that I feel I ought to speak on the matter of reparations. You see, I would like to inspire others who know what I know to do as I am doing, to speak for themselves on the matter of reparations.

Indeed, I am very much speaking to you, my friend and fellow traveler. I am inviting you to speak in chorus with me on the matter of reparations, in spite of the fact that no one has asked us to speak and so few care if we do. As I see it, all radical cultural transformations begin when those who are supposed to remain silent and be spoken for begin to stand up and speak for themselves, taking great care to articulate what they know as best they know how. Ay, and the making of reparations, as I imagine them, would be the most radical of cultural transformations.

So, here goes nothing, I shall speak for myself as best I know how...

America presently appears to be in the midst of a low-intensity civil war. This apparent civil war is being fought between two rival factions: let us call them the white nationalist faction and the liberal globalist faction. As I see it, both of these factions are expressions of the unraveling American capitalist supremacy.

America was founded on white supremacy, on the genocide of indigenous peoples and the enslavement of black peoples, and the white nationalist faction in America's apparent civil war embraces white supremacy as the central foundation of American identity. Against the white nationalists, the liberal globalist faction repudiates white supremacy, not because white supremacy is a bad thing in and of itself, but because white supremacy no longer offers American capitalism the meaningful advantages that it used to. The liberal globalists would ditch white supremacy for an ethno-cultural pluralism that is more compatible with capitalist globalization. This is not to say, however, that the liberal globalists mean to make meaningful reparations for any atrocities committed in the name of white supremacy. Rather to the contrary, liberal globalists hold that making meaningful reparations would disadvantage American capitalism far more than the maintenance of white supremacy would. Indeed, rather than making reparations, the liberal globalists want to put the atrocities of white supremacy behind them as quickly as they possibly can.

The liberal globalists claim that the white nationalists are backwards looking reactionaries and they denounce the white nationalists for holding America back. In turn, the white nationalists call the liberal globalists traitorous opportunists and hypocrites, and they denounce the liberal globalists for turning their backs on their nation's white supremacist past while reaping the rewards of this very same past. The white nationalists, protesting against ethno-cultural pluralism, berate the liberal globalists, "You would be nothing without us and we will not be so easily forgotten! You owe us everything!"

Those who have been oppressed by white supremacy in America are caught between a rock and a hard place. On one front, oppressed peoples must protect themselves from white nationalists, who threaten to compound past oppressions with further oppressions in the present and future. On the other front, oppressed peoples must confront the liberal globalists, who believe that they can continue to capitalize on past oppressions without contributing to further oppressions in the present and the future. These liberal globalists refuse to admit that to capitalize on past oppressions is, in effect, to contribute to further oppressions in the present and future. Indeed, oppressed peoples who see through liberal obfuscations agree with the white nationalists on one fundamental point: the liberal globalists are hypocritical opportunists.

The liberal globalists are smug in their hypocrisy. The liberal globalists tell oppressed peoples that they only have two options available to them: either (i) seek protection from a progressive global capitalism and endure its hypocrisies or (ii) fall prey to a regressive white supremacy and its atrocities. Either way, the liberal globalists tell us, reparations are not an option, "You need to move on. What's done is done. What has been broken either cannot be repaired, or, if it can be repaired, doing so is not worth the effort." Indeed, from the perspective of the liberal globalist, the oppressed peoples of the world who seek reparations are even more backwards looking than the white nationalists.

What the liberal globalists refuse to understand, of course, is that abolition and decolonization without reparations is a misnomer, a contradiction in terms: America will remain a white supremacist nation, a nation defined by genocide and chattel slavery, until it makes reparations. The liberal globalists who say otherwise are either white supremacists in denial or apologists for white supremacy. To put a very fine point on the matter, until America makes reparations, to be pro-American without pronounced reservations is to be pro-genocide and pro-slavery.

The white nationalist hears the word "reparations" and understands the word to mean "an eye for an eye, a tooth for a tooth": they fear that the tables will be turned on them and that white peoples will be re-educated, enslaved and/or exterminated by black and indigenous peoples. The liberal globalist hears the word "reparations" and understands the word to mean "compensation", sums of money paid by the oppressor to the oppressed for their oppression, like the paying of back wages. Neither of these cold and calculating notions of reparations are what I have in mind here. When I use the term reparations, I am referring to an art of making amends rather than a science of finding equivalents. Indeed, I am referring to a very specific art of making amends that eschews the finding of equivalents: the sublime art of making reparations, as I imagine it, is the art of kintsugi writ large as a metaphor for radical cultural transformation.

sublime (adj.) · from Latin sublimis "uplifted, high, borne aloft, lofty, exalted, eminent, distinguished," from sub "up to" + limen "lintel, threshold, sill".

reparation (n.) from Latin reparare "restore, repair," from re- "again" + parare "make ready"

kintsugi (n.) · unadapted borrowing from Japanese 金継ぎ, from 金 (kin, "gold") + 継ぎ (tsugi, "repairing, mending; joining"). Referring to the practice of repairing broken ceramics by gathering their fragments, re-assembling them, and gluing them together using a lacquer mixed with powdered gold. "There should be no attempt to disguise the damage, the point is to render the fault-lines [sublime] and strong. The precious veins of gold are there to emphasise that breaks have a philosophically-rich merit all of their own."

Let me put it this way: to make reparations is to make repairs, and repairs can be either made artfully or artlessly. The white supremacists and the liberal globalists would only ever conceive of artless reparations, of artless repairs. Those who call for abolition and decolonization, by contrast, would conceive of artful reparations, artful repairs. The question that follows from this is, of course, "How does one differentiate artful from artless repairs?"

Christopher Alexander, writing in *The Timeless Way of Building*, answers this question admirably by distinguishing between a common sense use of the word repair and a more novel use of the word.

> In the [common sense] use of the word repair, we assume that when we repair something, we are essentially trying to get it back to its original state. This kind of repair is patching, conservative, static.
>
> But in this new use of the word repair, we assume, instead, that everything is changing constantly: and that at every moment we use the defects of the present state as the starting point for the definition of the new state.
>
> When we repair something in this new sense, we assume that we are going to transform it, that new wholes will be born, that indeed, the entire whole which is being repaired will become a different whole as the result of the repair.
>
> In this sense, the idea of repair is creative, dynamic, open.

What Alexander calls "patching, conservative, static" repair is the making of artless reparations. What Alexander calls "creative, dynamic, open," repair is the making of artful reparations.

Those who call for abolition and decolonization are the exponents of artful reparations. White supremacists are the enemies of all reparations, no matter whether artful or artless. Liberal globalists claim to sympathize with calls for reparations but they refuse to admit that artful reparations are possible and they argue that all reparations are artless. The liberal globalist speaks of brave new peoples for whom the past is dead and the future is a boundless frontier.

Exhausted by the liberal globalists' speeches, those who call for abolition and decolonization retort, "The past is never dead. It's not even past. The past is still alive in the present but it is living in fragments and it is becoming ever more fragmented. Brave are those peoples who *(re-)create the past anew*, taking great care to piece together every recoverable fragment of the past that they have access to."

To (re-)create the past anew. — The sublime art of making reparations hinges on this paradoxical phrase. In this essay, I hope to help you imagine what this phrase means, but I must first give you a clear idea of what this phrase does not mean.

To be brief, to (re-)create the past anew does not mean indulging in wishful thinking and defensive rationalizations that cover up disturbing realities.

The student of psychoanalysis will tell you that the psyche disavows disturbing realities in and through the construction of two different kinds of fantasies. To quote Alan Bass, a profound interpreter of the work of Sigmund Freud, "One [way] is to replace something disagreeable with something pleasant – this is wish fulfillment. The other [way] is to eliminate the disturbance by attempting to render it nonexistent – this is defense."

Wish fulfillment is exemplified by the battered wife who says, "He hit me, and it felt like a kiss. Beating me, he teaches me the true meaning of love."

Defense is exemplified by the battered wife who says, "I know, I know: it looks like he hit me, but it isn't what it looks like. It was an accident. He didn't really hit me; I stumbled into his fist."

A wishful fantasy is a (mis)representation that acknowledges the character of the disturbing event, "He hit me", but disavows the disturbing affect accompanying the event, substituting a pleasing affect for the disturbing one, "And it felt like a kiss."

A defensive fantasy, by contrast, is a (mis)representation that acknowledges the disturbing affect but disavows the character of the disturbing event, "It was an accident. He didn't really hit me; I stumbled into his fist."

Wish fulfillment and defense are, together, the primary processes that enable a person (e.g., a battered spouse) to avoid confronting disturbing realities.

Returning to the subject of genocide and chattel slavery in America, I want to take some time to recognize the wish fulfillments and defenses that are employed by the oppressed and their oppressor in America today.

Keeping the example of the battered wife in mind, let us first consider the oppressed, the indigenous and black peoples of America in particular.

You must recognize that it is difficult, extremely difficult, for indigenous and black peoples in America to acknowledge the disturbing events that have shaped and continue to shape the American experience for them. Indeed, for indigenous and black peoples, it is an almost unbearably disturbing reality that America has refused to make reparations for genocide and chattel slavery and that white Americans continue to reap the rewards of genocide and chattel slavery. This reality is most unbearable for those indigenous and black people who would "get ahead" in the service of America's most powerful political-economic institutions.

To "get ahead" in America, many indigenous and black persons engage in wish fulfillment, "America beat us, but it felt like a kiss. In and through genocide and slavery, America has taught us the true meaning of freedom and democracy." Other indigenous and black persons seeking to "get ahead" engage in defense, "I know, I know: it looks like America was built on genocide and slavery, but it isn't what it looks like. These were accidents of history. White settlers stumbled upon indigenous and black peoples in a fit of absent-mindedness. An ensuing series of horrible misunderstandings, fueled by mutual fear and ignorance, eventually lead to genocide and slavery. In other words, we stumbled into the White Man's guns, germs, and steel."

Shifting our focus from the oppressed to the oppressor, the very same processes, wish fulfillment and defense, are at work in the oppressor's refusal to empathize with the oppressed.

It is wish fulfillment that allows the white nationalist to believe that the horrors of genocide and chattel slavery are part and parcel of either a "divine plan" or the "natural order" of things. The white nationalist in the guise of the Christian fascist proclaims, "Genocide and chattel slavery are horrors, yes, but they are like the horror of original sin: they are part of God's plan." Alternatively, the white nationalist as scientific racist proclaims, "Genocide and chattel slavery are horrors, yes, but the lion hunting the gazelle is also a horror. It is only natural for higher races to either dominate, educate, or exterminate lower races whenever it is pleasing and profitable for them to do so."

Defense, by contrast, allows the liberal globalist to deny that America has been and continues to be shaped by genocide and chattel slavery, echoing the defenses of the oppressed, "I know, I know: it looks like America was built on genocide and chattel slavery, but it isn't what it looks like. These were accidents of history. White settlers stumbled upon indigenous and black peoples in a fit of absent-mindedness. An ensuing series of horrible misunderstandings, fueled by mutual fear and ignorance, eventually lead to genocide and chattel slavery. In short, black and indigenous peoples stumbled into our guns, germs, and steel."

Having given you an idea of what (re-)creating the past anew does not entail, I now feel prepared to tell you what (re-)creating the past anew does entail.

To be brief, as I understand it, the sublime art of making reparations, of (re-)creating the past anew, is a two-step process. The first step, preparing to make reparations, is the artful *deconstruction* of wish fulfillments and defenses so as to enable us to acknowledge that which disturbs us. The second step, making reparations, is the sublimation of disturbances via the artful *reconstruction* of that which has been disturbed.

As I see it, we who call for abolition and decolonization are still in the midst of the first step in this process. The wishful fantasies of white nationalism — the fantasy of God's design and the fantasy of the white man's natural superiority — no longer prevail in America as they used to, but they are prevalent enough. What's more, the decline of the wishful fantasies of white nationalists has only ushered in the rise of the liberal globalists' defensive fantasy of "guns, germs, and steel". Those who call for abolition and decolonization have certainly done remarkable work to "see through" wishful and defensive fantasies that cover up the deeply disturbing realities of genocide and slavery, but there is a great deal of work still to be done with respect to artfully deconstructing these fantasies and uncovering the deeply disturbing realities of genocide and slavery, so that we no longer have to "see through" a cover up.

At this point, I feel that I ought to state for the record what I regard to be the deeply disturbing realities of genocide and chattel slavery.

Above all else, the wishful fantasies of white supremacists and the defensive fantasies of liberal globalists try to convince us that there is a divine plan, a natural order, or a historical accident beyond pleasurable and profitable cultural artifice that could explain genocide and chattel slavery in America. As I know it, however, the extermination indigenous peoples and the enslavement of black peoples was not a part of God's plan, nor was it a part of the natural order, nor was it a historical accident. Much to the contrary, genocide and chattel slavery are both forms of pleasurable and profitable cultural artifice, and white Americans exterminated indigenous peoples and enslaved black peoples for pleasure and for profit. In other words, white Americans proposed, perpetrated, and perpetuated the cultural artifices of extermination and enslavement in order to get off and to get ahead.

Going further and digging deeper, the cultural artifices of extermination and enslavement did not emerge in a vacuum, but were constructed atop other, preexisting cultural artifices in order to enhance pleasures and profits derived thereby. Indeed, as I understand it, (i) the pleasures enhanced by the cultural artifices of extermination and enslavement were, first and foremost, the pleasures derived from the cultural artifices of patriarchy, and (ii) the profits enhanced by the cultural artifices of extermination and enslavement were, first and foremost, the profits derived from the cultural artifices of capitalism. It follows from this that the wishful and defensive fantasies that disavow the deeply disturbing realities of genocide and chattel slavery are but secondary elaborations of the wishful and defensive fantasies that disavow the deeply disturbing realities of patriarchy and capitalism. Just as there is no divine plan, no natural order, and no historical accident beyond pleasurable and profitable cultural artifice that could explain genocide and chattel slavery, there is no divine plan, no natural order, and no historical accident beyond pleasurable and profitable cultural artifice that could explain patriarchy and capitalism.

It follows from this that the sublime art of making reparations as practiced by those calling for abolition and decolonization is a secondary elaboration of the same art as practiced by feminists and anti-capitalists.

Indeed, the reality of the matter is this: if reparations are to be made for the horrors genocide and chattel slavery, reparations will also need to be made for the horrors of patriarchy and capitalism.

It is no wonder that the liberal globalist wants to repudiate white supremacy without making reparations for it: making reparations for genocide and chattel slavery would call capitalism into question.

It is also no wonder that the white nationalist is also a misogynist: the pleasures that they take in oppressing peoples of other races are built on the pleasures that they take in oppressing women.

The example of the battered wife that I used to introduce wish fulfillment and defense earlier was not chosen arbitrarily. As I see it, the deeply disturbing character of men who dominate women using threats of deprivation and violence are at the root of capitalism, genocide, and chattel slavery.

Capitalist oligarchs are, above all else, men endowed with the means to take advantage of women threatened by poverty. Some capitalist oligarchs use their endowments for their own direct pleasure. Others take indirect pleasure in hoarding and lording their endowments over men who are not so well endowed, brandishing their *stockpiles of wealth* as if they formed an oversized phallus.

Genocidal murderers are, above all else, men endowed with the means to take advantage of women threatened with extermination. Some genocidal murderers use their endowments for their own direct pleasure. Others take indirect pleasure in hoarding and lording their endowments over men who are not so well endowed, brandishing their *stockpiles of weapons* as if they formed an oversized phallus.

Slave masters are, above all else, men endowed with the means to take advantage of enslaved women. Some slave masters use their endowments for their own direct pleasure. Others take indirect pleasure in hoarding and lording their endowments over men who are not so well endowed, brandishing their *retinues of docile bodies* as if they formed an oversized phallus.

Before making any meaningful reparations for slavery and genocide, we will need to uncover the reality that so many of our customs and institutions are cultural artifices that enable men to take direct and indirect pleasure in the domination of women. Again, it is not enough to "see through" the wishful and defensive fantasies that cover up this disturbing reality: this disturbing reality must be uncovered and exposed so that we no longer have to "see through" a cover up. Going further, we must recognize that the uncovering of disturbing realities is but a first step. The art of making reparations must go beyond uncovering disturbing realities concealed by wishful and defensive fantasies; it must also (re-)create fantasies that (re-)integrate and (re-)frame disturbing realities.

The art of making reparations is not hostile to fantasies in general; it is only hostile to wishful and defensive fantasies that cover up disturbing realities. Fantasies that (re-)integrate and (re-)frame disturbing realities, instead of covering them up, are called *sublimating fantasies*, and the art of making reparations appreciates and enables such fantasies.

Sublimating fantasies are the gold powdered lacquer used to glue together the fragments of the shattered vessel: they do far more than simply expose the disturbing realities that wishful fantasies and defensive fantasies cover up. Sublimating fantasies draw our attention to disturbances, yes, but they also draw our attention to the fragility of that which has been disturbed. Going further still, sublimating fantasies draw our attention to the fact that we can and should take care to artfully repair the precious vessel that has been disturbed and broken, for there are wonders to be had in doing so. That being said, however, it is important to stress that sublimating fantasies do not prevent future disturbances and breakages. The vessel that has been shattered can always be shattered again and again, by unforeseeable accident, by negligence, or by design.

Let me put all my cards on the table now. As I see it, the precious vessel that has been shattered by the advance of patriarchal capitalism is the vessel of *primitive matriarchal communism*. Ay, and the sublime art of making reparations that I am proposing here is the art of (re-)creating primitive matriarchal communism anew.

Again, however, you must understand that the art of making reparations never returns anything to back its original primitive state; rather, it is the art of establishing a new primitive state, a "neo-primitive" state. The art of making reparations is not patching, conservative, static; rather, it is creative, dynamic, open. To (re-)create primitive matriarchal communism anew is to transform it, and the result of the art of making reparations would be a *queer hybrid* vessel that both defers to primitive matriarchal communism and differs from it. It is, of course, true that every repair tends to an original primitive structure that precedes it but, as Christopher Alexander writes, "[artful] repair not only patches [primitive structures] — it also modifies [them], transforms [them], sets [them] on the road to becoming something else, entirely new."

The art of making reparations is not what white nationalists imagine it to be: it is not the tit-for-tat revenge of primitive matriarchal communists against "advanced" patriarchal capitalists. Neither is the art of making reparations what liberal globalists imagine it to be: it is not compensation paid by those who have profited under "advanced" patriarchal capitalism to those who would have profited under primitive matriarchal communism. To the contrary, the art of making reparations would transform existing forms of cultural artifice so as to (re-)create primitive matriarchal communism anew, restoring the *potentials* of primitive matriarchal communism.

The art of making reparations is, above all else, the art of transforming customs and institutions.

Tit-for-tat revenge and compensatory pay-offs will never (re-)create primitive matriarchal communism anew because they are not transformations of customs and institutions. Let us, instead deconstruct those customs and institutions that conceal the disturbing realities of "advanced" patriarchal capitalism and it (re-)construct customs and institutions in order to restore the potentials of primitive matriarchal communism.

Sublimating fantasies of a return to primitive matriarchal communism are the fantasies that will enable us to restore and renew the potentials of primitive matriarchal communism.

White men sneer at fantasies of a return to primitive matriarchal communism. They are sneering at me now as they read this. Projecting their own bad conscience onto others, white men make such fantasies out to be wishful and/or defensive fantasies, much like their own fantasies of primal fathers dominating their harems and hordes.

Certainly, some fantasies of a return to primitive matriarchal communism are wishful and some are defensive, but that does allow us to dismiss all such fantasies *tout court*. White men who indulge in patriarchal capitalist fantasies but are quick to dismiss fantasies of primitive matriarchal communism are, of course, apologists for patriarchal capitalism. These white men are deathly afraid of encountering a sublimating fantasy of primitive matriarchal communism that would expose and draw attention to disturbing realities that they are desperate to keep covered up.

Sublimating fantasies of primitive matriarchal communism reveal that there is nothing divine, nothing natural, and nothing accidental about patriarchy, capitalism, genocide, and slavery: these are cultural artifices proposed, perpetrated, and perpetuated by violent and rapacious men who take pleasure in dominating women. At the same time, however, sublimating fantasies of primitive matriarchal communism also reveal that there is nothing divine, nothing natural, and nothing accidental about primitive matriarchal communism: primitive matriarchal communism is nothing other than the cultural artifice of peoples who take pleasure in (re-)creating and nurturing life.

The apparent civil war between white nationalists and liberal globalists in America is a reaction against the fact that oppressed peoples have successfully begun to artfully deconstruct their own wishful and defensive fantasies and to uncover the disturbing realities of patriarchy, capitalism, genocide, and slavery and, what's more, the oppressed are also (re-)constructing sublimating fantasies of primitive matriarchal communisms. Indeed, the apparent civil war revolves around determining (i) what is the best way to keep these disturbing realities covered up and (ii) what is the best way to repress sublimating fantasies of primitive matriarchal communisms.

The liberal globalist faction in this apparent war has forsaken offensive wishful fantasies and embraced the defensive fantasy of historical accident, of "guns, germs, and steel". Liberal globalists tend to be rich white men for whom deprivation is a better means of oppression than violence, and the defensive fantasy of "guns, germs, and steel" protects what is most vital for rich white men: the cultural artifices that endow rich men with the means to take advantage of women threatened by poverty.

The white nationalist faction, by contrast, has doubled down on the offensive wishful fantasies of divine dispensation and natural superiority. White nationalists tend to be poorer white men, those who can only oppress women and others if they have recourse to displays of violence. That being said, however, there are many rich white men in the white nationalist camp: these rich white men side with poorer white men because they have a penchant for violent behavior and cannot find gratification through subjecting others to deprivation alone. The offensive wishful fantasies of divine dispensation and natural superiority protect what is most vital for poorer white men and rich white men with a penchant for violence; they protect the cultural artifices that endow these men with the means to threaten women with displays of violence.

Putting all of this together, America's apparent civil war is revealed to be a class war amongst white men: too many rich white men have ditched the offensive wishful fantasies of divine dispensation and natural superiority for the defensive fantasy of "guns, germs, and steel" and, in so doing, these rich white men are threatening to deprive poorer white men of their patriarchal powers.

Oppressed peoples are compelled to become proxies for rich white men in this apparent civil war: rich white men have hypocritically claimed to repudiate the offensive wishful fantasies of divine dispensation and natural superiority in the name of oppressed peoples; poor white men are avenging themselves against rich white men by attacking the oppressed peoples that rich white men claim to champion; and oppressed peoples of all races and sexes are being persuaded and pressured to make common cause with rich white men in order to defend themselves against poor white men.

Rich white men persuade the "best" amongst the oppressed (i.e., the most "professional" and most "marketable" amongst the oppressed) by "helping" them "earn" more and more money. The liberal globalist holds (i) that non-white men who "earn" enough money should be allowed to exercise the same patriarchal powers over poor women that rich white men do, and (ii) that women of all races who "earn" enough money should be protected against the indignities endured by women haven't "earned" enough.

Rich white men pressure the "rest" of the oppressed peoples, the "wretched of the earth", by "helping" them "learn" that the experience of deprivation under liberal globalism beats the alternative, the experience of violence under white nationalism.

These two ways in which rich white men persuade and pressure oppressed peoples—"helping" oppressed peoples to "learn" and to "earn" the goods of patriarchal capitalism—constitute "philanthropy" under liberal globalism.

Rich white men will be even better off if things go their way. Those who have "earned" the title of "best of the oppressed" will live comfortably beside respectable rich white men, they will apologize for rich white men, and they will make rich white men's "philanthropic" practices their own. The "rest of the oppressed" will turn to rich white men and their sycophantic apologists for protection from a new untouchable caste of poor, backwards, and violent white men. Poor white men have, of course, a sense that they are becoming a new untouchable caste but, alas, this has made a good portion of them cling more tightly to wishful fantasies of divine dispensation and natural superiority, and this is music to the ears of rich white men.

It should be clear to you now why America's civil war is only "apparent".

From the vantage point of oppressed peoples who can see disturbing realities through a cover up, this apparent civil war over the uncovering of patriarchal capitalism's disturbing realities is itself, in actuality, only a new way of covering up the disturbing realities of patriarchal capitalism.

The student of psychoanalysis will also recognize this fact. A good Freudian will tell you that the psyche tends to create false conflicts between wishful and defensive fantasies when disturbing realities become more and more difficult to cover up. What's more, a good Freudian will also tell you that a psychoanalysis often stalls and becomes interminable when its subject becomes increasingly skilled at playing wishfulness and defensiveness against each other in order to cover up disturbing realities that a psychoanalysis threatens to uncover.

We who would practice the sublime art of making reparations are in a position similar to that of a psychoanalyst in this regard: we have managed to artfully deconstruct many of the old wishful fantasies and a few of the newer defensive fantasies that have separately worked to cover up the disturbing realities of patriarchal capitalism, but we have not yet managed to artfully deconstruct the apparent conflicts between these wishful and defensive fantasies which are now working to cover up the very same disturbing realities.

Ay, and our preparations for the making of artful reparations have stalled and become interminable as a result.

Delighted at the fact that our preparations for the making of artful reparations have stalled, the liberal globalists are doubling down on their argument. Liberal globalists are telling us that now is not an auspicious time to radically transform prevailing customs and institutions because these flawed and fragile customs and institutions are the only thing keeping the white nationalists at bay. The question is, however, has there ever been and will there ever be an auspicious time to radically transform prevailing customs and institutions? Going further, mustn't the sublime art of reparations always be an untimely art?

If we are practicing an untimely art, there is no reason why we shouldn't persist in our efforts to artfully deconstruct the wishful and defensive fantasies that condition prevailing customs and institutions, and we should continue to insist upon sublimating fantasies as we endeavor to reconstruct prevailing customs and institutions otherwise. Rich white men and their sycophantic apologists of all races and sexes will snarl and snap at us, but they will always snarl and snap at those who persist in pointing out the disturbing realities of patriarchal capitalism and insist upon making artful reparations.

The reader will, no doubt, have realized that this essay is itself a small contribution to the artful deconstruction of the apparent conflict between liberal globalism and white nationalism that defines American politics today. For those of us calling for abolition and decolonization, this apparent conflict is a devious trap, and I have written this text in order to help myself and my fellow travelers better recognize this trap.

We must avoid and disarm the trap set by the splitting of the white-supremacist ego in order to pursue the work of abolition and decolonization: the work of exposing the disturbing realities of patriarchal capitalism and restoring the potentials of the most primitive of matriarchal communisms, the general economy of leakiness and superfluity that animates the (de-/re-)composition of Mother Earth.

Essay Two

Leaky Designs & Superfluities

Thinking about Race with and through Schizoanalysis

"The strata are judgments of God; stratification in general is the entire system of judgments of God (but the earth, or the body without organs, constantly eludes that judgment, flees and becomes destratified, decoded, deterritorialized)."

— Gilles Deleuze & Felix Guattari from *A Thousand Plateaus*

Thinking about race with and through schizoanalysis, I am struck by the fact that race is not a fluent matter. Rather, race is a code, it is a way of filtering and channeling fluent matter(s).

Schizoanalysis has taught me a great deal about flows and codes. First and foremost, it has taught me that codes are the filters and channels through which flows pass. Codes filter out determinate elements from the flows that pass through them and then channel these determinate elements in different directions. Codes do not transcend the flows that they filter and channel but are immanent to the flows that they filter and channel: they are the "intra-actions" of flows, expositions of fluent matter(s) as opposed to impositions on fluent matter(s).

Going further, schizoanalysis has taught me that fluent matter(s) are indeterminate until they are coded. Coding, or the filtering and channeling of flows, is the process of generating determinate elements from otherwise indeterminate matter(s). This is to say, in other words, that the determinate elements that are filtered and channeled from a given flow via different codings do not exist as determinate elements until after a given flow has been filtered and channeled.

Thinking about race with and through schizoanalysis, I am struck by the fact that neither black individuals nor white individuals are determined as such prior to their racial coding, prior to the filtering and channeling of flows by race. Prior the racial coding of flows there only exist fluent matter(s) of an indeterminate race or, in other words, racially determined individuals only ever come into being as the result of the racial coding of matters that are otherwise racially indeterminate. The existence of individuals of determinate races, e.g. white individuals and black individuals, is an effect of the racial coding of otherwise racially indeterminate matter(s) flowing into and over a social body.

Going even further still, schizoanalysis has also taught me about stratification. It has taught me that the filtering and channeling of fluent matter(s) can but does not necessarily lead to stratification.

To be brief, stratification only takes place when determinate elements are filtered out and channeled from an indeterminate flow in a way that minimizes or reduces their confluencing and their (re-)mixing. Which is to say, in other words, that stratification does not take place when determinate elements that have been filtered out from a flow are promptly channeled back to a confluence where they are (re-)mixed together into an indeterminate flow.

Thinking about race with and through schizoanalysis, I am struck by the fact that the racial stratification of black individuals and white individuals, which privileges the latter over the former, only exists (and persists) insofar as black individuals and white individuals are filtered out from otherwise racially indeterminate flows and channeled apart in ways that minimize or reduce their confluencing and (re-)mixing.

What's more, thinking about race in its broader social context, I am struck by the fact that social stratification by race is compounded with and through social stratification by sex, by wealth, by education, by nationality, and other such codings. Alongside the codes that filter black from white and channel them apart, we must also deal with the codes that filter and channel apart men from women, rich from poor, educated from uneducated, First World nationals from Third World nationals, etc.

Artful reparations, as I imagine them, would deconstruct the many different social strata that characterize our societies in order to (re-)create confluences where men and women, black and white, rich and poor, educated and uneducated, First World and Third World are (re-)mixed together into indeterminately queer and créole flows.

That being said however, artful reparations, as I imagine them, would not create a world in which all social distinctions have been eliminated. To the contrary, artful reparations are *artful* because they do not deconstruct all filters and channels that create social distinctions but, instead, select for deconstruction only those specific filters and channels that create and maintain separate social strata.

Put differently, all social stratifications are the products of *pipelines*—streamlined designs that filter and channel determinate elements apart from each other for extended periods of time—and the art of making reparations turns upon the deconstruction of pipelines.

The concept of a "pipeline" is my own: it is not a schizoanalytic concept, but it is informed by the schizoanalytic concepts of "territorialization" and "deterritorialization".

What schizoanalysis calls "territorialization" is the *extension* of the duration for which one sort of determinate element is filtered and channeled apart from other sorts. What schizoanalysis calls "deterritorialization" is the *compression* of the duration for which one sort of determinate element is filtered and channeled apart from other sorts. Stratification occurs when the duration of a determinate element's separation from others is extended beyond a critical point so as to break the determinate element's fluent connection to the indeterminate flow from which it was parted. Ay, and a pipeline is just that: it is a channel reserved for a determinate element that has been extended beyond a critical point, breaking that determinate element's fluent connection to the indeterminate flow from which it was parted.

Let us take, for instance, the pipelines that convey the richest and most "educated" white men of the First World to lives of leisure and luxury and the pipelines that convey the poorest and least "educated" black women of the Third World to lives of service and squalor.

These pipelines break the fluent connections between rich white men of the First World and poor black women of the Third World so that the two feel no empathy and responsibility for one another.

Rich white men of the First World only "care" about poor black women of the Third World in order to signal their own virtues to other rich white men of the First World. The charitable and philanthropic efforts of rich white men of the First World do not repair broken connections between them and the poor black women of the Third World but, rather, cover up the fact that the connections are broken.

Artful reparations, as opposed to charity and philanthropy, would deconstruct the pipelines that have broken the fluent connections between rich white men of the First World and poor black women of the Third World, and artful reparations would repair these broken connections so as to (re-)create mutual empathy and responsibility between rich white men of the First World and poor black women of the Third World.

In this essay, I want focus on black-white racial stratification in America, and I will take as my primary example the manner in which the "white progressive" perpetuates racial stratification.

The white progressive believes that "there are poor blacks who deserve better", and the white progressive endeavors to construct pipelines that convey "poor but deserving blacks" to institutions of "higher learning" and to "lucrative" careers.

Thinking with and through schizoanalysis, I am struck by the fact that the white progressive's "noble" endeavors effectively reinforce stratification by race, by education, and by wealth. The endeavors of the white progressive effectively maintain the filters and channels that generate pools of poor blacks and, taking these pools for granted, the white progressive endeavors to filter out "deserving blacks" from these pools and channel these "deserving blacks" along pipelines to privilege, leaving "undeserving blacks" to stew in poverty.

Going one step further, the white progressive also endeavors to filter out "undeserving whites" from pipelines to privilege and to channel these "undeserving whites" into poverty alongside "undeserving blacks".

The results of these endeavors are perverse.

"Undeserving whites" being filtered out of pipelines to privilege and into poverty watch as "deserving blacks" are filtered out of pools of poor blacks and channeled into privilege, and, as a result, many of these "undeserving whites" become resentful of "deserving blacks".

Meanwhile, "deserving blacks" become self-righteous at being found "deserving" and, here's the rub, white progressives become doubly self-righteous for being counted amongst "deserving whites" and for being the benefactors of "deserving blacks".

America's leading political parties devote a great deal of attention to the pipelines that are supposed to channel "deserving blacks" from poverty into privilege.

The Republican party appeals to the resentment of "undeserving whites" who have been filtered and channeled out of pipelines to privilege. Republicans demand the narrowing or the elimination of the pipelines channeling "deserving blacks" to privilege, arguing that too many "undeserving blacks" are being "mistakenly" channeled from poverty into privilege, taking the place of more deserving whites.

The Democratic party, by contrast, appeals to the hopes of poor blacks, the self-righteousness of white progressives, and to the gratitude of "deserving blacks". The Democratic party wants to broaden and multiply the pipelines to privilege for "deserving blacks", arguing that there are more "deserving blacks" than the existing pipelines can presently handle and, what's more, there are too many "undeserving whites" still being pipelined to privilege. Both the Republicans and Democrats, in spite of their differences, take racial stratification for granted. The question for both parties is how best to deal with "deserving blacks" and "undeserving whites": neither party cares to actually disrupt racial stratification.

Those who would make artful reparations and disrupt racial stratification are those who would deconstruct pipelines in order to (re-)create *leaky designs*. The filters and channels that lead to stratification are precisely those that aim to prohibit or preclude leakiness: pipelines effectively work to keep segregated flows from polluting and being polluted by one another. *But whereas a pipeline prevents pollution by maintaining segregation, a leaky design dilutes flows in order to undermine the conditions of possibility for pollution.* Recognizing that over-concentration is the process that turns an otherwise benign element into a malignant pollutant that must be separated from others, leaky designs are filters and channels that are (de)constructed so as to dilute over-concentrations, enabling determinate flows to course openly and confluently, to spill over into one another, and to safely (re-)mix together and back into indeterminate flows. Leaky designs thereby deconstruct fixed social strata and (re-)construct fluid social distinctions in their place.

Returning to the issue of black-white racial stratification in America, both the Republicans and the Democrats haven't simply failed to prevent over-concentrations of wealth and privilege, they have promoted over-concentrations of wealth and privilege. Hence their fear of leakiness and pollution.

On the one hand, the Republicans and the Democrats are both concerned that the flows filling the pools of the privileged will be polluted by the "undeserving", white and black. On the other hand, the Republicans and the Democrats are both concerned that the flows filling the pools of the poor will be polluted by the "deserving", white and black. What's more, both Democrats and Republicans take it for granted that it means one thing for blacks to be "deserving" and that it means something different for whites to be "deserving", which, in turn, means that there ought to be different pipelines, one for "deserving blacks" and one for "deserving whites".

The two political parties mainly differ with respect to their definitions of "deserving blacks" and "deserving whites"; they do not differ on the point that the "deserving" need to be pipelined to the pools of the privileged and that the pools of the privileged mustn't be polluted by the "undeserving". Thus, the two parties are both organized against leaky designs that would allow the deserving-and-undeserving, black-and-white, to be (re-)mixed together and back into indeterminate flows wherein neither one can be strictly distinguished from the other.

The need to strictly distinguish the deserving from the undeserving is, above all else, justified by (the appearance of) scarcity.

We are told, "There is not enough to go around, so we need to know who deserves a livelihood and who is undeserving. The right resources need to go to the right people, to those who rightly deserve them." This logic tells us that leaky designs are to be disparaged for squandering scarce resources on the undeserving. Thinking with and through schizoanalysis, however, I believe that we should disparage (the appearance of) scarcity as opposed to leaky designs.

Those who endeavor to fight against leaky designs but don't bother to fight against (the appearance of) scarcity are not to be esteemed: they are the friends of scarcity and the champions of stratification. Indeed, the Republicans and the Democrats are but two factions of the friends of scarcity, two factions of the champions of stratification.

By contrast, the champions of leaky designs are, above all else, the enemies of (the appearance of) scarcity. The champions of leaky designs want, above all else, to create a superfluity of livelihoods so that there is no longer any need to strictly differentiate the deserving from the undeserving.

Indulge me, if you will, by attending to a rather specific problem: to the problem of making a livelihood as an artist in America.

As I am sure you know, one can scarcely find a livelihood as an artist in America, and the general assumption is that there are those who deserve a livelihood as an artist and there are those who do not. Many "activists" will point, with one hand, to the undeserving white artists pipelined to the privileged pools of career artists, and then, with the other hand, point to the deserving black artists pipelined to the pools of the impoverished, unable to make a living as an artist. These "activists" argue that the right thing to do is to channel undeserving (white) artists out of pipelines to privilege and to channel deserving (black) artists into pipelines to privilege.

Thinking with and through schizoanalysis, I propose that we ask more fundamental questions, "Why can one scarcely find a livelihood as an artist in America? Why can't there be an abundance of artistic livelihoods in America? How can we create a abundance of artistic livelihoods in America?"

These questions do not diminish the importance of anti-racist activism. To the contrary, they heighten the importance of anti-racist activism. It ought to be clear that white supremacist racism is one reason why artistic livelihoods are scarce: white supremacist racism survives and thrives by promoting (the appearance of) scarcity, by making livelihoods (appear) scarce, and by claiming to guarantee scarce livelihoods to whites who "truly deserve" them. What's more, it ought to be clear that white supremacist racism is allied with other "-isms" (e.g., sexism, capitalism) in promoting (the appearance of) scarcity. For instance, white supremacist racism and capitalism are allied when it comes to creating (apparent) scarcities of livelihoods because capitalism revolves around profiting from (apparent) scarcities of resources and opportunities. That being said, however, capitalism is a fair weather friend of white supremacist racism because capitalism can accept the filtering out of "undeserving whites" and the filtering in of "deserving blacks" as long as this filtering out and filtering in does nothing to prevent (the appearance of) scarcities.

If we aim to create a greater abundance of artistic livelihoods in America, I would propose that we deconstruct pipelines to artistic livelihoods and (re-)create leaky designs that render artistic livelihoods superfluous .

It would be a mistake to create an abundance of artistic livelihoods exclusively for "deserving (black) artists" and to regard "undeserving (white) artists" as contaminants to be filtered and channeled out of the pools of artists that can make a living by practicing their art. Instead, let us create a superfluity of livelihoods for artists, so that artists whom we consider undeserving can just as easily make a living as those that we consider deserving, so that there can be no reason for any one group to resent any other group's definition of "being deserving". This does not mean creating more and more jobs for specialists in the arts but, rather, it means encouraging art-making to spillover into increasingly more livelihoods, into livelihoods that would otherwise be considered non-artistic.

Artists in America are, unfortunately, conditioned to over-concentrate in art and to live in fear of scarcity. They are conditioned to continually prove that they "deserve" to make a living as an artist in order to gain access to pipelines for dedicated career artists, and they do not endeavor to create a superfluity of artistic livelihoods for all. This conditioning runs so deep that many American artists who do make decent livelihoods and who could further the (re-)creation of leaky designs, choose instead to hoard opportunities for themselves and the few they believe to be "deserving": transforming themselves and their cliques into new pipelines for "deserving" artists.

Let me finish this text by citing myself as a case study. I am a black artist in America who has yet to find a livelihood for himself as an artist: I have never even approached the possibility of feeding and housing myself and my family with my art. It follows that I am desperate to prove that I "deserve" to be an artist: I am desperately seeking access to an artistic career through the pipelines available to me.

Thus far, I have failed on three fronts:
1. My art is not "marketable", so it has not been found "deserving" by the commercial pipelines to artistic careers.
2. The academic pipelines to artistic careers, supported by grant seeking and teaching, are closed to me because I have no credentials and, at least for now, I refuse to become a glorified debt peon in order to "earn" credentials in the arts that can hardly assure me a livelihood.
3. What's more, I have, thus far, been shut out of the pipelines for "deserving black artists" due in no small part to my lack of marketability and credentials but also, in part, due to the fact my art has not, until now, directly addressed my "being black".

Having no proper pipelines to an artistic career, I have been looking for ways in which I might surreptitiously seep into a pipeline that wouldn't otherwise have me. To be specific, recognizing that I could pass for an academic artist in spite of my lack of credentials, I have been seeking out the faults and fissures in the academic pipelines to an artistic career so that I might improperly convey myself to a livelihood as an artist.

But I wonder... Could I do something more radical? Seeping through the faults and fissures in the academic pipelines does not seem very radical to me. Although I am not accessing the academic pipelines through the proper filters and channels, I am still working to prove that I "deserve" an artistic livelihood to those who are accessing the academic pipelines through the proper filters and channels. Indeed, all that I am really doing is asking proper artist-academics to recognize me as "deserving" and to let me in on their pipelines to scarce livelihoods through improper side-channels. In other words, I am only accepting and navigating the (apparent) scarcity of livelihoods available to artists: I am not (re-)creating leaky designs so that art-making spills over into increasingly more livelihoods.

So, of course, I am now wondering how I might (re-)create leaky designs so that art-making spills over into increasingly more livelihoods. Or, in other words, I am wondering how to develop an artistic practice that makes non-artistic livelihoods increasingly more artistic, so that I need not judge myself or other artists as "deserving" or "undeserving". In the same vein, being a black man in America, I am wondering how I might do something other than accept and navigate the (apparent) scarcity of livelihoods available to black people, how I might do something other than prove myself a "deserving" black person who should be filtered out from the pool of "undeserving" black people and pipelined to privilege. Indeed, I am wondering how I might (re-)create leaky designs so that my livelihood needn't depend on my being judged "deserving" or "undeserving" according to a double standard that discriminates by race.

Considering the above, I hope that it now makes sense to you, dear reader, why I have come to formulate a concept of artful reparations. All of my ideas regarding the "art of making reparations" betray my desire that art-making spillover into labors that deconstruct social strata and repair broken connections between different social elements kept apart by social stratification. In other words, the ideas expressed in this essay and the preceding essay betray my desire to confuse my aesthetics and my politics. Ay, and I hope you realize that my confusion of aesthetics and politics is not the flaw that mars my ideas but the sought after feature that defines the ideas that matter most to me.

Essay Three

Revaluation & Reparative Economy

The Idea of Money, the Fluidity of Value, and the Swapping of Options

"The reasons why anthropologists haven't been able to come up with a simple, compelling story for the origins of money is because there's no reason to believe there could be one. Money was no more ever 'invented' than music or mathematics or jewelry. What we call 'money' isn't a 'thing' at all, it's a way of comparing things mathematically, as proportions: of saying one of X is equivalent to six of Y. As such it is probably as old as human thought."

— David Graeber from *Debt : The First 5,000 Years*

Let me begin this essay by proposing that money is an idea.

The proposition that money is an idea is, in and of itself, neither a novel nor a controversial proposition. Indeed, the proposition has currency in many academic and political milieus. At the same time, however, this proposition is, more often than not, qualified in ways that dismiss money's significance as an idea. It is often said that "money is just an idea" or that "money is a mere idea", with the qualifiers "just" and "mere" serving to indicate that the idea of money is not itself significant but, rather, that the idea of money signifies something of greater significance: e.g., Marxian "relations of production" or Foucauldian "power formations".

I propose, however, that there is no such thing as a "mere" idea, that no idea is "just" an idea. Indeed, I propose that ideas are signified by other things rather than being signifiers of other things. The dollar notes, euro notes, pound notes, or yen notes that you may have in your wallet are not themselves money but, rather, they are signifiers of the idea of money, or, to be rather more precise, they are things that promise to be of monetary significance.

What economists call the four functions of money are, in light of my proposition, four ways in which things promise to be of monetary significance. This is to say, in other words, that a thing promises to be of monetary significance when it functions as (i) a unit of account, (ii) a store of value, (iii) a means of payment, or (iv) a standard of deferred payment.

That being said, however, a promise to be of monetary significance is just that: a promise. A thing may promise to be of monetary significance by functioning in one or more of the four aforementioned ways but it may never actually deliver on its promise. Thus, the question for me is never, "Is X, Y, or Z money?" Instead, the question is, "What are the conditions under which X, Y or Z promises to be of monetary significance and actually delivers on its promise?"

Let me pause here and consider an idea other than the idea of money in order to clarify what I mean when I say that something is an idea.

Say, for instance, that you have an idea for redecorating your living room in a mid-century modern style. In light of your idea for redecorating, every piece of furniture that you encounter that is of mid-century modern design, or that bears a resemblance to something of mid-century modern design, or that might complement pieces of mid-century modern design will promise to be of significance with respect to your idea for redecorating. These pieces of furniture will lure you in and you will notice them in light of your idea for redecorating. If you hadn't any ideas for redecorating, you either wouldn't notice these pieces or you would notice them differently.

Going further, some of these pieces of furniture promise to be of significance in more senses than others: e.g., the piece that promises to fit snugly in the northwest corner of your room, the piece that promises to complement the stain of the wood paneling in your room, and the pieces that promise to fit within your redecorating budget — each of these pieces could be said to have promised to signify your idea in more senses than other pieces. That being said, however, it is only after you select certain pieces of furniture that are promising and attempt to redecorate your living room with them that you discover whether or not the selected pieces of furniture deliver on their promise to be of significance with respect to your idea for redecorating. If the pieces of furniture that you select do not deliver or if they deliver less than what you bargained for—by not fitting the room quite right— the selected pieces fail to signify your idea for redecorating, and you may decide to return them, to resell them, to give them away, to put them in storage, or to live with them in spite of their failed promise. If the pieces of furniture that you selected do deliver or deliver more than you bargained for—fitting perfectly in your living room and looking quite stylish—the selected pieces are said to succeed in signifying your idea for redecorating.

Let us now return to the idea of money.

The idea of money, as I understand it, is the idea of using one good or service to take a measure of the value contained in another good or service. Thus, any and every good or service that promises to be of monetary significance is a good or service that might be able to take a measure of the value contained in another good or service. But a promise is only a promise: we only discover whether or not a selected good and service delivers on its promise to be of monetary significance after we attempt to use the good or service to take a measure of the value contained in other goods and services.

Those goods and services that we have come to call money are those goods and services that have delivered on their promise to be of monetary significance so often that we have come to "fetishize" them and identify them with the idea of money. Indeed, many of the goods and services that have become "fetishes" for money are goods and services that have been designed to serve no other purpose than to express the idea of money. Still, however, even if these goods and services have been designed for no other purpose than expressing the idea of money, to say that these goods and services are themselves money and nothing more, is like saying that a 1-pound object designed for no other purpose than to measure the weight of another object is itself a weight and nothing more. Certainly, speaking casually, we do call a 1-pound object designed to measure weights a "weight" but, in practice, we know better than to treat it as if it was "weight itself" rather than a particular expression of the idea of weight. Similarly, although we casually refer to goods and services designed for the express purpose of taking measures of value as "money", in practice, we should know better than to treat these goods and services as if they were themselves money rather than particular expressions of the idea of money.

Consider, for instance, the fact that a "weight" labeled "one pound" might promise to weigh one pound, but this "weight" may fail to deliver on its promise if it does not balance a scale when measured against other "weights" that we hold to be one pound weights. Similarly, the "money" in terms of which a good or service has been priced might promise to be of monetary significance, but this "money" only fulfills its promise to be of monetary significance when someone actually pays the price in question for a good or service using such "money".

There is, of course, nothing wrong with using the terms "weight" and "money" casually, without quotations. In fact, I will use the term "money" quite casually, without quotations, throughout this text. The problem is only in assuming that what is casually called money will always deliver on its promise to be of monetary significance.

As I have already stated above, goods and services commonly promise to be of monetary significance by either functioning as a unit of account, a store of value, a means of payment, or as a standard of deferred payment. Indeed, it can be said that a good or service that functions in all four of these ways promises to be of monetary significance in every common sense of the idea of money. That being said, however, depending upon the circumstances at play, a good or service may only function in one of these common senses in order to promise to be of monetary significance, and it is possible that a good or service can function in none of these common senses and still promise to be of monetary significance. What's more, a good or service that functions in every common sense might still fail to deliver on its promise to be of monetary significance, while a good that does not function in any common sense might successfully deliver on its promise to be of monetary significance.

How is this possible?

That which promises (from *pro* "before" + *mittere* "to release, let go; send, throw") is that which *sets out* in some way. That which delivers (from *de* "away" + Latin *liberare* "to free," from *liber* "free, unrestricted, unimpeded") on a promise is that which *sets out and makes it*, having overcome *encumbrances* (from *in-* "in" + *combrus* "barricade, obstacle") along its way. In light of these etymological and tropological ideas, I find that a useful metaphor with respect to any idea of "promising" and "delivering", of "setting out" and "making it", is the sending and receiving of letters by post. Ay, and, with respect to the idea of money, I hold that the issues involved in posting letters (dis-)simulate the issues involved in promises of monetary significance in the most profound ways.

The posted letter promises and sets out to convey a message to its addressee and the letter conveys its message when it is delivered and makes it to its addressee intact. Similarly, the good or service which promises to be of monetary significance sets out to take a measure of the value contained in other goods and services, and it delivers on its promise to be of monetary significance if and when it makes it and takes a measure of the value contained in another good or service. But just as letters don't post themselves alone, the good or service that promises to be of monetary significance does not take measures of value itself alone. In other words, just as the posting of a letter assumes the existence of *postal services*, the promise to be of monetary significance assumes the existence of *financial services*. Indeed, what economists have called the four functions of money are, in fact, only the four most common financial services: accounting services, payment processing services, debt services, and value storing services.

An unscrupulous postal service provider can wreak havoc by intentionally mis-delivering letters and by taking advantage of the information conveyed in letters. Similarly, an unscrupulous financial service provider can wreak havoc by mis-delivering on promises of monetary significance and by taking advantage of the value conveyed in promises of monetary significance. Those who claim that money is the root of all evil by citing the bad behavior of unscrupulous financial service providers, are like people claiming that letters are the root of all evil by citing the bad behavior of unscrupulous postal service providers. The benefits of being able to post letters are immense and, knowing the great harm that can be done by unscrupulous postal service providers, we have developed social conventions that enable us to recognize and seek reparations from unscrupulous postal service providers. Similarly, the benefits of being able to take measures of value are immense, and we have also developed social conventions that enable us to recognize and seek reparations from unscrupulous financial service providers.

If we complain that money is the root of all evil but do not complain about letters in the same breath, this is because the social conventions that we have developed around postal services are effective at outing unscrupulous postal service providers but those that we have developed around financial services are ineffective at outing unscrupulous financial service providers. Unscrupulous financial service providers are, of course, happy to have us believe that it is money that corrupts because, in fact, it is they who use money to corrupt, systematically biasing measures of value and tipping the scales to their own advantage.

Many societies today have built public infrastructures to guarantee a modicum capable and scrupulous postal services at a fair cost for all, but very few societies today have built public infrastructures to guarantee a modicum of capable and scrupulous financial services at a fair cost for all.

Imagine if all letters addressed to the underprivileged and powerless were held for ransom by postal service providers until their ransom victims overpaid to receive them or took out usurious loans from postal service providers in order to receive them. Ay, that is how the underprivileged and powerless often relate to financial service providers. Goods and services that promise to be of monetary significance for the underprivileged and powerless are often held for ransom by financial service providers and the underprivileged and powerless overpay and take on debt in order to receive them. What's more, financial service providers curry favor with powerful and privileged actors who are not themselves in the business of providing financial services, helping these actors maintain and extend their power and privilege via investments in exploitative financial services. It is as if postal services not only held the letters of the underprivileged and powerless for ransom but also read letters held for ransom in order to inform the privileged and powerful of goings on amongst the underprivileged and powerless.

Privilege and power maintained and extended by way of financial services that exploit the underprivileged and powerless; this is precisely what has been called the "financialization of everyday life" and it is the basis for the "inverted totalitarianism" of liberal globalism. Today, many of us are shocked by *Abteilung* M – Department M of the Stasi, which monitored letters posted in German Democratic Republic in order to find out the vulnerabilities of the East Germans. Tomorrow, our descendants will be shocked by the Big Three Credit Bureaus in America which monitor the financial histories of Americans so that financial firms can find out which Americans are financially vulnerable and exploit their vulnerabilities, making it more costly for financially vulnerable Americans to gain access to financial services and making less costly for rich Americans to gain access to financial services.

While I recognize that the idea of money is the condition of possibility for the wretched actions of unscrupulous financiers, I also recognize that the idea of money is no more responsible for the wretchedness of unscrupulous financiers than the idea of the letter is responsible for the wretchedness of blackmailers who hold purloined letters over their victims. The idea of the letter is the condition of possibility for exploitative miseries, like the holding of letters for ransom, as well as for creative marvels, like epistolary literature; similarly, the idea of money is the condition of possibility for both exploitative miseries and creative marvels. In and through this essay, I hope to encourage the creative marvels that the idea of money makes possible and to discourage the exploitative miseries that the idea of money makes possible. The exploitative miseries in and through which the unscrupulous financier consolidates power and privilege are what I shall call *artless* expressions of the idea of money or *exploitative* financial services. What I shall call *artful* expressions of the idea of money, or *reparative* financial services, are the creative marvels that would counter the exploitative miseries of the financialization of everyday life and dissipate power and privilege thereby.

"The [financialization] of daily life means the imposition of impersonal rules and regulations; impersonal rules and regulations, in turn, can only operate if they are backed up by the threat of force. And indeed, in this most recent phase of [financialization], we've seen security cameras, police scooters, issuers of temporary ID cards, and men and women in a variety of uniforms acting in either public or private capacities, trained in tactics of menacing, intimidating, and ultimately deploying physical violence, appear just about everywhere—even in places such as playgrounds, primary schools, college campuses, hospitals, libraries, parks, or beach resorts, where fifty years ago their presence would have been considered scandalous, or simply weird."
— David Graeber, from *The Utopia of Rules*

Imagine, if you will, a river flowing through a valley, a fluid in flux, feeding fauna, flora, and fungi along its course. Imagine walking up to this river and dipping a vessel into it, a small cup. In doing so, you take a measure of water from the river. You now possess a cup of water that you may drink, hold onto, or give away. At the same time, in and through dipping the cup into the river and taking a measure of water, you have also generated some spillage, some overflow. As you walk away from the river and up the hillside with your measure of water, you will notice that, along the course that you take up the hillside, water drips and drops from the cup and from your hands, leaving behind little puddles, droplets, and rivulets that feed fauna, flora, and fungi that happen across them.

Now, imagine that you have walked from the river to the hilltop that overlooks it and, having reached the hilltop, you drink the measure of water that you took from the river. After drinking this measure of water, while in the midst of enjoying the hilltop view, very suddenly, you suffer a heart attack and you die. Over the next few hours, days, weeks, scavengers and decomposers consume your dead body, each of them taking from your body some measure of the measure of water that you took from the river. Ay, and each and every scavenger and decomposer produces some spillage, some overflow as they take a measure of your water, leaving a trail of drippings and droppings behind them as they abandon your carcass, and these drippings and droppings feed fauna, flora, and fungi that happen across them.

Then comes the rain. What remains of the puddles, droplets, and rivulets of water that you left behind you as you walked uphill, what remains of the drippings and droppings of the creatures who consumed and decomposed your corpse, and what remains of your last gulp of water in your decomposing carcass—all of this flows back down the hill and returns to the very river from which you took your last measure of water, feeding fauna, flora, and fungi on the re-course, on the return journey to the river.

Let us stop here and take a step back.

Reflecting upon this scenario, you will recognize that a cup's capacity to take a measure of water from a stream or reservoir can serve five different purposes, can function in five different ways:

· First, a cup can be used to take and hold a measure of water from a stream or reservoir: that is to say, the cup can serve as a store of water.

· Second, a cup can serve as a *unit of account* for measures of water taken from a stream or reservoir: for instance, water taken from a river may measure one cup, or a $\frac{1}{2}$ cup, or a $\frac{1}{4}$ cup, etc.

· Third, one can give a cup containing a measure of water to someone else in exchange for something else: that is, the cup can serve as a means of payment.

· Fourth, I can give you a full cup of water now if you promise to take the cup back down hill to the stream and bring back an equal measure of water for me: that is to say, the cup can function as a standard of deferred payment.

· Fifth, and finally, one can let water overflow and spill from the cup as it takes a measure of water, and one can leave a fortuitous trail of drippings and droppings as one conveys this measure of water elsewhere: that is to say, the cup can serve as a dissipator of water thanks to its in-ability to contain all that it draws in and its ability to leave behind a trail of fortuitous drippings and droppings wherever it goes.

Let us stop here and take another step back and make two realizations.

First, let us realize that what economists call "value" is the fluid that sustains living cultures, and it is akin to water the fluid that sustains living creatures. Second, let us realize that a good or service that promises to be of monetary significance is a receptacle with the capacity to take measures of value from streams and reservoirs of value, akin to a receptacle with the capacity to take measures of water from streams and reservoirs of water. For now, let us not speculate on the nature (or artifice) that characterizes the fluidity of value, as our focus is economics rather than metaphysics. Knowing full well that our focus leaves much to be desired, let us hope that the idea of the fluidity of value enables us to take note of things that we would have otherwise overlooked.

In light of the idea of the fluidity of value, I would first like to reconsider what it means to possess value. Water courses through the different ecologies that make up the "bio-sphere", our global ecology, in such a way that no one person can truly claim ownership over streams and reservoirs of water. Similarly, value courses over and through the different economies that make up the "value-sphere", our global economy, in such a way that no one person can truly claim ownership over streams and reservoirs of value. That being said, however, people do claim ownership over streams and reservoirs of water and of value, and they maintain such claims with threats of violence. Indeed, one can only claim ownership over streams and reservoirs of water and of value in and through denying others access to streams and reservoirs of water and of value: a billionaire's claim to possess certain streams and reservoirs of value is a false claim that is maintained with threats of violence, akin to the threats of violence with which a despot makes a false claim to possess certain streams and reservoirs of water. *It is might that makes property rights over streams and reservoirs of value and of water.*

Next, I want to re-consider what it means to determine the amount of value in a stream or reservoir of value. We *speculate* the measure of water flowing through the biosphere to be 326 million trillion gallons without being able to actually *deposit* all of the water in the biosphere in actual gallon jugs. Similarly, we *speculate* the measure of value flowing through the global economy to be 87,752 trillion American dollars without being able to convert the global economy into American dollars that can be *deposited* in an account. Going further still, a significant measure of the water in the biosphere is contained in lifeforms and cannot be converted into actual gallons of water without *liquidating* lifeforms, without killing living creatures. Similarly, a significant measure of the value of the global economy is contained in lifeways and cannot be converted into deposits, without *liquidating* lifeways, without killing living cultures.

David Graeber, in Debt: The First 5,000 Years, has pointed out that throughout human history periods during which deposits (as opposed to speculations) form the basis for economic activity are periods during which lifeways are constantly under threat of liquidation and periods during which speculations (as opposed to deposits) form the basis for economic activity are periods during which lifeways are spared so many threats of liquidation. In other words, those who are compelled to make deposits are often compelled to liquidate their lifeways, while those who can speculate instead of making deposits are rarely compelled to liquidate their lifeways.

In light of all of the above, I shall speak of three different kinds of financial services.

- First, I shall speak of financial services that enable people to gain access to and draw value from streams and reservoirs of value: these financial services are what I call "valueworks" by analogy with "waterworks".

- Second, I shall speak of financial services that compel people to liquidate their lifeways so as to make deposits (as opposed to speculating): these financial services are what I call "devaluations".

- Third, I shall speak of financial services that enable people to sustain their lifeways by speculating (as opposed to making deposits): these financial services are called "transvaluations".

Rather than considering the four sorts of financial services that economists attend to (accounting services, payment processing services, debt services, and value storing services), I would rather consider whether and how different financial services contribute to valueworks, to devaluations, and to transvaluations. Ay, and I say that a financial service is *artless* to the degree that it contributes to devaluations, and that it is *artful* to the degree that it contributes to transvaluations. Contributing to valueworks in and of itself neither makes a financial service artless nor artful, but contributing to valueworks in a way that promotes devaluations makes a financial service artless, and doing so in a way that promotes transvaluations makes a financial service artful.

59

The financialization of everyday life in America is defined by artless financial services that devalue the lifeways of the underprivileged and powerless multitudes. The financial services that prevail in America today give privileged and powerful capitalist oligarchs exclusive access to bountiful streams and reservoirs of value, such that these privileged and powerful oligarchs are never in desperate need of deposits, but these very same financial services only allow the underprivileged and powerless multitudes to access meager streams and reservoirs of value that cannot be easily drawn from and, as a result, the underprivileged and powerless multitudes are constantly facing pressures to devalue and liquidate their lifeways to come up with deposits.

Devaluation wreaks havoc on lifeways akin to the manner in which desertification wreaks havoc on lifeforms. Just as desertification creates natural landscapes in which deposits of water become harder and harder to find, devaluation creates cultural landscapes in which deposits of value become harder and harder to find.

Today, as a result of the financialization of everyday life, powerful and privileged oligarchs and their retinues live in value oases with plentiful deposits of value that are manufactured and maintained by artless valueworks. In turn, the underprivileged and powerless multitudes live in growing value deserts with meager deposits of value, and these value deserts are manufactured and maintained by the same artless valueworks that maintain the value oases of the powerful and privileged.

Exploitative financial services that devalue cultural landscapes need to be countered by reparative financial services that revalue cultural landscapes.

Revaluing a cultural landscape that has undergone devaluation is like rewilding a natural landscape that has undergone desertification. A natural landscape cannot return to what was before being undone by desertification. Similarly, a cultural landscape cannot return to what was before being undone by devaluation.

Rewilding and revaluation both tend to and mend what has come before, yes, but in so doing they also amend what has come before and create something new and different. Rewilding (re-)creates natural landscapes anew, weaving delicate and intricate webs of differing and deferring lifeforms anew. Similarly, revaluation (re-) creates cultural landscapes anew, weaving delicate and intricate webs of differing and deferring lifeways anew.

Revaluations are those valueworks that make more transvaluations possible and make fewer devaluations necessary. Valueworks that do the opposite, that make more devaluations necessary and fewer transvaluations possible, are what I call *overvaluations-and-undervaluations.* All revaluations begin by deconstructing overvaluations-and-undervaluations and then proceed to (re-)construct potentials for transvaluations.

Let me describe this two step process step-by-step.

The deconstruction of overvaluations-and-undervaluations begins with the recognition that every overvaluation is the flip side of an undervaluation.

For instance, there are exploitative valueworks that overvalue computing services performed by men, giving men engaged in computing exclusive access to bountiful streams and reservoirs of value. These exploitative valueworks simultaneously undervalue house cleaning services performed by women, denying women engaged in house cleaning access to bountiful streams and reservoirs of value and only giving these women access to meager streams and reservoirs of value. Thanks to these exploitative valueworks, these overvaluations-and-undervaluations, women engaged in providing house cleaning services face greater pressure to devalue and liquidate their lifeways whenever they are compelled to come up with deposits, while men engaged in providing computing services are safe in their lifeways.

Imagine, if you will, a Haitian cleaning lady named Grace who cleans the homes of Silicon Valley tech bros. Imagine that, this year, Grace needs to come up with some money to pay for a medical procedure. Every year before this one, Grace had traveled back to Haiti in December to visit her aging mother for the Christmas holiday but, in order to make money to pay for her medical procedure, Grace has devalued and liquidated this custom this year in order to work through the month of December and make some extra money. The following January, however, Grace's mother in Haiti passes away suddenly from a stroke, and Grace realizes that she devalued her last opportunity to spend Christmas in Haiti with her beloved mother. Still reeling from the news of her mother's death, but also still working hard to make money for her procedure, our protagonist stumbles upon a bank statement that one of her tech bro employers, Doug, carelessly left out for her to see. Reviewing the bank statement, Grace discovers just how easily Doug could have both paid for her medical procedure and her annual trip to Haiti and still had deposits to spare.

This imagined scenario, the overvaluation of the tech bro and the undervaluation of the cleaning lady, is a prime example of how an artless expression of the idea of money leads to tragic devaluations and liquidations of living customs.

How might we make artful reparations for such an artless expression of the idea of money? How might we revalue Grace's custom of visiting her mother in Haiti every December, especially now that her mother is dead and gone? Going further, how might we transvalue this custom after it has been revalued so that Grace might afford the medical procedure that she needs?

I do not intend to answer these questions fully in this essay. I only hope to convince you that these are the kinds of questions that we ought to be asking ourselves if we are interested in artful expressions of the idea of money and in reparative financial services.

We are asking artless questions (i) when we ask how we can subsidize healthcare for people performing low paying "menial" labor, and (ii) when we ask how we might retrain the workforce in order to create more highly paid "hi-tech" laborers.

The artful question to ask is how to revalue delicate and intricate webs of lifeways so that overvaluations-and-undervaluations do not lead to devaluations and liquidations. In the specific scenario above, we might rephrase the artful question as follows, "How might we revalue the custom of periodically visiting far away family members so that overvaluations-and-undervaluations do not precipitate the devaluation and liquidation of the custom?"

Again, I do not intend to answer this question fully in this essay. That being said, however, I will imagine the beginnings of a possible answer in order to spark your imagination.

As I imagine them, reparations for Grace would deconstruct the exclusive property rights that her Silicon Valley tech bro employers have over streams and reservoirs of value, and they would give Grace, as their employee, *options* to access these very same streams and reservoirs of value in the event that she needs to pay for an expensive medical procedure, or in the event of her annual visit to Haiti in the winter, or in accord with some other ordinary and extraordinary events that one can *speculate* upon.

Indeed, revaluations, as I imagine them, would transform all economic relations (e.g., the employer-employee relation, landlord-tenant relation, and creditor-debtor relation) by (re-)founding them anew on the basis of options instead of property rights. Revaluations would deconstruct exclusive property rights on streams and reservoirs of value that are held by employers, landlords, and creditors, and they would give employees, tenants, and debtors options to access and draw from these very same streams and reservoirs of value in accord with ordinary and extraordinary events that can be speculated upon by the employer and employee, the landlord and tenant, the creditor and debtor.

As a result of the revaluations that I imagine, employer-employee, landlord-tenant, creditor-debtor, and all other kinds of economic relations would be founded on options that precede, exceed, and succeed any and all payments and property rights, and the transvaluations that would follow from such revaluations would be *swaps of options*.

In finance, a swap of options is a speculative arrangement between two counterparties to exchange options on different streams and reservoirs of value in accord with ordinary and extraordinary events that can be speculated upon. For instance, an employee of a small business concern might swap options for a time with a friend or relative who is employed by a large business concern in the event that they require a medical procedure that they could not have paid for by drawing from the streams and reservoirs available to them via the small business concern. In the meantime, the friend or relative involved in the swap will meet their own needs by accessing and drawing from the streams and reservoirs of the small business concern which they gained access to in the swap.

In effect, swaps of options create confluences and crossings between different streams and reservoirs of value, allowing value to flow more freely over a given cultural landscape. Indeed, swaps and options together are what you might call leakily designed financial services or dissipators of value.

The practice of designing options and swaps, as I understand it, revolves around speculating upon the events that govern the terms of options and swaps. Insofar I aim to revalue and transvalue lifeways, I hold that the events that govern the terms options and swaps ought to be life-events that are integral to lifeways: either (i) life-events conditioned by lifeways or (ii) life-events that condition lifeways. Options and swaps that are governed by no more than the passage of time, like an option for a period of twelve months or a swap for a period of twelve weeks, are art-less options and swaps because of the fact that their terms do not specify any life-events that are integral to lifeways. By contrast, art-ful options and swaps are contracted for intervals between specified life-events and, as such, they revalue and transvalue the lifeways that specified life-events are integral to. Life-events integral to lifeways that could govern the terms of options and swaps could include births, deaths, meals, comings of age, illnesses, extreme weather events, marriages, divorces, vacations, hirings, firings, retirings, quitings, relocatings, reunions, and more.

Putting options and swaps aside, the point is this: Grace and others like her will never have reparations for lifeways that they have had to devalue and liquidate for as long as they know that, when misfortune strikes again, they will have no option other than to devalue and liquidate their lifeways again and again in order to make deposits. I have only imagined one possible way by which Grace might have reparations by being given options to avoid devaluations, but there are many, many other ways that can be imagined. I invite you to imagine alternative ways for yourself and I challenge you to try and bring them into being.

Essay Four

Rewilding & Reparative Ecology

Towards a Neoprimitivism

"We tried ruling the world; we tried acting as God's steward, then we tried ushering in the human revolution, the age of reason and isolation. We failed in all of it, and our failure destroyed more than we were even aware of. The time for civilisation is past. Uncivilisation, which knows its flaws because it has participated in them; which sees unflinchingly and bites down hard as it records – this is the project we must embark on now."

— Paul Kingsnorth and Douglas Hine from *Uncivilization*

Is there any reality that is more disturbing than that of the ongoing rape and abuse of Mother Earth?

This reality disturbs me more than genocide, more than slavery, more than the rape and abuse of women — and these realities already disturb me to no end.

I imagine that I am so deeply disturbed by the rape and abuse of Mother Earth because I sense somehow that this reality conditions the rape and abuse of women which, in turn, conditions genocide and slavery.

The reality of the ongoing rape and abuse of Mother Earth has become so violent and extreme over the past two-and-a-half centuries that no one can effectively deny it anymore. It has been noted that the sum total of the harm inflicted on Mother Earth since the Second World War, the last "hot" war to consume the entire globe, exceeds the ravages that another world consuming war would have left behind. Yet still, in spite of its obviousness, the reality of the ongoing rape and abuse of Mother Earth is still spoken of in euphemisms: so few of us speak openly and honestly of ongoing ecocide.

What's more, most of our customs and institutions still express wishful and defensive fantasies that bunglingly attempt to cover up and deny the ongoing rape and abuse of Mother Earth; this is to say, in other words, that most of our customs and institutions perpetuate forms of anthropocentrism and anthropodenial.

Anthropocentrism is the wishful fantasy of human beings who would deny the reality of the ongoing rape and abuse of Mother Earth. Anthropocentrism and its privileged customs and institutions tell us that Man's dominion over the Earth is a matter of divine dispensation or of natural superiority. Anthropocentric customs and institutions hold that either (i) God made the Earth for Man's pleasure or (ii) Man has conquered the Earth because Man is a conqueror by nature. Either way, Man can and should have his way with Earth because the Earth is Man's property.

Anthropodenial is the defensive fantasy that attempts to cover up the rape and abuse of Mother Earth. Anthropodenial and its privileged customs and institutions tell us that human beings can't have an abusive relationship with Mother Earth because there is no such thing as Mother Earth. Anthropodenial claims that the idea of Mother Earth is a primitive anthropomorphism, a superstition that human beings need to put behind them in order to meet their "Sustainable Development Goals". Those who engage in anthropodenial will tell you that the Earth does not have feelings and, as such, the Earth cannot be raped and abused. The Earth can only be used or misused: that is to say, it can be used effectively and efficiently or it can be used ineffectively and inefficiently. The "Sustainable Development Goals" that anthropodenialists hold dear are primarily concerned with making more effective and efficient use of the Earth, choosing success over failure in order to avoid collapse. These goals do not aim to develop ever deeper and ever more meaningful relations with Mother Earth.

Anthropocentrism as wishful fantasy and anthropodenial as defensive fantasy are both "human, all too human" or art*less* anthropomorphisms: they anthropomorphize humans and de-anthropomorphize non-human so as to keep humans from meaningfully relating to non-humans. Opposed to anthropocentrism and anthropodenial, those who would acknowledge and make reparations for the rape and abuse of Mother Earth find meaning and purpose in animisms.

Animisms are "beyond human" or art*ful* anthropomorphisms. Animisms anthropomorphize non-humans and de-anthropomorphize humans so that humans can relate to non-humans in increasingly more meaningful ways, flipping the script of anthropocentrism and anthropodenial. Animisms tell us that we have feelings for the Earth and that the Earth has feelings for us, and animisms invite us to take care not to hurt the Earth's feelings and to make amends for having hurt the Earth's feelings. This is to say, in other words, that animisms are sublimating fantasies that enable human beings to better acknowledge and make reparations for the harm that they have done to non-human others.

I hear the anthropocentrists and the anthropodenialsts sneering at me, accusing me of "vain superstition and womanish pity" when I talk about Mother Earth's feelings. Indeed, I hear them quoting Spinoza at me, aware of how fond I am of the 17th-century rationalist, "The rational quest of what is useful teaches us the necessity of associating ourselves with our fellow men, but not with beasts, or things, whose nature is different from our own."

The disdain that anthropocentrists and the anthropodenialsts have for the animisms of primitive peoples is but an expression their refusal to admit the reality of ongoing rape and abuse of Mother Earth. Anthropocentrists and anthropodenialists would find it difficult to live with themselves if they made an earnest effort to imagine how Mother Earth feels and to express the feelings they imagine. Anthropocentrists and anthropodenialsts cannot claim that it is impossible to imagine how Mother Earth feels because primitive peoples have proven again and again that it is possible to imagine how Mother Earth feels in ways that are credibly meaningful. Instead, anthropocentrists and anthropodenialsts argue that imagining Mother Earth's feelings is an irrational activity, a waste of time, and they claim that primitive peoples are irrational peoples with too much time on their hands. "Be smart," say the anthropocentrists and anthropodenialsts, "Do not waste our time and yours, for we have important things to do."

To their chagrin, I and others like me continue to persist in our idiocy and we insist upon wasting everyone's time with sentimental stories about Mother Earth. This is because we believe that making reparations for the rape and abuse of Mother Earth must involve (re-)creating primitive animisms anew. Indeed, my fellow travelers and I, in our endeavors to (re-)create primitive animisms anew, are what you might call neo-primitives.

Switching from the psychoanalytic register to the schizoanalytic register, we neo-primitives find that modern human societies are defined by increasingly streamlined designs, by proliferations of pipelines dedicated to conveying human wants and needs hither and thither apart from the wants and needs non-humans. These streamlined designs are breaking fluent connections between human and non-human wants and needs, and anthropocentrism and anthropodenial are, above all else, expressions of the fact that fluent connections between human and non-human wants and needs have been broken.

In endeavoring to (re-)create primitive animisms anew, we neo-primitives aim to deconstruct "advanced" patriarchal capitalism's streamlined designs and to (re-)construct leaky designs in their place, enabling human and non-human wants and needs to become confluent again. As we neo-primitives see it, the animisms of ur-primitive peoples were expressions of their societies' leaky designs and the confluences of human and non-human wants and needs that their societies enabled. We neo-primitives aim to (re-)create primitive animisms anew by (re-)creating the potentials that yielded primitive animisms: by (re-)creating human societies with leaky designs so as to (re-)generate confluences humans and non-human wants and needs.

The eco-modernism of liberal globalism is the foil of neo-primitivism. Eco-modernism is the extreme form of anthropodenial that is the logical endpoint of our "Sustainable Development Goals". Eco-modernism aims to decouple the global economy from the ecology of the biosphere and, in so doing, it would sever whatever fluent connections still remain between the wants and needs of humans and non-humans. Eco-modernism would take streamlined designs to new heights, plugging up every fault and fissure to be found in existing pipelines and creating new seamless pipelines that would ensure that human wants and needs do not leak out into and pollute non-human environments. Indeed, this is what the eco-modernist calls environmental conservation.

Instead of working to conserve environments, neo-primitives work to rewild the world.

Rewilding is not a matter of removing humans from nature and letting nature do its thing. Humans, so long as they exist, are inextricable from nature, and nature cannot become wild again without human beings also becoming wild again—unless, of course, the human species becomes extinct. Rewilding, insofar as it is a human practice, is about (re)creating confluences of human and non-human wants and needs.

The eco-modernist snarls and snaps, "Luddites! Neo-primitives are the enemies of progress, science, and technology!"

I implore you not to take them seriously. Neo-primitives are in no way the enemies of science and technology, unless science and technology are definitively characterized by seamless and streamlined designs. If there are sciences and technologies that can be characterized by seamful and leaky designs—and I assure you there are—then there are neo-primitive sciences and technologies.

Rewilding, as the neo-primitive understands and practices it, is only about eschewing the seamless and streamlined and embracing the seamful and leaky. In light of this, the neo-primitive finds that making the world wild again is not the impossible feat that "advanced" capitalist man makes it out to be. The mistake is to think that rewilding is about sustaining nature as it is or returning nature to what it was. When undertaken by neo-primitives, however, rewilding is about making nature differ wildly again, it is about (re-)creating potentials for things to wildly differ. Indeed, going even further, we neo-primitives find life's meaning and purpose in asking and answering the following question,

"How can we defer to what wildly differs?"

NIETZSCHE

THE WAR ON TERRA & THE NEW UNDERGROUND RAILROAD

I have been a close reader of the work of Friedrich Nietzsche since I first encountered his books as a teenager. Though I now find the man, his life, and his philosophical project rather sad, I still find his works most illuminating. It was Nietzsche's writings that helped me develop the tools that I needed to question Western civilization from my wretched place within it, and so I shall be forever thankful to him and to his work.

When I read Nietzsche now, I recognize him as one thoroughly aware of the fact that modern European peoples' justifications for their "supremacy" were baseless. Nietzsche knew that modern European peoples hadn't conquered as a result of divine dispensation, or natural superiority, or historical good fortune. Nietzsche knew that modern European peoples had conquered thanks to their extreme willingness to murder, rape, steal from, and enslave others. What's more, Nietzsche knew that modern European peoples had become willing to murder, rape, steal from, and enslave others to an extreme degree because they had learned to lie to themselves to an extreme degree: they had stopped recognizing murder, rape, theft, and slavery for what they are.

Nietzsche's philosophical project was about getting modern European peoples to stop lying to themselves and to affirm murder, rape, theft, and slavery with a good conscience. Nietzsche did not want to condemn murder, rape, theft, and slavery and seek reparations for victims. Rather, Nietzsche wanted to nurture "good Europeans" who could admit to themselves and to the world that they committed atrocities for the sake of their own enjoyment: neither God, nor Nature, nor History made them do what they did.

Nietzsche calls weak and slavish those peoples who justify their atrocities with appeals to God, Nature, and History. Nietzsche calls strong and masterful those peoples for whom being implicated in atrocities is admittedly a matter of taste. Nietzsche's artful deconstructions of the concepts of divine dispensation, natural superiority, historical good fortune are perhaps the most clear and powerful philosophical writings that I have ever read in my entire life.

That being said, however, I read Nietzsche now and I find that his writings are remarkable expressions of powerlessness in the face of suffering. Nietzsche seems to have felt that he was powerless to do anything about the murder, rape, theft, and slavery that was the condition of possibility for his existence as a modern European. He believed that all he could do was learn to affirm with a "good conscience" the atrocities that made his existence possible.

What makes Nietzsche such a sad character is the fact that Nietzsche believed that affirming life meant affirming murder, rape, theft, and slavery. He could not imagine care and compassion getting the better of conquest, domination, and exploitation so as to yield creative wonders that affirm life. Again and again, Nietzsche makes the case that creative wonders are only made possible by "aristocratic" peoples that risk themselves to conquer, dominate, and exploit others; he cannot fathom that creative wonders have been made possible by "communistic" peoples that risk themselves to show care for and compassion towards others.

Nietzsche is said to have suffered a mental breakdown after witnessing a street scene in which a man mercilessly whipped a horse raw for refusing to work. It is said that Nietzsche intervened to stop the spiteful man from beating the proud horse any further and that Nietzsche then embraced the horse and wept. It is said that Nietzsche's final words before his "madness" made him mute were, "Mutter, ich bin dumm" ("mother, I am stupid").

I have come to read this mental breakdown as a philosophical breakthrough, and I have come to read all of Nietzsche's works in light of this breakdown. What Nietzsche realized in this dramatic moment of clarity was that he could not affirm atrocities with a good conscience, he was not powerless to stop atrocities, he could risk himself and affirm life by caring for and being compassionate towards another living creature. He realized that neither he nor anyone else had a taste for the atrocities that conditioned modern Europe's conquests; for these atrocities were not matters of taste but the consequences of addictions.

A good conscience actually demanded that Nietzsche either (i) speak with care and compassion against the atrocities that conditioned his existence and the addictions that motivated these atrocities or (ii) that he keep silent.

He kept silent. I forgive him for keeping silent. Just consider where Western Civilization's addictions were heading: world wars, weapons of mass destruction, more genocides, and planetary ecocide. Having written all that he had already written, Nietzsche's silence following the scene with the proud horse and spiteful master speaks volumes to me, like the philosophical stunts of Diogenes the Cynic, like the antics of Zen masters related in koans.

In this essay, I would like to interpret Nietzsche's silence for others.

To the "Four Great Errors" that Nietzsche identified in his written works, Nietzsche performative silence adds a fifth error: his own error, the error of confusing matters of taste with the consequences of addiction.

Before his silence, Nietzsche had sought to divide the world into two kinds of people: into noble pushers and common addicts or, to use his own parlance, into masters and slaves. What Nietzsche called the morality of the slave is more aptly termed the mentality of the addict; and what he called the morality of the master is more aptly termed the mentality of the pusher — the pusher being that exploiter of addicts who is themself but another kind of addict, a "nobler" kind of addict: one who is addicted to exercising power over addicts. What Nietzsche called the corruption of master morality by slave morality is more aptly described as the pusher's becoming addicted to the product that they push; and what he called the triumph of slave morality is more aptly described as noble pusher's transformation into a common addict, a noble addiction to power yielding to a common addiction to a product.

Nietzsche was concerned most by three different "pushers of illusions": the artist who pushes illusions of beauty and sublimity; the philosopher who pushes illusions of truth and meaning; and the scientist who pushes illusions of empirical reality and intelligible matter. His remarks on artists, philosophers, and scientists can be summed up as follows: the noble artist deals in illusions of beauty and sublimity but doesn't crave such illusions themselves, only the common artist craves beauty and sublimity; the noble philosopher deals in illusions of truth and meaning but doesn't crave such illusions themselves, only the common philosopher craves truth and meaning; the noble scientist deals in illusions of empirical reality and intelligible matter but doesn't crave such illusions themselves, only the common scientist craves empirical realities and intelligible matters.

Before his silence, Nietzsche's aim was to keep the noble pushers (masters) from becoming common addicts (slaves). To that end, Nietzsche told the artist to abstain from overindulging in beauty and sublimity in order to better deal in beauty and sublimity; he told the philosopher to abstain from overindulging in truth and meaning in order to better deal in truth and meaning; and he told the scientist to abstain from overindulging in empirical realities and intelligible matters in order to better deal in empirical realities and intelligible matters.

Nietzsche did not want to heal addicts and addictions. To the contrary, what he wanted to create an "order of rank", a segregated hierarchy of addicts. He wanted to keep the noble power-addicted pushers apart from and above their common product-addicted clients. He argued that the noble pusher's addiction to exercising power over addicts, their "Will to Power", ought not be corrupted by an addiction to the products that they push. To that end, he affirmed a kind of asceticism and sobriety that would keep the noble pusher from indulging in the products that they push, keeping their "Will to Power" as pure as can be.

Affirming Nietzsche's silence over and above what he wrote, I am interested in the treatment of addicts of all kinds: power-addicted pushers and their product-addicted clients alike. Like food, sex, and medicine, the illusions pushed by artists, philosophers, and scientists are not bad things in and of themselves but they can become the focus of addictions under certain conditions. Indeed, even power is not a bad thing in and of itself but, rather, it can become the focus of an addiction under certain conditions. I am interested in creating the conditions under which one can indulge in one's tastes for illusions (and even for the power) without fostering addictions that motivate destructive behaviors.

The focus of one's addiction may be a matter of taste, but one's becoming an addict is certainly not a matter of taste. A noted writer on the topic of addiction, Dr. Gabor Maté proposes the following:

> [A]ddiction is neither a choice nor primarily a disease. It originates in a human being's desperate attempt to solve a problem: the problem of emotional pain, of overwhelming stress, of lost connection, of loss of control, of a deep discomfort with the self. In short, it is a forlorn attempt to solve the problem of human pain. All drugs—and all behaviours of addiction, substance-dependent or not, whether to gambling, food, sex, alcohol, cigarettes, the internet or cocaine—either soothe pain directly or distract from it. Hence my mantra: "The question is not why the addiction, but why the pain."

One becomes addicted to beauty and sublimity, or to truth and meaning, or to empirical reality and intelligible matter, or power in order to escape the burdens of pain, stress, loneliness, self-loathing. Ay, and one can only overcome one's addictions by sharing one's burdens with others and receiving non-judgmental care and compassion from others. This is what Nietzsche could not fathom until his breakdown and breakthrough.

While Nietzsche was focused on pushers of art, philosophy, and science, there are more specific and dangerous pushers that I am confronted with and that I wish to attend to. I refer, of course, to those pushers that enable imperialisms, only some of which are pushers of art, philosophy, and science.

In the book *Tools for Conviviality*, Ivan Illich described three different sorts of imperialism, each successive one being more insidious and intractable than the last. First, he described a nationalist imperialism that is characterized by "the pernicious spread of one nation beyond its boundaries." Second, he described a capitalist imperialism that is characterized by "the omnipresent influence of multinational corporations." Third, and finally, he described a careerist imperialism, the most insidious and intractable of the three, characterized by "the mushrooming of professional monopolies over production." It is an addiction to national symbols and national security measures that yields a nationalist imperialism, an addiction to economic "growth and progress" that yields a capitalist imperialism; and an addiction to "human resources" and "professional development" that yields a careerist imperialism. These three entangled addictions are the most destructive addictions that humankind has ever succumbed to: they have yielded weapons of mass destruction, outrageously exploitative inequities in global opportunities and wealth, and, worst of all, planetary ecocide.

The power-addicted pushers of nationalisms, capitalisms, and careerisms are, to wax Nietzschean, "ignoble" pushers. They themselves overindulge in the products they push and cannot be neatly distinguished from their product-addicted clients. Nevertheless, Nietzsche's distinctions do bear fruit on this point: they teach us that a power-addiction may become inextricable from a product-addiction but the two addictions will have different affects and effects and they will require different therapies, even if these therapies must work cooperatively and run concurrently.

Recognizing that nationalist, capitalist, and careerist imperialisms are the consequences of addictions, Illich wrote, "Withdrawal from these mania[s] will be painful, but mostly for members of the generation which has to experience the transition and above all for those most disabled by consumption. If their plight could be vividly remembered, it might help the next generation avoid what they know would enslave them." This is the arduous task confronting generations now living: to take pains to withdraw from these imperious, all-consuming, ecocidal addictions and to create vivid documents of how we got over as lessons and warnings for future generations.

(DE-/RE-) CON- STRUCT- ING WORLDS

THE WAR ON TERRA & THE NEW UNDERGROUND RAILROAD

Radical Everydayness

My favorite Sherlock Holmes story by Sir Arthur Conan Doyle has long been "A Case of Identity", published as the third story in *The Adventures of Sherlock Holmes* in 1892. Curious as it may seem, the titular case of identity upon which the story turns is not what makes it my favorite Sherlock Holmes story. Rather, what makes the story my favorite is the brief philosophical dialogue between Holmes and Watson that frames the titular case. This brief dialogue is, in my humble and idiosyncratic opinion, one of the most profound philosophical dialogues ever written.

The main part of the dialogue runs as follows:

> Holmes: My dear fellow, life is infinitely stranger than anything which the mind of man could invent. We would not dare to conceive the things which are really mere commonplaces of existence. If we could fly out of that window hand in hand, hover over this great city, gently remove the roofs, and peep in at the queer things which are going on, the strange coincidences, the plannings, the cross-purposes, the wonderful chains of events, working through generations, and leading to the most *outrè* results, it would make all fiction with its conventionalities and foreseen conclusions most stale and unprofitable.

> Watson: And yet I am not convinced of it, the cases which come to light in the papers are, as a rule, bald enough, and vulgar enough. We have in our police reports realism pushed to its extreme limits, and yet the result is, it must be confessed, neither fascinating nor artistic.

> Holmes: A certain selection and discretion must be used in producing a realistic effect. This is wanting in the police report, where more stress is laid, perhaps, upon the platitudes of the magistrate than upon the details, which to an observer contain the vital essence of the whole matter. Depend upon it, there is nothing so unnatural as the commonplace.

So, you ask me, "What profound insight is to be gained from this dialogue?"

Well, as I have come to read it, Holmes is reproaching Watson for believing that what is "common sense" is coterminous with what is "commonplace" when, and this is the proud insight, what is "commonplace" tends to defy "common sense".

Readers of my works will note that I have used the term "common" quite often in my writings and, more often than not, I have used the term negatively. This is because I almost always use the term "common" to refer to the "conventionalities" and "foreseen conclusions" that constitute "common sense". I have only very rarely used the term "common" to refer to the "wonderful chains of events" and "*outrè* results" that are "commonplace". That being said, however, I must admit that I have, like Watson, too often mistaken the common sense for the commonplace.

A major part of the (De-/Re-)Constructing Worlds project, as I have conceived of it, will be about taking care not to mistake the common sense for the commonplace. For while the project aims to forsake what is common sense, the project also aims to embrace what is commonplace. To put it differently — reserving the term "common" for that which is common sense, as I have in previous writings, and employing the term "everyday" to refer to that which is commonplace — I say that the (De-/Re-)Constructing Worlds project aims to forsake the common in order to embrace the everyday.

The (De-/Re-)Constructing Worlds project is about (de-/re-)constructing statements, implements, and environments so as to make everyday sense — this as opposed to making common sense and as opposed to appealing to higher senses and reasons. Which is to say, in other words, that the project is both opposed to the populisms of common sense and opposed to the elitisms of higher senses and reasons.

Indeed, as I see it, the populisms of common sense and the elitisms of higher senses and reasons are two sides of the same coin. Aristocratic and meritocratic elites impose a common sense upon everyday words, things, and places in order to claim that singularity and spontaneity of expression are the scarce possessions of those who have cultivated higher senses and reasons. In turn, the populists who celebrate common sense and disparage higher senses and reasons are doing little more than expressing their *ressentiment* towards elites who have robbed people of everyday sense and who have claimed higher senses and reasons as the means and the ends of privilege.

Radical resistance to common sense, as I would practice it, is resistance to the conventionalities and foreseen conclusions that aristocratic and meritocratic elites impose upon everyday words, things, and places in their bid to claim singularity and spontaneity of expression as aristocratic and meritocratic privileges. What's more, going further, radical resistance to common sense is about making everyday sense, which means making sense of the fact that singularity and spontaneity of expression are commonplaces as opposed to privileges.

So, you now ask me, "What makes everyday sense?"

Well, I say that statements, implements, and environments that make everyday sense are those that stand the test of everyday use and repair. In this I follow Soetsu Yanagi, the Japanese philosopher and aesthete, who writes in an essay translated as "The Beauty of Miscellaneous Things":

> [Everyday statements, implements, and environments] cannot be fragile, lavishly decorated, or intricately made; such will not do. Thick, strong, and durable, that is what is needed. [Statements, implements, and environments] for everyday use are not averse to rough handling [...] They cannot be flimsy or frail of nature; neither can they be overly refined. They must be true and steadfast to their use. They must be ready for any type of handling, for use by any individual. Pretentious ornamentation is not permitted; dishonesty of any type is rejected. They must bear every trial and test.

This does not mean, however, that everyday statements, implements, and environments are things that lack beauty. Very much to the contrary, they are beautiful because they are stripped of pretentious artifice and bear the traces of everyday use and repair. Indeed, in lieu of pretentious artifice, the traces of everyday use and repair become baroque decorations and ornamentations, and these traces constitute the beauty of everyday statements, implements, and environments.

Yanagi continues:

Since [everyday statements, implements, and environments] have [commonplace tasks] to perform, they are dressed, so to speak, in modest wear and lead quiet lives. In them one can almost feel a sense of satisfaction as they greet each day with a smile. They work thoughtlessly and unselfishly, carrying out effortlessly and inconspicuously whatever duty comes their way. They possess a genuine, unmovable beauty. On the other hand, of course, there is also delicate beauty, beauty that quakes at the slightest perturbation. Yet isn't beauty that remains unfazed by a hard knock or two all the more amazing?

Moreover, this type of beauty grows with each passing day. [Everyday statements, implements, and environments] become more beautiful the more they are used, and the more beautiful they become, the more they are used. Users and the used have exchanged a vow: the more an [everyday statement implement, or environment] is used the more beautiful it will become, and the more the user uses an [everyday statement implement, or environment], the more that [statement implement, or environment] will be loved.

Statements, implements, and environments that only make common sense (as opposed to making everyday sense) are expendable: they are meant to be used, abused, and thrown away. That which is common sense fails the test of everyday use because it is not meant to be improved upon in and through its everyday use and repair. Rather, what is common sense is meant to be disposed of after falling into disrepair or disrepute. You can be sure that you are dealing with a word, thing, or place that makes common sense whenever you find that the word, thing, or place is easily exchanged for another one just like it when it falls into disrepair or disrepute.

Statements, implements, and environments that appeal to higher senses and reasons (as opposed to making everyday sense) are not meant for everyday use: they are meant to be used by special persons for special purposes at specially appointed places and times. You can be sure that you are dealing with a word, thing, or place that appeals to higher senses and reasons when rules and regulations must be formalized and authorities established to prevent the word, thing, or place from being used by people who do not "deserve" the privilege.

Statements, implements, and environments that make everyday sense bear the traces of their everyday use and repair with beauty and grace: the more they are used and repaired in different ways by different people, the more beautiful and useful they become. You can be sure that you are dealing with a word, thing, or place that makes everyday sense when it begs to be used and repaired again and again by different people and in different ways in order to enhance both its beauty and its usefulness.

The statements, implements, and environments that we have access to are what make us what we are.

- Those who are made into slavish commoners are those who only have access to statements, implements, and environments that make common sense. This is to say, in other words, that expendable words, things, and places make for expendable people.

- Those who are made into aristocratic and meritocratic masters are those who "earn" special privileges and "deserve" access to statements, implements, and environments that appeal to higher senses and reasons. This is to say, in other words, that words, things, and places that are refined for a "higher purpose" make for people who believe that they have been refined for a "higher purpose" that the common people cannot serve.

- Those who are made into everyday people, who become neither masters nor slaves, are those who have access to statements, implements, and environments that make everyday sense. This is to say, in other words, that words, things, and places that become more beautiful and useful in and through everyday use and repair are what make for people who create increasingly beautiful and useful words, things, and places by living their everyday lives.

We live in a world in which the production and proliferation of expendable statements, implements, and environments prevails. This means that we live in a world in which people are being made expendable.

Some submit to being made expendable, others resist. Alas, many who resist being made expendable are desperately grasping for special privileges and for access to statements, implements, and environments that appeal to higher senses and reasons. Those who manage to grasp special privileges for themselves fear the *ressentiment* of those still grasping and coming up empty handed: the privileged fear that the have-nots are resolved to wrest special privileges away from those who have, and they fear that some have-nots are resolved to wreck what they aren't able to wrest from the haves. It follows that many social struggles in our world are defined by the desperate grasping of those wanting special privileges and by the apprehensive clinging of those holding onto special privileges.

Ay, but there is also a radical resistance to expendability that would neither desperately grasp at nor apprehensively cling to special privileges. This radical resistance to expendability would promote and participate in the production and proliferation of statements, implements, and environments that make everyday sense.

I call such radical resistance to expendability a "radical everydayness", and I have conceived of (De-/Re-)Constructing Worlds as a project in radical everydayness.

Abolition

The (De-/Re)Constructing Worlds project will consider different ways in which we may *deconstruct the industrialized world* and *(re-)construct convivial worlds*. You ask , "How does deconstructing the industrialized world and (re-)constructing convivial worlds contribute to the project of abolition?"

Well, the industrialized world, as I have come to regard it, is a world constructed on the hypothesis that machines can replace slaves or, rather more precisely, that new machine slaves could be gradually made to replace the human slaves of old, and that a "temporary" and "voluntary" sort of human slavery, wage slavery, will suffice in the interim between the old human driven order and the new machine driven order — the imperative being that the wage slave uses their wage labor as a stepping-stone to small proprietorship.

The logic of slavery is built into the "deep structure" of the environments, implements, and statements that characterize the industrialized world. Indeed, the pervasiveness of this logic is such that many do not fully appreciate the horrors endured by the enslaved. Many believe that the work slaves are forced to perform is "essential work" that someone or something must be made to perform and they believe that what makes slavery wrong is the fact that slaves are not properly compensated for the "essential work" that they are made to perform. The fact is, however, that slaves are, by definition, forced to perform excessive, superfluous work for the sake of the master's pleasure and profit.

Our so-called "higher senses" and "reasons" have misled us into thinking that slavery is an unfortunate solution to a real problem and that industrialization is the better solution this problem. Exposing the falsehoods of our "higher senses" and "reasons", everyday sense reveals to us that slavery is, in fact, a bad solution to a false problem—the false problem of "who (or what) can be made to work for us". Going further, everyday sense reveals to us that industrialization is but another bad solution to this same false problem.

What's more, and going even further still, everyday sense reveals to us that we will not be able to confront the global economic and ecological crises that we are living through today unless we learn to see beyond the false problem of "making others work *for* us" and learn to confront the real problem of "finding ways to work *with* others".

Ivan Illich puts a fine point on the matter in the book Tools for Conviviality:

> [Our crises] can be solved only if we learn to invert the present deep structure of tools; if we give people tools that [...] [eliminate] the need for either slaves or masters and [enhance] each person's range of freedom. People need new tools to work with rather than tools that work for them. They need technology to make the most of the energy and imagination each has, rather than more well-programmed energy [and information] slaves. [...] Neither a dictatorial proletariat nor a leisure mass can escape the dominion of constantly expanding industrial tools.

Abolition, as I conceive of it, is about (re-)constructing a world in which the prevailing working relation amongst peoples, implements, and environments is that of working-*with* as opposed to working-*for*. From this perspective, eliminating chattel slavery, the most egregious form of working-for, could only ever be the beginning of abolition.

Indeed, as a project in abolition thusly understood, the recurring question throughout the (De-/Re)Constructing Worlds project will be this, "How can we deconstruct statements, implements, and environments that facilitate relations of working-for, and how can we (re)construct statements, environments, and implements that facilitate relations of working-with?"

Industrialization in its latest and most extreme phase is about constructing a world in which artificially intelligent machines perform intellectual labor *for* their masters and in which robotic machines perform physical labor *for* their masters. This is to say, in other words, that industrialization today seeks to construct a world in which slavery has been perfected. In this brave new hyper-industrialized world, the biggest problem that the new masters of machines will have to confront is what to do with human beings who are expendable, who are neither masters nor overseers of the perfect slaves, fully automated and artificially intelligent robots.

We all know, of course, that those peoples most likely to be counted amongst the expendable are those who once were slaves and those who were displaced and dispossessed by the advance of slaveholding and industrial societies. It follows that, in the United States of America where I live, black and indigenous peoples are those most likely to be counted amongst the expendable.

robot (n.) from Czech *robotnik* "forced worker," from *robota* "forced labor, compulsory service, drudgery," from *robotiti* "to work, drudge," from an Old Czech source akin to Old Church Slavonic *rabota* "servitude," from *rabu* "slave"

Working *with* the aid of a technical implement and a built environment is not the same thing as having a technical implement and a built environment that works *for* you. The difference between implements and environments that you work with and those that work for you is the difference between augmentation and automation, between the prosthetic and the robotic.

The (De-/Re-)Constructing Worlds project aims (i) to encourage augmentation and the proliferation of prosthetic implements and environments which would multiply our senses for the world around us, and, concomitantly, (ii) to discourage automation and the proliferation of robotic implements and environments which would increasingly rationalize the world around us. But promoting the prosthetic above and beyond the robotic is not enough. Promoting working-with above and beyond working-for also means promoting collective prostheses above and beyond individual prostheses. Working-with means producing prostheses that bring bodies together as opposed to prostheses that set bodies apart from one another.

Working-with means producing prostheses that invite two or more different bodies to aid one another and work together, this as opposed to producing prostheses designed exclusively for a single body to operate alone without the aid of others.

But favoring working-with above and beyond working-for does not at all mean favoring the simple above and beyond the complex. Some of the collective prostheses that I might cite as furthering working-with are quite complex. Take, for instance, the marvelous work of a friend and mentor, Sha Xin Wei, who creates "responsive environments" in which "computationally augmented tangible media respond to the improvised gesture and activity of their inhabitants" so as to enable "participatory sense-making" and the "steering of complex adaptive systems". Yet other collective prostheses that I might cite as examples are so simple that they can easily be taken for granted. Take, for instance, a simple two person rowboat.

As I conceive of it, advancing abolition in defiance of hyper-industrialization is not about advancing simplicity above and beyond complexity. Rather, it is about advancing a prosthetics (i.e., a technics of augmentation) that enables an increasing diversity of bodies to form collectives and to work with one another—this as opposed to advancing a robotics (i.e., a technics of automation) that would work for privileged bodies and that would enable privileged bodies to insulate themselves from collective work.

Overturning Humanism

The story that I want to tell in this essay is the story of how and why it is that courses in the humanities taught at American schools, colleges, and universities tend to motivate some groups of American students and demotivate others. To be more specific, I want to tell the story of how and why courses in the humanities tend to motivate White American and European Males and their imitators, and the story of how and why these courses demotivate non-Whites and non-Males who refuse to put White American and European Males on pedestals.

This story is not a new story. It has been told many times before, and my telling of this story is very much inspired by and indebted to previous tellings.

Nearly a century ago, in the early 1930s, Carter G. Woodson wrote in *The Mis-Education of the Negro*:

> The same educational process which inspires and stimulates the oppressor with the thought that he is everything and has accomplished everything worthwhile, depresses and crushes at the same time the spark of genius in the Negro by making him feel that his race does not amount to much and never will measure up to the standards of other peoples... Negroes are taught to admire the Hebrew, the Greek, the Latin, and the Teuton and to despise the African... The thought of the inferiority of the Negro is drilled into him in almost every book that he studies. It is strange then that the friends of truth... have not risen up against the present propaganda in the school... This crusade is much more important that the anti-lynching movement — because there would be no lynching if it did not start in the classroom. Why not exploit, enslave or exterminate a class that everybody is taught to regard as inferior.

Following Woodson, here is Sylvia Wynter from the book *Do Not Call Us Negroes*, written in the 1990s, reflecting upon the education that I, myself, endured during my childhood and young adulthood:

> The representation of Afro (Black) inferiority and Euro (White) superiority that Woodson has identified are not mere "slights" against the "special interests" of Black Americans which can be rectified by either the "equal time" or "equal glory" approach.
>
> Adding a few more Black individuals would not be any more effective than the attempts of the lay intelligentsia of 14th and 15th century Europe to apply their "fallen reason" unaided by theology to overcome the doctrine of the infallibility of the Divine Truth of Clergy.
>
> Nothing less than the cultural-intellectual revolution of humanism and the "entire upheaval of the Renaissance" could free them of those prescriptive modes.
>
> Equally, it will take the emancipation of our present mainstream mode of social knowledge [...] in order to rid ourselves of the stubborn persistence of the representations which Woodson found 60 years ago.

Woodson and Wynter's writings speak loudly and clearly to me, for I was one of those students depressed and crushed by what I learned in courses in the humanities at American schools, colleges, and universities. The courses that I took in the history of art, philosophy, and science primarily served to teach me the "truth" of America's race, class, and gender hierarchies. I was taught that the White American and European Male historical continuum was the world's primary and defining historical continuum, and I was taught that all other historical continua were secondary add-ons and supplements. The histories of non-Whites and non-Males were either marginalized for being matters of "special interest" or they were reduced to histories of being "discovered" by and then assimilated into the history of White American and European Males.

In being taught how White American and European Males "discovered" and learned to embrace the humanity non-Whites and non-Males, I was essentially being taught that the accomplishments of non-Whites and non-Males did not belong to them but, rather, that these accomplishments belonged to the White American and European Males who "discovered" the humanity in them. This is to say, in other words, that I was being taught that my own accomplishments would never be my own but would always belong to White American and European Males, to whom I had to appeal and entreat to recognize my humanity. "Equal time" and "equal glory" may be given to the accomplishments of non-Whites and non-Males, but White American and European Males maintained the privilege of defining what does and doesn't count as a real accomplishment. It follows that non-Whites and non-Males who want their accomplishments to be recognized by history must do, make, say, and think in a manner that compliments and complements the accomplishments of White American and European Males.

For instance, I was taught that the accomplishments of African sculptors belonged to the European avant-gardes who discovered and incorporated aspects of African sculpture into the European tradition, and I was taught that the accomplishments of Black American blues and jazz musicians were proven by the irresistible appeal of their music to White American and European audiences. What African sculpture meant for African sculptors and what blues and jazz meant for Black American musicians was a matter of secondary importance. The matter of primary importance was that African sculptures and Black American blues and jazz had an impact on White American and European history. The lesson to be drawn for me as a young Black person aspiring to do creative work was that, in order to accomplish anything of historical merit, I had to create work that appealed to and invited appropriation by White Americans and Europeans.

At some point early on in my life, I decided for myself that I would not bid for universality by creating work that appealed to White Americans and Europeans. That being said, however, in and through refusing to appeal to White Americans and Europeans, I also wanted to reject the racial identity that had been imposed upon me by White American and Europeans. This is to say, in other words, I had also decided for myself that I would not create work that took my being "Black" for granted.

To this end, I embarked upon a series of philosophical investigations in order to decide to whom I would appeal and how I would appeal to them. My published books are documents of these philosophical investigations. First, in my *Triptych*, I wondered how I might become what I am, and I documented my endeavors to dispense with the identities imposed upon me and to (re-)create myself otherwise. Next, in *Other Related Matters*, I wondered how I might relate to others, and I documented my search for a way to appeal to others who, like me, sought to dispense with the identities imposed upon them and to (re-)create themselves otherwise.

Building on the philosophical investigations documented in these books, my two most recent projects, my *Four Essays on Reparations* and the (De-/Re-)Constructing Worlds project, are my attempts to contribute to the cultural-intellectual revolution that Sylvia Wynter called for in the above quoted passage: the cultural-intellectual revolution against the stubborn persistence of White supremacist, colonialist, and capitalist modes of social knowledge.

The cultural-intellectual revolution of humanism against the Divine Truth of the Clergy, which Wynter cited as her informative anecdote, took the form of a revival and renewal of ways of knowing that belonged to classical civilizations — the expansive, militaristic, slave-holding, and coin-circulating agrarian empires of the ancient Greeks and Romans. Similarly but differently, I believe that the cultural-intellectual revolution against white supremacy, colonialism, and capitalism — the revolution that I have taken to calling *neoprimitivism* — will assume the form of a revival and renewal of ways of knowing belonging to those who have been called "uncivilized" peoples by White Americans and Europeans — indigenous hunter-gatherers, horticulturalists, and pastoralists.

The cultural-intellectual revolution of neoprimitivism, as I conceive of it, is the overturning of humanism. The fundamental assumption of humanism is that Man triumphs over nature because Man is possessed of higher senses and reasons. Ay, and the humanist project is all about celebrating Man's higher senses and reasons and his triumphs over nature. The White American and European Man who has conquered and overcome nature with his science and industry is the apotheosis of Man according to humanism, and non-Whites and non-Males are goaded by humanism to prove their humanity, their manliness, by demonstrating that they too are willing and able to use science and industry to conquer and overcome nature.

Humanism deems "primitive" all those peoples who resist the goad and who refuse to use science and industry to conquer and overcome nature. This is to say, in other words, that humanism deems "primitive" all those peoples who would persist in deferring to nature instead of dominating nature like Real Men, like White Men. Ay, and because they persist in deferring nature, "primitive" peoples are, like nature, ripe for conquest by Real Men, for conquest by White Men and their imitators. It follows that, from a humanist perspective, those peoples who use science and industry to conquer other peoples are to be considered more advanced and less primitive, while those peoples who are conquered are to be considered underdeveloped and more primitive.

The cultural-intellectual revolution of neoprimitivism, the overturning of humanism, would champion those who resist the temptation to conquer and overcome nature and who instead persist in deferring to nature. The humanist will no doubt argue that neoprimitivism, thusly conceived, is the denial of human freedom: for the humanist believes that Man can only be free after having conquered and overcome nature. The neoprimitivist response to this argument is that limiting "human freedom" means (re-)gaining the freedom of nature, what the Japanese philosopher and aesthete Soetsu Yanagi would call (re-)gaining "freedomless freedom". Conversely, when nature is conquered and overcome, the "human freedom" that one gains thereby is what Yanagi called a "free freedomlessness".

Writing about the manufacture of kasuri (絣) cloth, Yanagi writes marvelously of the freedom of nature:

> In one sense, it can be said that the fact that the pattern edges don't align perfectly is due to human ineptitude, to a lack of mastery of the technique. In another sense, given that the result is the same regardless of who undertakes the task, it can be said that some deeper process is at work, that this nonalignment is an inevitable natural outcome, that the smudging and rubbing of kasuri is nature taking its course. That is, the kasuri effect is a technique originating in nature, not a human manipulation.

> This is strikingly similar to the blurring effect that occurs in calligraphy as a result of natural processes, not as an intentional human augmentation. Interestingly, the fact that this adds immensely to the beauty of calligraphy evinces the power of nature as opposed to human contrivance. Consequently, if one were to try intentionally to produce this effect, the result would, conversely, be unnatural and result in a loss of beauty, the upshot of going against nature.

> [...] Human restriction is nature's freedom; this is the essence of kasuri, its origin. To understand this truth more fully, think of the artist who in unshackled, unrestrained freedom creates a pictorial design. Some good pictures will result from this endeavor, but also a great many that are unsightly. Since humans are imperfect beings, they cannot wholly escape from committing mistakes. However, let's look at the state of standard kasuri. To my way of thinking, the case is entirely the opposite of the above: as long as kasuri adheres to standard procedure, almost nothing is produced that is positively ugly. Why should this be? The reason lies in the fact that many of the techniques involved are carried out under the aegis of nature, leaving little room for human error.

What Yanagi calls the "aegis of nature" in the quoted passage is what scientists like to call "random error" or "noise", and what Yanagi calls "human error" is what scientists like to call "systematic error" or "bias". It follows that, speaking scientifically, we may say that humanism, the affirmation of "free fredomlessness", is about reducing noise by introducing bias, "making Man the measure of all things". Ay, and we may say neoprimitivism, the affirmation of "freedomless freedom", is about reducing bias by welcoming noise, "letting nature to do its thing".

Taking things one step further, we may say that the humanist maintains that White Americans and Europeans are the apotheosis of Man because White Americans and Europeans have excelled most at biasing the world in their favor. Indeed, this is essentially what I was taught in my humanities courses. I was taught that to be human one must make oneself the measure of all things, and I was taught that the White Man was the exemplar of the human in this regard because, in and through conquest and the imposition of capitalism and colonialism, the White Man has excelled most at making himself the measure of all things. Thus, to become human was to become more like the White Man in one of two different senses: either (i) by measuring up to the White Man or (ii) by following the White Man's example and endeavoring to make oneself the measure of all things.

Alas, there are oppressed peoples who have fallen into humanisms trap. Some have taken to writing "separate but equal" histories (e.g., Black histories, Women's histories, and Indigenous histories) that strive to prove either that they can measure up to the White Man or that they can displace the White Man as the measure of all things. In doing so, these oppressed peoples have written histories that uphold the White Man's definition of human history, maintaining the White Man's privileged place in human history as he who defined human history.

The overturning of humanism, the cultural-intellectual revolution of neoprimitivism encourages us to radically differ from the White Man by radically deferring to nature. As opposed to measuring up to the White Man and as opposed to displacing the White Man as the measure of all things, the neoprimitivist invites nature to make increasingly more noise and to increasingly vary the measures of things. From a neoprimitivist perspective, the more noise that one is able to welcome, the more that one has accomplished. This is to say, in other words, that accomplishment does not mean signaling oneself out from the noise (which is what the White Man has done in constructing himself and his history). Instead, much to the contrary, accomplishment means adding one's own signal to the noise in such a way that one's own signal becomes part and parcel of the noise and the noise becomes part and parcel of one's own signal.

To this end, the neoprimitivist aims to (re-)construct confluent genealogies and to deconstruct "separate but equal" histories. Instead of constructing a separate Black history, Women's history, or Indigenous history that stands in opposition to the White Man's history, the neoprimitivist aims to (re-)construct queer and creole genealogies in and through which many different histories become confused and no one history can be clearly signaled out from the noise. From a neoprimitivist perspective, it is a badge of honor to be told by a White European philosopher that one belongs to a people without a definite history of their own. Indeed, the neoprimitivist ought to reply to the White European philosopher, "If we have our way, soon enough your people will no longer have a definite history of their own to lord over others, and we will all be better off for it."

World-Making

The artist makes sensations in a given world. — The artist composes sights (visual sensations), sounds (aural sensations), smells (olfactory sensations), tastes (gustatory sensations), touches (tactile sensations), etc.

The philosopher makes conceptions of a given world. — The philosopher establishes the significance, the whither and the wherefore, of different sights, sounds, smells, tastes, touches, etc.

The scientist makes predictions about a given world. — The scientist figures out whether and how likely it is that one will encounter different sights, sounds, smells, tastes, touches, etc.

But neither the artist, nor the philosopher, nor the scientist can be said to make a world. — The making of a world precedes, exceeds, and succeeds the making of sensations, conceptions, and predictions. The world that we come to sense in and through art, and to conceive of in and through philosophy, and to make predictions about in and through science is a world that is taken for granted by the artist, the philosopher, and the scientist.

Relations are the makings of worlds, which is to say, in other words, that making a world means making relations. — Sensations, conceptions, and predictions articulate relations that precede, exceed, and succeed them. The figure of the artist enables us to *sense* existing relations, the figure of the philosopher enables us to *conceive* of existing relations, and the figure of the scientist enables us to make *predictions* about existing relations, but none of these figures actually make relations. *Making relations is an extra-artistic affair for the artist, an extra-philosophical affair for the philosopher, and an extra-scientific affair for the scientist.*

A world-making project is neither an artistic project, nor a philosophical project, nor scientific project. Rather, a world-making project is the condition for artistic, philosophical, and scientific projects. Thus, artists, philosophers, and scientists who cannot take the world that conditions their practices for granted find that they must act as world-makers *in addition to* acting as artists, philosophers, and scientists: they find that they must make the worlds that their artistic, philosophical, and scientific practices will then take for granted.

Only the most privileged artists, philosophers, and scientists working in our time can take their world for granted. The world news today is always bleak — Economic Crisis, Climate Disaster, the Great Thinning of Nature, and the Sixth Extinction — but don't get it twisted: it is not our world that is dying. Rather, it is our world that is killing us: the world that we have made, some of us willingly but most unwillingly, is poised to destroy the greater part of life as we know it. Our arts make sense of this deathly reality, our philosophies conceive of this deathly reality, and our sciences enable us to make predictions about this deathly reality. Ay, but our arts, philosophies, and sciences can do nothing in and of themselves to stop the unfolding of this deathly reality.

Art-qua-art, philosophy-qua-philosophy, and science-qua-science cannot, in and of themselves, make a better world. Better art, better philosophy, and better science in and of themselves will only better our awareness of the catastrophe that is this deathly world that we have made. To escape this catastrophe, we need better relations first, foremost, and above all else. Which is to say, in other words, that better art, better philosophy, and better science will either be the consequence of better relations or they will not be.

To do art, philosophy, and science alone is to do no more than run diagnostics on our relations. Running diagnostics and treating an illness are not at all the same thing. Refusing to invest in art, science, and philosophy means being unable to diagnose the ills of our relations, yes, but investing in art, philosophy, and science without regard for world-making will do nothing to treat the ills of our relations. Ay, and it seems to me that the diagnosis is in and has been in for a half century, if not two and a half centuries. What we need now is to treat the ills of our relations: to further refine our diagnosis without regard for finding treatments is dithering.

It is no wonder that many artists, philosophers, and scientists today are finding themselves called to be world-makers first and to be artists, philosophers, and scientists second. Which is to say, they are finding that they must put more time and energy into making relations and less into making sensations, conceptions, and predictions.

But what is a relation and how does it differ from a sensation, a conception, a prediction?

The wind whips across your face. You sense your face in relation to the wind, you sense the wind in relation to your face, you sense a world in which the wind and your face are related.

This particular sensation of the wind whipping your face is but one expression of the world in which the wind and your face are related, and this one expression of this relation does not exhaust the relation. The sensation of the wind gently caressing your face is another, different expression of the world in which the wind and your face are related.

Indeed, the world in which the wind and your face are related is the set of all the different possible sensations of the-wind-in-your-face/your-face-in-the-wind, of which the whipping wind and the caressing wind are but two of the possible sensations making up the set.

- The act of world making, the act of making relations, opens up or forecloses this set of possible sensations.

- The artistic act, the act of making of sensations, is the act of exploring this set of possible sensations by realizing some of its possibilities.

- The philosophical act, the act of making of conceptions, is the act of establishing priorities, deciding which sensations to realize from this set of possible sensations and in what order to realize them.

- The scientific act, the act of making of predictions, is the act of figuring probabilities, the act figuring out the likelihood that certain sensations within this set of possible sensations will be actualized.

Whether begrudgingly or exuberantly, no artist is exempted from doing philosophy and science, no philosopher is exempted from doing art and science, and no scientist is exempted from doing art and philosophy.

Indeed, before specialization made us believe that art, philosophy, and science could be separate and distinct disciplines, the artistic act, the philosophical act, and the scientific act were often performed together, with a single fluid gesture, by ritual figures like that of the medicine man, the oracle, the shaman, and the witch.

The specialization of the artist, the philosopher, and the scientist in our time is responsible for the mistaken impression, held by many, that art, philosophy, and science are practices that can make worlds in and of themselves.

In our world, those who have been made to specialize in the different disciplines must compete for scarce resources, and this competition compels them to claim that their own specific discipline is the one that grounds all the others. The specialist in art is compelled to claim that art grounds philosophy and science; the specialist in philosophy is compelled to claim that philosophy grounds art and science; and the specialist in the sciences is compelled to claim that their science grounds art and philosophy.

What gets lost in these competing claims is the practice of world-making, which is the proper ground of art, philosophy, and science. It is when the artistic act, the philosophical act, and the scientific act are performed together, with a single fluid gesture, that we realize that we must find the ground of art and philosophy and science elsewhere, in world-making.

The act of world-making is the act of making of statements ("epistemic relations"), making of implements ("technical relations"), and making of environments ("spatiotemporal relations") that taken together condition the makings of sensations, conceptions, and predictions.

Figures like the medicine man, the oracle, the shaman, and the witch tend not only to act as artists, philosophers, and scientists all at once but, more profoundly still, these figures tend to act as world-makers first, foremost, and above all else — making statements, implements, and environments together, with a single fluid gesture, prior to making sensations, conceptions, and predictions with a subsequent gesture. The "charms" of the medicine man, the oracle, the shaman, and the witch are the "sleights of hand" in and through which their primary world-making gestures deftly anticipate the secondary gestures with which they make sensations in, conceptions of, and predictions about the worlds that they have made.

Today, as many who previously specialized in art, philosophy, and science find themselves called to be world-makers first and to be artists, philosophers, and scientists second, it is no wonder that many are coming to regard the "charms" of medicine men, oracles, shamans, and witches with less prejudice and incredulity and with more wonder and appreciation.

The makings of statements, implements, and environments together constitute the makings of worlds.

A statement, or "epistemic relation", is a set of possible senses of understanding.

- Art realizes different senses of understanding, philosophy prioritizes different senses of understanding, science figures the likelihood of realizing different senses of understanding, but art, philosophy, and science always take certain statements as given in doing so.
- The making of statements — the act of world-making which opens up or forecloses different possible senses of understanding — is an extra-artistic, extra-philosophical, and extra-scientific affair. World making gives us statements rather than taking them as given.

An implement, or "technical relation", is a set of possible senses of affordance.

- Art realizes different senses of affordance, philosophy prioritizes different senses of affordance, science figures the likelihood of realizing different senses of affordance, but art, philosophy, and science always take certain implements as given in doing so.
- The making of implements — the act of world-making which opens up or forecloses different possible senses of affordance — is an extra-artistic, extra-philosophical, and extra-scientific affair. World making gives us implements rather than taking them as given.

An environment, or "spatiotemporal relation", is a set of possible senses of place.

- Art realizes different senses of place, philosophy prioritizes different senses of place, science figures the likelihood of realizing different senses of place, but, art, philosophy, and science always take certain environments as given in doing so.
- The making of environments — the act of world-making which opens up or forecloses different possible senses of place — is an extra-artistic, extra-philosophical, and extra-scientific affair. World making gives us environments rather than taking them as given.

Regard the laboratory of a scientist, which is one world amongst others. Before the scientist can conduct science there, the world of the laboratory has to be made in and through the making statements, implements, and environments.

What people call the "difference between the laboratory and the real world" is a misnomer because the world of the laboratory is as real as any other. The "difference between the lab and the outside world" is perhaps a little less of a misnomer, but it is still a misnomer because there is more than one world outside of the laboratory. We should instead speak of the difference between the world of lab and the plurality of worlds outside the lab. The plurality of worlds outside the lab are no less constructed than the world of the lab: the plurality of worlds outside of the lab are composed of statements, implements, and environments, like the lab but different. Indeed, what differentiates lab results from "real world" results are the differences between those statements, implements, and environments that compose the lab and those that compose worlds outside of the lab.

The construction of the laboratory is the construction of a world in which a certain scientific results can be achieved, ipso facto, achieving a scientific result outside of the laboratory means constructing worlds outside of the laboratory that are more and more like the world of the laboratory. The scientist who is deeply concerned with doing science in worlds outside of their lab is the scientist who is called to be a world-maker first and a scientist second. The same could be said of the artist who is deeply concerned with doing art in worlds outside of their studio and of the philosopher who is deeply concerned with doing philosophy in worlds outside of their study — such artists and philosophers are called to be world-makers first and artists and philosophers second. But these calls to make worlds should not simply be calls to make outside worlds more and more like the world inside of one's lab, or studio, or study. Rather, these calls to make worlds should be calls to (de-/re-)construct the world of one's lab, studio, or seminar room so as to prefigure worlds that one would like to (de-/re-)construct outside of one's lab, studio, or seminar room.

Beyond Disciplines

When I first began thinking up the (De-/Re-)Constructing Worlds project, I felt compelled to return to the book *Hold Everything Dear* by John Berger and to a particular passage that has been and continues to be decisive for me. This passage, from the essay "Where Are We?", is quoted at length below.

> People everywhere – under very different conditions – are asking themselves – where are we? The question is historical, not geographical. What are we living through? Where are we being taken? What have we lost? How to continue without a plausible vision of the future? Why have we lost any view of what is beyond a lifetime?
>
> The well-heeled experts answer: Globalization. Post-Modernism. Communications Revolution. Economic Liberalism. The terms are tautological and evasive. To the anguished question of *Where are we?* the experts murmur: Nowhere!
>
> Might it not be better to see and declare that we are living through the most tyrannical – because the most pervasive – chaos that has ever existed? It's not easy to grasp the nature of the tyranny, for its power structure (ranging from the 200 largest multinational corporations to the Pentagon) is interlocking yet diffuse, dictatorial yet anonymous, ubiquitous yet placeless. It tyrannizes from offshore – not only in terms of fiscal law, but in terms of any political control beyond its own. Its aim is to delocalize the entire world. Its ideological strategy [...] is to undermine the existent so that everything collapses into its special version of the virtual, from the realm of which – and this is the tyranny's credo – there will be a never-ending source of profit. It sounds stupid. Tyrannies are stupid. This one is destroying at every level the life of the planet on which it operates.

[...] Most analyses and prognoses about what is happening are understandably presented and studied within the framework of their separate disciplines: economics, politics, media studies, public health, ecology, national defence, criminology, education, etc. In reality each of these separate fields is joined to another to make up the real terrain of what is being lived. It happens that in their lives, people suffer from wrongs which are classified in separate categories, whereas they suffer them simultaneously and inseparably.

A current example: some Kurds, who fled last week to Cherbourg and have been refused asylum by the French government and risk being repatriated to Turkey, are poor, politically undesirable, landless, exhausted, illegal and the clients of nobody. And they suffer each of these conditions at one and the same second!

To take in what is happening, an interdisciplinary vision is necessary in order to connect the 'fields' which are institutionally kept separate. And any such vision is bound to be (in the original sense of the word) political. The precondition for thinking politically on a global scale is to see the unity of the unnecessary suffering taking place.

Today, I am writing to you about what I think Berger meant when he called for "an interdisciplinary vision" that is "bound to be political". I am writing about this today because most of what passes for inter-disciplinary or trans-disciplinary thinking in our time does not approach what Berger called for, and I would like do my small part to change that.

When Berger wrote that, "we are living through the most tyrannical – because the most pervasive – chaos that has ever existed", Berger was recognizing a fact that has only become more and more obvious in the two decades since he wrote it. The increasingly obvious fact is that crisis has become the primary mode of government in our world. Crisis as a mode of government works by conceiving of the world in terms of so many different crises that are to be studied separately by "subject matter experts" in different fields, and then managed separately or in tandem by so many different specialized bureaucracies.

Crisis as a mode of government demands that the public health crisis be given its own experts and specialized bureaucracies, that the climate crisis be given its own, that the migrant and refugee crisis be given its own, that the unemployment and underemployment crises be given their own, and so on and so forth.

As Berger notes, however, in reality each of these separate crises is joined to another to make up the real terrain of the chaos that we are living in and through. We live all of these crises "simultaneously and inseparably" but the specialization of our tools, our knowledges, and our institutions conspire to keep us from addressing these crises in connection with one another. This is to say, in other words, that our tools, our knowledges, and our institutions force us to address each of these crises separately, dismembering and dissecting our lives. This manner of managing crises leaves each of us with the nearly impossible task of re-animating our lives from so many disparate parts: we somehow have to suture together what our specialized tools, knowledges, and institutions have butchered, and then we have to try and shock the resulting assemblage into life.

On the one hand, for the poor, crisis as a mode of government looks like going from one social service provider to the next, having your life dismembered and dissected, piece by piece, and then having to find some way to maintain the disparate pieces that have been handed back to you. The poor person goes from the housing services provider charged with addressing the housing crisis, to the unemployment services provider charged with addressing the employment crisis, to the healthcare services provider charged with addressing the public health crisis, to the immigration services provider charged with addressing the migration and refugee crisis, to the nutrition assistance provider charged with addressing the hunger crisis, to the education and training services provider charged with addressing the skills gap crisis. And is it any wonder that the poor are constantly struggling to keep themselves together?

On the other hand, for the rich, crisis as a mode of government looks like being able to hire so many specialists — some human, some algorithmic — to maintain your dismembered and dissected life for you. Which is to say, in other words, that the rich person pays others to keep it all together for them. Today, the relatively rich person trying to keep it together can say, "I've got an app for that." And the really rich person can say, "I'll put my people on it."

Either way, for rich and poor alike in today's world, life and its sufferings are dismembered and dissected into separate parts that are tended to separately and then put back together. Against all these dismemberments and dissections, I hold fast to what Berger called a political vision which presupposes the unity of life and its sufferings. This vision demands that we (de-/re-)construct our tools, knowledges, and institutions so as to enable us tend to life and its sufferings in their unity. Indeed, as I see it, and as Berger saw it before me, the tyrannical chaos that we are living through is the result of prioritizing our specialized tools, knowledges, and institutions over and above the unity of life and its sufferings. Going further, I hold that the prioritization of specialized tools, knowledges, and institutions yields the mistaken belief that many of life's present sufferings are not only unavoidable but are necessary, whether to promote "economic growth" or "technological progress" or "national security" or "fairness". By contrast, as Berger writes, tending to the unity of life and its sufferings above all else means affirming "the contestation (which we all acknowledge somewhere but, out of powerlessness, dismiss) that much of the present suffering could be alleviated or avoided if certain realistic and relatively simple decisions were taken."

So, the obvious next question is, how does one tend to the unity of life and its sufferings? Well, I would like to propose that one tends to the unity of life and its sufferings like one tends to the unity of the body and its organs.

My body as a unit and my left hand as a part of my body are not identical with one another. To the contrary, they are obviously different from one another: my left hand can be severed from my body, and my body can survive the severing of my left hand if properly tended to. At the same time, however, my left hand will remain integral to my body even after having been severed from it: my severed left hand will haunt my body, as a phantom limb, for as long as my body survives it.

Our specialized tools, knowledges, and institutions first dismember and dissect our bodies and then they concern themselves with maintaining the organs they have separated out, apart from our bodies. They do not concern themselves with our bodies, which suffer the organs that have been parted from them. Many, if not most, inter-disciplinary and trans-disciplinary projects fail to grasp this and, thus, lack a political vision.

Failed inter-disciplinary and trans-disciplinary projects take the existence of so many organs without bodies for granted and try to construct "complex systems" from these various dissociated organs. These projects do not recognize that the organs they take for granted were parted from bodies that preceded and exceeded them. Moreover, these projects do not recognize that these bodies may survive and suffer the organs that have been parted from them. Ay, and these projects do not recognize that these surviving and suffering bodies deserve far greater attention than the organs that have been parted from them.

Rather than taking so many organs without bodies for granted, a political vision primarily attends to suffering bodies, to bodies without organs, bodies haunted by the organs that they are deprived of.

For example, rather than asking how we can make connections between the separate organs that are charged with, say, addressing the housing crisis on one hand and the public health crisis on the other, we should instead ask from what body have these two organs been parted and how can we tend to that suffering body. Tending to that suffering body might mean re-connecting one or both of these organs back to the suffering body or it might mean enabling the suffering body to survive without one or both of these organs. In other words, it may be that the organs addressing the housing crisis and the organs addressing the public health crisis have both become so detached and remote from the suffering social body that these organs need to be given up. Indeed, perhaps there are other organs closer to and still connected to the suffering social body that we might turn to so as to ease the sufferings of the body in lieu of these detached and remote organs.

The mistake is to prioritize connecting separate organs to one another, because this means prioritizing the maintenance of the parted organs over and above the sufferings of the body from which they were parted. Imagine two doctors, one whose top priority is keeping patients' hearts beating and the other whose top priority is keeping patients' lungs breathing. Imagine that, when these doctors collaborate, neither one tends to the well-being of patients' suffering bodies, that they only work together to ensure that the patients' hearts and lungs work in tandem.

Imagine the unfortunate results of these collaborations: so many braindead bodies otherwise wasting away but connected to machines and attended to by servants that keep their hearts beating and their lungs breathing in tandem. This is precisely what many have taken to calling inter-disciplinary and trans-disciplinary thinking.

To avoid this deathly mistake means prioritizing the suffering body first and foremost, and this sometimes means sacrificing the maintenance of organs that can be parted from the body. It follows from this that inter-disciplinary and trans-disciplinary thinking shouldn't be about connecting more and more disparate disciplines together. Rather, it should be about re-connecting disciplines back to suffering bodies. Ay, and if a discipline cannot be re-connected to any suffering bodies so as to ease their suffering, then inter-disciplinary and trans-disciplinary thinking should recommend sacrificing discipline in order to tend to suffering bodies.

Living Worlds

A LIVING WORLD respects the unity of life and its sufferings, and it maintains and multiplies the wholeness of life.

A DEATHLY WORLD dismembers and dissects life and its sufferings, and it maintains and multiplies the parts that it plucks from life without respect for the wholeness of life.

The architect Christopher Alexander has proposed that the fundamental characteristic of a living world is that it is composed of "strong centers" or, to use an alternative term much more to my liking, Alexander has proposed that a living world is composed of STRONG FOCI. These strong foci are themselves, in turn, composed by and through processes that Alexander calls "structure preserving transformations". Alexander finds fifteen of these processes in sum total, though he does not find that all fifteen of them are always needed to create a living world.

Being an architect, Alexander is primarily concerned with applying these "structure preserving transformations" to built environments in order to deconstruct deathly worlds and (re-)construct living worlds. Thinking through and beyond Alexander, I hold that the makings of meaningful statements and useful implements alongside built environments are, together, what constitute the makings of worlds. Consequently, I am interested in applying "structure preserving transformations" to meaningful statements and useful implements alongside built environments in order to deconstruct deathly worlds and (re-)construct living worlds.

The text below provides Alexander's own definitions of the fifteen structure preserving transformations that he identified. In the bullet points below each of Alexander's definitions, you will also find my own thoughts about the ways in which these processes apply not only to built environments but also to useful implements and to meaningful statements.

LEVELS OF SCALE is "the way that a strong focus is made stronger partly by smaller foci contained in it, and partly by larger foci which contain it and relate it to other foci on its level."

· With respect to a given built environment — take an apartment building for instance — there are the several different "sub-environments" that are features of the given built environment — e.g., the hallways, stairwells, common use areas, parking garages, and the different apartments and their rooms. And then, of course, there are the "super-environments" or "encompassing landscapes" that count the given built environment as but one feature alongside others — the neighborhood that contains our apartment building, for instance, will have many other buildings in it and there will be built spaces between the many buildings in the neighborhood. Levels of scale are constructed (i) when the placements of the features within a given environment strengthen the foci of the given environment, and (ii) when the placements of the given environment relative to other environments in its encompassing landscape also strengthen the foci of the given environment.

· With respect to a given useful implement — take a hammer, for instance — there are the different features that make up the given implement — e.g., the hammer's handle, its neck, its face, its claw. And then there are the encompassing toolkits that count the given implement as but one feature amongst others — the toolkit containing the hammer, for instance, may also contain screwdrivers, pliers, a tape measure, etc. Levels of scale are constructed (i) when the affordances of the features of the given implement strengthen the focus of the given implement, and (ii) when the affordances of the given implement relative to those of other implements in its encompassing toolkit also strengthen the focus of the given implement.

· With respect to a meaningful statement — the "series of letters, A, Z, E, R, T, listed in a [French] typewriting manual" — there are the signifiers that are features of the given statement — e.g., "A", "Z", "E", "R", and "T". And then there are the encompassing discourses that count the given statement as but one feature amongst others — a discourse around French typewriting might also contain a number of tables denoting of how prevalent accented letters and ligatures are in commonly written French words. Levels of scale are constructed (i) when the interpretations of the features of the given statement strengthen the focus of the statement, and (ii) when the interpretations of the given statement relative to other statements in its encompassing discourse also strengthen the focus of the given statement.

115

LEVELS OF SCALE
"... the small foci intensify the large ones ...
the large foci also intensify the small ones
..."

STRONG CENTERS
"The great courtyard, the large dome, the smaller dome, the individual battlements,
the steps, the entrance, the individual arches, even the segments on the roof ... the
sequence of three domes, each one higher than the other, leading up to the main dome
as a pinnacle. The entire structure builds up to the main dome ..."

STRONG CENTERS defines "the way that a strong focus requires a special field-like effect, created by other foci, as the primary source of its strength."

- "Strong centers" are constructed when a built environment that has a strong focus itself becomes the focus of a series of supporting environments in its encompassing landscape.

- "Strong centers" are constructed when a useful implement that has a strong focus itself becomes the focus of a series of supporting implements in its encompassing toolkit.

- "Strong centers" are constructed when a meaningful statement that has a strong focus itself becomes the focus of a series supporting statements in its encompassing discourse.

BOUNDARIES

"The door as a focus is intensified by placing a beautiful frame of foci around that door. The smaller foci in the boundary are also intensified, reciprocally, by the larger focus which they surround ..."

BOUNDARIES defines "the way in which the field-like effect of a focus is strengthened by the creation of a ring-like focus, made of supporting foci which surround and intensify the first. The boundary also unites the focus with the foci beyond it, thus strengthening it further."

- Again, a built environment that has a strong focus will become the focus of other supporting environments in its encompassing landscape. Boundaries are constructed when these supporting environments circumscribe the environment that is the primary focus. This is to say, in other words, that the placement of the primary environment come to be circumscribed by the placement of its supporting environments, and the placement of supporting environments also relates the primary environment to other environments that do not necessarily support the primary environment.

- Again, a useful implement that has a strong focus will become the focus of other supporting implements in its encompassing toolkit. Boundaries are constructed when these supporting implements circumscribe the implement that is the primary focus. This is to say, in other words, that the affordances of the primary implement come to be circumscribed by the affordances of its supporting implements, and the affordances of supporting implements also relates the primary implement to other implements that do not necessarily support the primary implement.

- Again, a meaningful statement that has a strong focus will become the focus of other supporting statements in its encompassing discourse. Boundaries are constructed when these supporting statements circumscribe the statement that is the primary focus. This is to say, in other words, that the interpretations of the primary statement come to be circumscribed by the interpretations of its supporting statements, and the interpretations of supporting statements also relate the primary statement to other statements that do not necessarily support the primary statement.

ALTERNATING REPETITION

"... in Brunelleschi's Foundling Hospital, the round medallions alternate within the columns and column bays. We see the columns repeating ... the arches repeating ... space of bays repeating ... triangular space between adjacent arches repeating ... ceramic roundels in these triangles repeating ... Each of these things ... is a profoundly formed and living focus. The result is beautifully harmonious and has life."

ALTERNATING REPETITION is "the way in which foci are strengthened when they repeat, by the insertion of other foci between the repeating ones."

- Alternated repetition is constructed by repeated placements of one built feature in alternation with other such features of a given environment or encompassing landscape.

- Alternated repetition is constructed by repeated uses of one useful feature in alternation with other such features of a given implement or encompassing toolkit.

- Alternated repetition is constructed by repeated articulations of one meaningful feature in alternation with other such features of a given statement or encompassing discourse

POSITIVE SPACE [AND TIME]

"In this plan each bit of every street is positive, the building masses are positive, the public interiors are positive. There is virtually no part of the whole which does not have definite and positive shape. This has come about, I think, because of how these spaces ... have been shaped over time by people who cared about them, and they have therefore taken a definite, cared for shape with meaning and purpose ..."

"In the present Western view ... we tend to see buildings floating in empty space ... the buildings ... have their own definite physical shape — but the space which they are floating in is shapeless, making the buildings almost meaningless in their isolation. This has a devastating effect: it makes our social space itself — the glue and playground of our common public world — incoherent, almost non-existent ..."

POSITIVE SPACE [AND TIME] is "the way that a given focus must draw its strength, in part, from the strength of other foci immediately adjacent to them."

· To create positive space [and time], a built feature must draw its strength of focus, in part, from the focus of other built features placed immediately beside them in space [and immediately before and after them in time].

· To create positive space [and time], a useful feature must draw its strength of focus, in part, from the focus of other useful features that are put to use immediately beside them in space [and immediately before and after them in time].

· To create positive space [and time], a meaningful feature must draw its strength of focus, in part, from the focus of other meaningful features interpreted immediately beside them in space [and immediately before and after them in time].

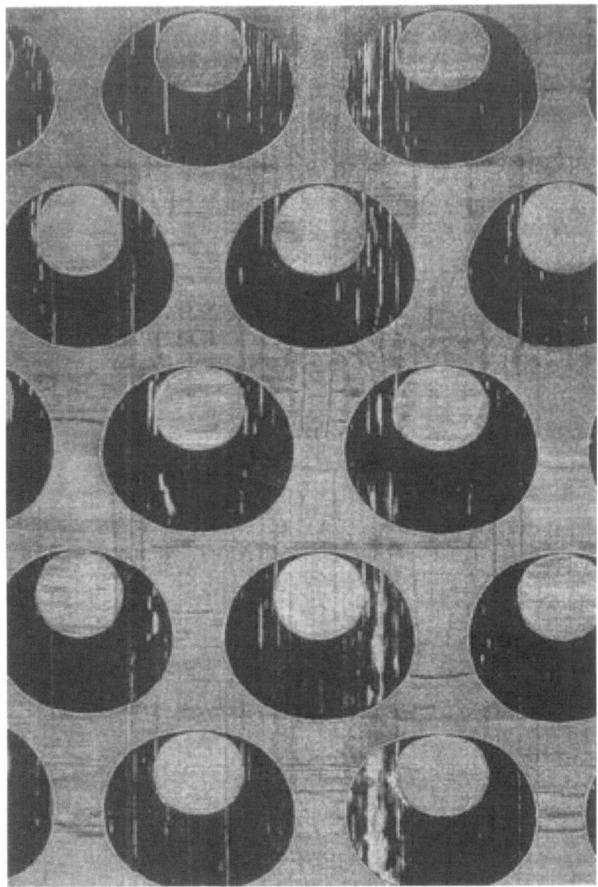

GOOD FORM

"The good form is an attribute of the whole configuration, not
of the parts; but it comes about when the whole is made of parts
that are themselves whole in this rather simple geometric sense
..."

"... The high degree of sophistication needed to make a circle
have good form is seen in the fabulous Ottoman velvet ... where
the two systems of circles are drawn slightly distorted so that the
moon shapes, the space between the circles, and the small circles
and large circles all work as foci."

GOOD FORM is "the way that the strength of a given focus depends on its actual form, and the way this effect requires that even the form, its boundary, and the space and time around it are made up of strong foci."

- To create good form, every built feature of a given environment or encompassing landscape should contribute to the strength of focus of other such features of its given environment or encompassing landscape.

- To create good form, every useful feature of a given implement or encompassing toolkit should contribute to the strength of focus of other such features of its given implement or toolkit.

- To create good form, every meaningful feature of a given statement or encompassing discourse should contribute to the strength of focus of other such features of its given statement or encompassing discourse.

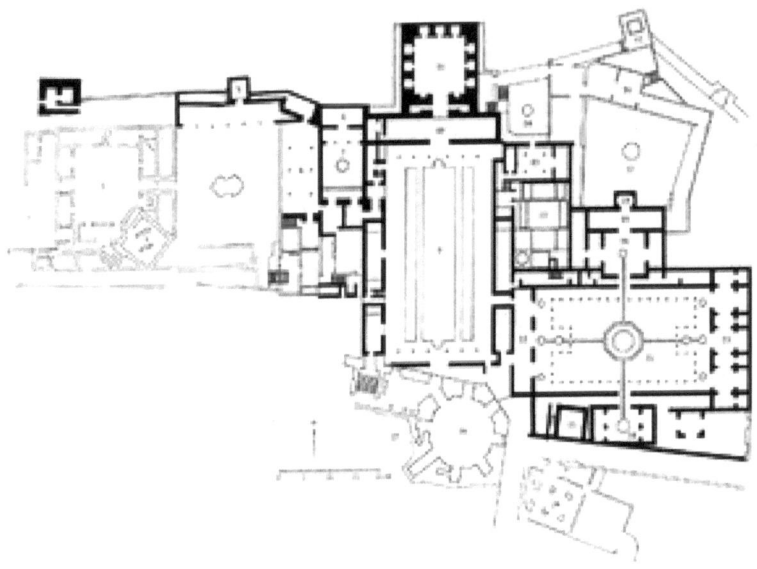

LOCAL SYMMETRIES

"We see this clearly in the Alhambra ... a marvel of living wholeness. It has no overall symmetry at all, but an amazing number of minor symmetries, which hold within limited pieces of the design, leaving the whole to be organic, flexible, adapted to the site."

LOCAL SYMMETRIES defines "the way that the intensity of a given focus is increased by the extent to which other smaller foci which it contains are themselves arranged in locally symmetrical groups."

- The built features of a given environment or encompassing landscape should be placed in such a way to create local symmetries amongst them.

- The useful features of a given implement or encompassing toolkit should be used in such a way to create local symmetries amongst them.

- The meaningful features of a given statement or encompassing discourse should be interpreted in such a way to create local symmetries amongst them .

DEEP INTERLOCK AND AMBIGUITY

"In a surprisingly large number of cases, living structures contain some form of interlock: situations where foci are 'hooked' into their surroundings. This has the effect of making it difficult to disentangle the focus from its surroundings."

"... a similar unification is accomplished through the creation of spatial ambiguity ... a common example ... is the house with a gallery or arcade round it ... the space in the gallery belongs to the outside world and yet simultaneously belongs to the building."

DEEP INTERLOCK AND AMBIGUITY is "the way in which the intensity of a given focus can be increased when it is attached to a nearby focus, through a third set of foci that ambiguously belong to both."

- Again, a built environment that has a strong focus will become the focus of other supporting environments in its encompassing landscape. These supporting environments should circumscribe the environment that is the primary focus. This is to say, in other words, that the placement of the primary environment ought to be circumscribed by the placement of its supporting environments, and the placement of supporting environments should also relate the primary environment to other environments that do not support the primary environment. Furthermore, these supporting environments should ambiguously belong to the primary environment and to the other non-supporting environments that they relate the primary environment to.

- Again, a useful implement that has a strong focus will become the focus of other supporting implements in its encompassing toolkit. These supporting implements should circumscribe the implement that is the primary focus. This is to say, in other words, that the affordances of the primary implement ought to be circumscribed by the affordances of its supporting implements, and the affordances of supporting implements should also relate the primary implement to other implements that do not support the primary implement. Furthermore, these supporting implements should ambiguously belong to the primary implement and to the other non-supporting implements that they relate the primary implement to.

- Again, a meaningful statement that has a strong focus will become the focus of other supporting statements in its encompassing discourse. These supporting statements should circumscribe the statement that is the primary focus. This is to say, in other words, that the interpretations of the primary statement ought to be circumscribed by the interpretations of its supporting statements, and the interpretations of supporting statements should also relate the primary statement to other statements that do not support the primary. Furthermore, these supporting statements should ambiguously belong to the primary statement and to the other non-supporting statements that they relates the primary statement to.

Contrast in a Shaker schoolroom

CONTRAST

"In the case of the Shaker classroom ... the two bands of wood above shoulder level, because of contrast, form a definite focus which would not be there or felt strongly — if the wood were pale ... The focus which is so formed helps the room to become one, unified ..."

CONTRAST is "the way that a foci is strengthened by the sharpness of the distinction between its character and the character of surrounding foci."

- The placements of the environment that is the primary focus should contrast with the placements of the environments that support and circumscribe it.

- The affordances of the implement that is a primary focus should contrast with the uses of the implements that support and circumscribe it.

- The interpretations of the statement that is a primary focus should contrast with the articulations of statements that support and circumscribe it.

GRADIENTS

"... Gradients must arise in the world when the world is in harmony with itself simply because conditions vary. Qualities vary, so foci which are adapted to them respond by varying in size, spacing, intensity and character. Daylight varies from the top floor of an urban building to the bottom floor: both windows and ceiling heights will probably have to vary to adapt to these conditions ..."

"... These gradients will also form foci because the field-like character which is needed to make every strong focus is precisely that oriented, changing condition which 'points' towards the focus of the focus ..."

"Buildings and artifacts without gradients are more mechanical. They have less life to them, because there is no slow variation which reveals the inner wholeness ..."

"... although gradients are commonplace in nature and in much traditional folk art, they are nearly non-existent in much of the modern environment. That is, I think, because the naive forms of standardization, mass production ... and regulation of sizes ... all work against the formation of gradients, and almost do not allow them to occur."

GRADIENTS defines "the way in which a focus is strengthened by a graded series of foci which then "point" to the new foci and intensify its field effect."

- The placements of the environments that are of primary focus should involve the placement of graded series of built features whose placements strengthen the primary focus.

- The affordances of the implements that are of primary focus should involve the affordances of graded series of useful features whose uses strengthen the primary focus..

- The interpretation of the statements that are of primary focus should involve the interpretations graded series of meaningful features whose articulations strengthen the primary focus.

ROUGHNESS

"... The seemingly rough arrangement is more precise because it comes from a much more careful guarding of the essential foci in the design."

"... Roughness can never be consciously or deliberately created. Then it is merely contrived. To make a thing live, its roughness must be the product of endlessness, the product of no will ... Roughness is always the product of abandon — it is created whenever a person is truly free, and doing only what is essential."

"... Roughness does not seek to superimpose an arbitrary order over a design, but instead lets the larger order be relaxed, modified according to the demands and constraints which happen locally in different parts of the design."

ROUGHNESS is "the way that the field effect of a given foci draws its strength, necessarily, from irregularities in the scales, forms and arrangements of other nearby foci."

- The environments that support and circumscribe a primary environment should have features that seem to vary randomly in their placements.

- The implements that support and circumscribe a primary implement should have features that seem to vary randomly in their affordances.

- The statements that support and circumscribe a primary statement should have features that seem to vary randomly in their interpretations.

ECHOES

"... in the Himalayan monastery all the parts — stones, caps, doors, and steps — are heavily square with a line and a shallow angle ... In Thyangboche, the monastery in the foothills of Everest, we feel in some profound and subtle way that this building is part of the mountains: part of the Himalayas themselves. The angles of the roofs, the way the small roof sits on the larger roof, the 'peak' on the largest roof, the band below the roof edge — all reflect or echo one another, and echo the structural feeling of the mountains themselves."

ECHOES defines "the way that the strength of a given foci depends on similarities of inclination and orientation and systems of foci forming characteristic inclinations thus forming larger foci, among the foci it contains."

- Relations between a primary environment and its supporting environments in a given landscape should echo the relations between other primary environments and their supporting environments in the given landscape.

- Relations between a primary implement and its supporting implements in a given toolkit should echo the relations between other primary implements and their supporting implements in the given toolkit.

- Relations between a primary statement and its supporting statements in a given discourse should echo the relations between other primary statements and their supporting statements in the given discourse.

THE VOID

"In the most profound foci which have perfect wholeness, there is at the heart a void which is like water, infinite in depth, surrounded by and contrasted with the clutter of the stuff and fabric all around it ..."

THE WAR ON TERRA & THE NEW UNDERGROUND RAILROAD

THE VOID is "the way that the intensity of every foci depends on the existence of a still place — an empty foci — somewhere in its field."

- Every built feature of a given environment or landscape should draw strength of focus from the unbuilt features that are a part of the given environment or landscape.

- Every useful feature of a given implement or toolkit should draw strength of focus from the useless features of the given statement or discourse.

- Every meaningful feature of a given statement or discourse should draw strength of focus from the meaningless features that are a part of the given statement or discourse.

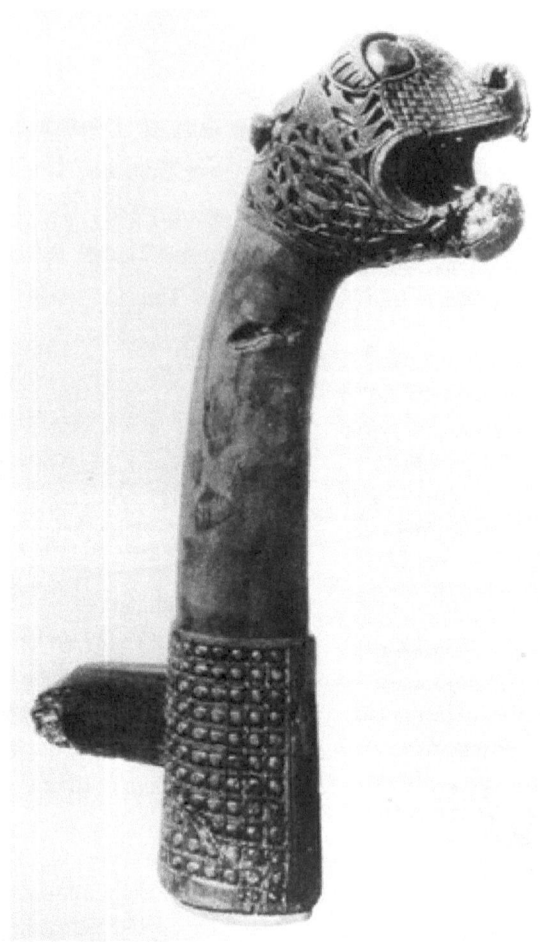

A carved Norwegian dragon. Very complex, but it still has inner calm.

SIMPLICITY AND INNER CALM

"The quality comes about when everything unnecessary is removed. All foci that are not actively supporting other foci are stripped out, cut out, excised. What is left, when boiled away, is the structure in a state of inner calm. It is essential that the great beauty and intricacy of ornament go only just far enough to bring this calm into being, and not so far that it destroys it ..."

"Simplicity and inner calm is not only to be produced by simplicity ... the wild Norwegian dragon ... has inner calm even though it is so complex ... So it is not true that outward simplicity creates inner calm; it is only inner simplicity."

THE WAR ON TERRA & THE NEW UNDERGROUND RAILROAD

SIMPLICITY AND INNER CALM is "the way the strength of a foci depends on its simplicity — on the process of reducing the number of different foci which exist in it, while increasing the strength of these foci to make them weigh more."

·   Aim to reduce the number of built features belonging to an environment and its encompassing landscape while also strengthening the foci of the environment and its encompassing landscape.

·   Aim to reduce the number of useful features belonging to an implement and its encompassing toolkit while also strengthening the foci of the implement and its encompassing toolkit.

·   Aim to reduce the number of meaningful features belonging to a statement and its encompassing discourses while also strengthening the foci of the statement and its encompassing discourse.

NOT-SEPARATENESS

"The correct connection to the world will only be made if you are conscious, willing, that the thing you make be indistinguishable from its surroundings, that, truly, you cannot tell where one ends and the next begins, and you do not even want to be able to do so."

"The sophisticated version of this rule, which comes about when we apply the rule recursively to its own products ... which ties the whole together inside itself, which never allows one part to be too proud, to stand out too sharp against the next, but assures that each part melts into its neighbors, just as the whole melts into its neighbors, too."

NOT-SEPARATENESS is "the way the life and strength of a focus depends on the extent to which that focus is merged smoothly — sometimes even indistinguishably — with the foci that form its surroundings."

- Each built feature of an environment or landscape should merge smoothly with the other built (and unbuilt) features in its vicinity.

- Each useful feature of an implement or toolkit should merge smoothly with the other useful (and useless) features in its vicinity.

- Each meaningful feature of a statement or discourse should merge smoothly with the other meaningful (and meaningless) features in its vicinity

Pivotal Processes

The previous dispatch examined the fifteen processes (or "structure preserving transformations") that the architect Christopher Alexander found to be pivotal to the deconstruction of deathly worlds and the (re-)construction of living worlds.

In considering the specific kinds of living worlds that I would (re-)construct, I have found that, while all fifteen of these processes have their place in my worlds, some are more pivotal to my worlds than others. The most pivotal processes to my worlds are the processes of (i) NOT-SEPARATENESS, (ii) DEEP INTERLOCK AND AMBIGUITY, (iii) ROUGHNESS, and (iv) SIMPLICITY AND INNER CALM. These four processes are the most pivotal to my worlds because they produce the defining features of my worlds in ways that would enable me superpose my worlds together.

The text below sketches out how and why it is that these four processes are the most pivotal to my worlds.

...worlds in which humanisms would be overturned and primitivisms would be revalued...

Humanisms have endeavored to separate culture from nature: they have celebrated the refinement of civilized cultures that have broken with nature, and they have denigrated the roughness of primitive cultures bound up with nature. In doing so, humanisms have decimated the deep interlocks and ambiguities that exist between culture and nature. The overturning of humanisms and the revaluation of primitivisms aims to further the NOT-SEPARATENESS of culture and nature by (i) embracing the ROUGHNESS of primitive cultures that are bound up with nature, and (ii) strengthening and multiplying the DEEP INTERLOCKS AND AMBIGUITIES that exist between culture and nature.

What's more, humanisms have wagered that the increasing complexities and neuroses that attend the refinement of civilized cultures are the necessary evils that attend all progress and development. The overturning of humanisms and the revaluing of primitivisms, by contrast, wagers that increasing SIMPLICITY AND INNER CALM is the sign of profound progress and development, while increasing complexity and neurosis is the sign of superficial progress and development.

...worlds in which the radicalism of everyday sense would counter both the populisms of common sense and the elitisms of higher senses and reasons...

Pivotal to radical everydayness is, first and foremost, ROUGHNESS. That which makes everyday sense is never exact in its measures because that which makes everyday sense must make do with whatever measures are available on any given day. Also pivotal to radical everydayness is SIMPLICITY AND INNER CALM. That which makes everyday sense is never exacting in its demands on the body and the psyche because that which makes everyday sense must be done day after day without doing irreparable harm to the body and the psyche.

...worlds in which working-for would be abolished in favor of working-with...

The most pivotal process to abolition is that of DEEP INTERLOCK AND AMBIGUITY. Abolition proceeds by creating ambiguity regarding who is working for who in any given scenario, so much so that the only meaningful way to describe the scenario would be to say that the parties involved are working with one another. The concomitant result of all of this is the NOT-SEPARATENESS of employer and employee, producer and consumer, of creditor and debtor, etc.

...worlds in which ecoregionalisms, communisms, and dilettantisms would counter nationalist, capitalist, and careerist imperialisms...

Ecoregionalism demands that biogeochemical flows and processes (in)form the BOUNDARIES of self-organized communities. The boundaries of ecoregions are coherent when they are drawn in accord with biogeochemical flows and processes that construct STRONG CENTERS and GOOD FORMS. In addition, CONTRASTS amongst neighboring ecoregions will give their boundaries greater coherence. That being said, it must be noted that, insofar as they are determined by natural processes, the boundaries of ecoregions will inevitably be characterized by ROUGHNESS and by DEEP INTERLOCKS AND AMBIGUITIES. This is to say, in other words, that there will be no way to disentangle a given ecoregion from its neighbors because their boundaries are roughly and ambiguously drawn in accord with the vagaries of biogeochemical flows and processes. As a result, different ecoregions will constantly have to cooperate and negotiate conflicts with one another about and around their boundaries, thereby ensuring their NOT-SEPARATENESS. But such conflict negotiation and cooperation will only be possible if each ecoregion can achieve SIMPLICITY AND INNER CALM thereby.

In principle, communism means "from each according to their abilities, to each according to their needs". In practice, communism means creating NOT-SEPARATENESS and DEEP INTERLOCKS AND AMBIGUITIES between one's abilities and another's needs and, vice versa, between one's needs and another's abilities. Insofar as abilities and needs both vary widely and wildly in their distribution, there will always be a ROUGHNESS about the matching of needs and abilities — one cannot hope to create a precise one-to-one match of abilities to needs. Rather, one can only construct so many rough matches amongst abilities and needs.

Pivotal to dilettantism is, first and foremost, the NOT-SEPARATENESS of the expert and the layperson and, concomitantly, a DEEP INTERLOCK AND AMBIGUITY between the expert and the layperson. Also pivotal to dilettantism is ROUGHNESS. Whereas the expert is at pains to refine their discipline into an exact science and to seek definitive proofs, the dilettante gladly lives with rough approximations and back-of-the-envelope calculations. This is to say, in other words, that dilettantism aims to construct a world in which exactness and definitive proofs are superfluous, which is, in other words, a world in which rough approximations and back-of-the-envelope calculations will always suffice. In so doing, a dilettantism tends to promote SIMPLICITY AND INNER CALM.

Countering Power

All power is power to mediate.

Power always mediates between contending factions.

The contending factions that a power mediates between may or may not precede the formation of a power. In other words, a power is either formed in response to the existence of contending factions or a power crafts contending factions as it form itself.

Taking racist powers as our informative anecdote, the contending factions that we call "races" did not precede the formation of the powers that mediate between them. Rather, "races" are constructs that racist powers create as they form themselves.

From this it follows that, on the one hand, to simply take the existence of races for granted is to take the workings of power for granted, and, on the other hand, to simply deny the existence of races is to make oneself oblivious to the workings of power.

Instead of simply taking the existence of races for granted or denying the existence of races, we must deconstruct the workings of power that bring races into existence.

Power, in order to perpetuate itself, must make "immediate relations" intolerable.

The power to mediate between factions becomes null and void if immediate relations between factions are tolerable, for then there is no call for there to be a mediator between factions.

The power to mediate between factions only functions when immediate relations between factions are made intolerable. Indeed, a power often forms itself by making immediate relations between existing factions intolerable or by crafting factions that are intolerant of one another. Power then functions by seizing upon intolerance between factions and mediating between them in the name of tolerance.

Returning to our informative anecdote, racist powers formed themselves by crafting factions, so-called "races", that were intolerant of one another. Racist powers will preach tolerance, yes, but they do so in order to make themselves the mediums and guarantors of tolerance.

Intolerance is the result of relative over-concentrations of properties amongst factions. Greater intolerance is generated when distributions of properties amongst factions are skewed so that one faction possesses desirable or undesirable properties in excess over others.

For example, there will be greater intolerance amongst whites and blacks if a desirable property, be it housing, education, or employment, is increasingly concentrated in white populations relative to black populations. A power formation can exploit this greater intolerance by casting itself as the means by which blacks can acquire the desirable property that they lack. Such a power formation does not endeavor to do away with lack but, rather, such a power formation endeavors to keep those suffering from an intolerable lack dependent upon it for a more tolerable existence.

An alternative example: there will be greater intolerance amongst whites and blacks if an undesirable property, like criminality, is increasingly concentrated in black populations relative to white populations. A power formation can exploit this greater intolerance by casting itself as the means by which the undesirable excesses of blacks can be pacified. Such a power formation does not endeavor to do away with the undesirable excesses but, rather, such a power formation endeavors to keep those who cannot tolerate undesirable excesses dependent upon it for a more tolerable existence.

149

To counter power is to make "immediate relations" tolerable and, thus, to obviate the want for a medium and guarantor of tolerance.

Taking "anti-racist criminal justice reforms" as our informative anecdote, one must be wary of attempts to create new commissions, offices, and task forces that will mediate between black populations and the police in order to guarantee that relations between black populations and the police become more tolerable: this approach redoubles our want for power instead of obviating it.

Whereas the power of the police pivots on blacks possessing the undesirable property of criminality in excess, the power of "social services" pivots on blacks lacking desirable properties like housing, education, and employment. Either way, both police and social service powers tell us that blacks have a problem: blacks are either excessive in their criminality or lacking in social niceties and necessities. Either way, both powers tell us that blacks will need more administration and greater supervision if they are going to live tolerably alongside whites. Both powers tell us that the freedom of blacks must be sacrificed, either to temper their excesses or to compensate for what they lack.

Intolerance is reduced and greater tolerance is achieved when distributions of properties amongst factions are varied in such a way that no property tends to be concentrated in any one faction. This dissipative variation of distributions is what liberates us from the want for power, from the want for more administration and greater supervision. Administration and supervision are all about identifying and separating out those factions that pose intolerable risks from those factions that cannot tolerate risks. Liberation, by contrast, is about sharing risks amongst different factions so that risks are made more tolerable for all the different factions, so that no faction needs to be identified and separated out from others for being a risk or for being at-risk.

Our age is defined by the ceaseless proliferation of administrative and supervisory organs that service "at-risk" populations, and this is a sign that our age is one in which "at-risk" populations are less free and more oppressed than in previous ages. This oppression may be less brazen than the oppressions of previous ages, yes, but this oppression is far more pervasive than the oppressions of previous ages. Indeed, oppression today can afford to be less brazen because it is so much more pervasive: e.g., the New Jim Crow can afford to be less brazen than the Old Jim Crow because it is far more pervasive than the Old Jim Crow.

Ruling powers are mediators that enable one faction to rule over others.

A ruling power is constituted by *ritualized spectacles* that organize subjugated factions according to a rule, the result being that the ruling faction stands out as an exception to the rule.

The sovereign stands, everybody else kneels: thus, the sovereign, as he who stands while others kneel, appears as the exception to the rule. The sovereign boldly demands taxes and tribute from his subjects, but everybody else receives the sovereign's beneficence: thus, the sovereign, as he who boldly demands while others humbly receive, appears as the exception to the rule.

The racism of the white supremacist invokes ruling powers. To put it in crude but accurate terms, the white supremacist wants all other races to kneel and pay tribute to the white race as a rule, the result being that the sovereign white race becomes the exception to the rule, standing tall and giving beneficence to the subject races.

It is important to note, however, that the ruling powers invoked by white supremacy do not belong to the sovereign white race but to the organs that administer and supervise the ritualized spectacles that maintain white supremacy. These mediating organs may or may not be serviced by white peoples. On the plantation, for instance, both the white overseer and the black "Uncle Tom" could effectively wield the ruling powers that maintained white supremacy.

Disciplinary powers are mediators that enable one faction to determine the norms that other factions are supposed to conform to.

Disciplinary powers are constituted by *routine examinations* that distinguish the stereotypical individuals belonging to a given faction from the atypical individuals belonging to the given faction.

The racism of the white meritocrat invokes disciplinary powers. The white meritocrat will make the untested anecdotal observation that the stereotypical black man has athletic ability but no mind for mathematics. As such, the white meritocrat, seeking to develop and exploit the "natural" talents of the stereotypical black man, will routinely send talent scouts and coaches to predominantly black high schools in order to examine for, discover, and develop those "natural" athletic talents stereotypically found in young black men. This same white meritocrat wouldn't bother sending talent scouts and coaches to examine for, discover, and develop talents for mathematics that are considered "unnatural" amongst black men: it is assumed that, because mathematical talents are not stereotypically found in black men, examining for mathematical talents in predominantly black schools is a waste of resources. Thus, the white meritocrat will only examine black students for the bare minimum of mathematical skill that is needed to "get by" in the modern workplace, and they will leave it up to the discretion of individual parents and teachers to bring black men with "unnatural" mathematical talents to their attention. The result is that black men who would become mathematicians will always need to take non-standard routes to do so, while black men who would become great athletes have standard routes to follow.

Again, it is important to note that the disciplinary powers invoked by white meritocrats belong to the organs that administer and supervise the routine examinations that maintain white meritocracy. These organs may or may not be serviced by white peoples: black coaches and black math teachers can wield the disciplinary powers that maintain white meritocracy as effectively as white coaches and white math teachers.

Normalizing powers are mediators that enable one faction to determine the distribution of another faction's probabilities.

Normalizing powers are constituted by *biased surveys* that substantiate and qualify stereotypes.

The racism of the conservative white technocrat invokes normalizing powers. The conservative white technocrat substantiates and qualifies the untested and anecdotal observations of the white meritocrat by carrying out biased surveys that are designed to verify the white meritocrat's untested and anecdotal observations. Thanks to the conservative white technocrat's biased surveys, it becomes a *technical fact* that predominantly black schools are less likely to produce mathematicians relative to predominantly white schools.

It must be stressed that the conservative white technocrat takes that which was an anecdotal observation and transforms it into a technical fact, which means altering environments, implements, and statements so as to ensure repeatability or test–retest reliability of the observation. Whereas the white meritocrat takes it for granted that predominantly black schools underachieve based on scant evidence, the conservative white technocrat needs to make certain that predominantly black schools underachieve by manufacturing a preponderance of evidence. Predominantly black schools that overachieved flew under the radar of the white meritocrat but they are subject to extreme scrutiny by the conservative white technocrat who needs to justify excluding them as outliers.

Again, it is important to note that the normalizing powers invoked by a conservative white technocrat belong to the organs that administer and supervise the biased surveys that maintain a conservative white technocracy. These organs may or may not be serviced by white peoples: the black social scientist can wield the normalizing powers that maintain conservative white meritocracies as effectively as the white social scientist.

Optimizing powers are mediators that enable one faction to modulate the distribution of another faction's probabilities.

Optimizing powers are constituted by *variable controls* that modulate a populations characteristics in predictable ways.

The racism of the progressive white technocrat invokes optimizing powers. Working from biased surveys which "prove" that predominantly black schools are less likely to produce mathematicians relative to predominantly white schools, the progressive white technocrat endeavors to make predominantly black schools "measure up" to predominantly white schools by "controlling for the confounding variables" that have favored predominantly white schools in the production of mathematicians over predominantly black schools.

Whereas the conservative white technocrat was content with making it a technical fact that predominantly black schools underachieve relative to predominantly white schools, the progressive technocrat subjects predominantly black schools to increased administration and supervision in order to make them "measure up". The end result is that educators at predominantly black schools are subject to more and more rational controls and they are given less and less freedom to educate their students in ways that make sense.

Again, it is important to note that the optimizing powers invoked by a progressive white technocrat belong to the organs that administer and supervise the variable controls that maintain a progressive white technocracy. These organs may or may not be serviced by white peoples: the black social reformer can wield the optimizing powers that maintain progressive white technocracies as effectively as the white social reformer.

Countering power is one thing, fighting those who seemingly benefit from power is another.

White technocrats, white meritocrats, and white supremacists do not always see eye to eye. The white technocrat, for instance, is dismissive of the white meritocrats' untested and anecdotal observations when there is no way that these observations can be substantiated, and, what's more, the white technocrat cries foul when white supremacists make claims without reference to any observations at all. Indeed, white technocrats are very often heard disparaging white meritocrats and white supremacists for their lack of scientific rigor. In response, the white supremacist and the white meritocrat will lament that the white technocrat wastes time and resources trying to prove that which needs no proof because it should be regarded as obvious or self-evident.

That being said, however, those who would counter racist powers must be careful not to side with white technocrats against white meritocrats and white supremacists, for the white technocrat is no less of a racist. Rather, the white technocrat is, in fact, only the most reserved and qualified white supremacist and white meritocrat.

What's more, it is one thing to fight against individual white supremacists, individual white meritocrats, and individual white technocrats; it is another thing to counter the ritualized spectacles that enable white supremacy, to counter routine examinations that enable white meritocracy, and to counter the biased surveys and variable controls that enable white technocracy. Naming, shaming, and maiming individual racists, however satisfying that may be, doesn't necessarily contribute in any direct or indirect way to countering racist powers. Much to the contrary, racist powers can feed off the naming, shaming, and maiming individual racists.

What power wants, above all else, is to craft definite and unambiguous distinctions: the ruling powers invoked by white supremacists use ritualized spectacles to craft definite and unambiguous distinctions between blacks and whites; the disciplinary powers invoked by white meritocrats use routine examinations to craft definite and unambiguous distinctions between stereotypical blacks and atypical blacks; the normalizing powers invoked by conservative white technocrats use biased surveys to craft definite and unambiguous distinctions between blacks that fall within the normal distribution and blacks that are outliers; the optimizing powers invoked by progressive white technocrats use variable controls to craft definite and unambiguous distinctions between blacks belonging to intervention groups and blacks belonging to control groups. In other words, individual racists will continue to proliferate for as long as racist powers are able to craft definite and unambiguous racial distinctions through ritualized spectacles, routine examinations, biased surveys, and variable controls. There will always be another racist to rise and take the place of a fallen racist as long as there are means to make definite and unambiguous racial distinctions.

To counter power is to prevent definite and unambiguous distinctions from being made, which means promoting ROUGHNESS, NOT-SEPARATENESS, and DEEP INTERLOCKS AND AMBIGUITIES amongst differing factions. To counter the ruling powers invoked by white supremacists is to make it so that there can only ever be rough and ambiguous distinctions drawn between blacks and whites. To counter the disciplinary powers invoked by white meritocrats is to make it so that there can only ever be rough and ambiguous distinctions drawn between stereotypical blacks and atypical blacks. To counter the normalizing powers invoked by conservative white technocrats is to make it so that there can only ever be rough and ambiguous distinctions drawn between blacks that fall within the normal distribution and blacks that are outliers. To counter the optimizing powers invoked by progressive white technocrats is to make it so that there can only ever be rough and ambiguous distinctions drawn between blacks belonging to intervention groups and blacks belonging to control groups.

That which liberates will only ever demand that people make rough and ambiguous distinctions between themselves and others; only that which oppresses demands that people make definite and unambiguous distinctions between themselves and others. Going further, that which liberates demands that even rough and ambiguous distinctions be made as sparingly as possible, promoting SIMPLICITY AND INNER CALM.

Power persists because feeling powerful and feeling powerless are addictive.

One who is addicted to feeling powerful is one who is addicted serving as a mediator. The person addicted to feeling powerful is one who feels compelled to stand between opposing factions and to play the role of medium and guarantor of tolerance.

One who is addicted to feeling powerless is one who is addicted to mediation, addicted to the services of the mediator. The person addicted to feeling powerless is one who feels compelled to identify themself with one faction over and against others, and, being intolerant of others, the person addicted to feeling powerless is compelled to seek out a mediating authority to stand between them and others.

Like all other addictions, the addiction to feeling powerful and the addiction to feeling powerless are ways of coping with pain. As a noted writer on the topic of addiction, Gabor Maté, writes:

> [A]ddiction is neither a choice nor primarily a disease. It originates in a human being's desperate attempt to solve a problem: the problem of emotional pain, of overwhelming stress, of lost connection, of loss of control, of a deep discomfort with the self. In short, it is a forlorn attempt to solve the problem of human pain. All drugs—and all behaviours of addiction, substance-dependent or not, whether to gambling, food, sex, alcohol, cigarettes, the internet or cocaine—either soothe pain directly or distract from it. Hence my mantra: "The question is not why the addiction, but why the pain."

Feeling powerful and feeling powerless are perhaps the most addictive of behaviors. Indeed, one will be hard pressed to find an addictive behavior that does not invoke the feeling of being powerful or the feeling of being powerless. It follows from this that one cannot effectively counter power unless one is able to effectively tend to the sufferings that drive people to take refuge in and to become addicted to the feeling of being powerful or that of being powerless.

The reverse is also true: a power cannot effectively maintain itself unless it is able to effectively aggravate the sufferings that drive people to take refuge in and to become addicted to the feeling of being powerful or powerless. Indeed, all powers — ruling powers, disciplinary powers, normalizing powers, and optimizing powers — maintain themselves by aggravating people's sufferings and by claiming that there is a higher sense or a reason that justifies the aggravation of people's sufferings. Those who seem to benefit from the maintenance of a power are always, in fact, suffering from the maintenance of the power that benefits them; it is only that they are able to distract themselves from their own suffering with the superficial consolations that power confers on them. Those who believe that power can provide anything more than superficial consolations are foolish and pitiable creatures: they do not recognize power provides short-term pleasures while aggravating long-term sufferings, making us crave power more and more.

The ceaseless proliferation of administrative and supervisory organs in our time betrays the fact that our age is the most power hungry of all ages. The arduous task confronting generations now living is to take pains to help each other withdraw and recover from our all-consuming addictions to power, to feelings of being powerful and powerless. In this, I find myself echoing Ivan Illich, who wrote in Tools for Conviviality, "Withdrawal from [our addiction for power] will be painful, but mostly for members of the generation which has to experience the transition and above all for those most disabled by [their addiction to power]. If their plight could be vividly remembered, it might help the next generation avoid what they know would enslave them."

Freeing Time

All powers first establish themselves over us by determining the rhythm and tempo of our lives. This is to say, in other words, that powers can only rule, discipline, normalize, and optimize our lives if they succeed in ruling, disciplining, normalizing, and optimizing the rhythm and tempo of our lives.

It follows from this that countering the powers that effectively determine the rhythm and tempo of our lives is decisive to countering any and all powers.

A *ruling power* first endeavors to create definite and unambiguous distinctions between different rhythms and tempos. Having made this distinction, the power then endeavors to give certain rhythms and tempos priority over others. For instance, a power ruling over music-making might contrive to create definite and unambiguous distinctions between straight time and swing time in order to prioritize one over the other. To do this, a ruling power will need to inhibit the making of music in which ambiguities between swing time and straight time arise.

A *disciplinary power* first endeavors to create definite and unambiguous distinctions between the variations on a given rhythm and tempo that are stereotypical and those that are atypical. Having made this distinction, the power then endeavors to promote conformity with the stereotypical over the atypical. For instance, a power that disciplines music-making might contrive to stereotype swing time by claiming that one particular variation on swing time is the stereotypical norm and that all others are atypical deviations. To do this, a ruling power will need to inhibit the making of music in which there are ambiguities between the variations that fit the stereotypical norm and the variations that are atypical for deviating from the norm.

A *normalizing power* first endeavors to create definite and unambiguous distinctions between the variations on a given rhythm and tempo that fall within a normal distribution and the variations that are outliers. Having made this distinction, the power then endeavors to exclude the latter, the outliers, from considerations and calculations. For instance, a power that normalizes music-making might contrive to exclude "outlying" variations on swing time from any and all compilations and curricula of swing music. To do this, a normalizing power will need to inhibit the making of music in which there are ambiguities between those variations on swing time that fall within the normal distribution and those variations that are outliers.

An *optimizing power* endeavors to create definite and unambiguous distinctions between the aspects of a variation that are confounding variables that must be controlled and the aspects of a variation that may be subject to varied interventions. For instance, a power that optimizes music-making might contrive to produce records with the optimal amount of swing. Such an optimizing power might have a drummer maintain a certain hi-hat figure, "ti-tshhh-SH", while otherwise allowing musicians to vary their playing however they want. Such a power will then ask audiences to rank which variations achieve the "most satisfying" swing while the hi-hat figure holds steady. The power will then try to optimize the production of music that swings by selecting for the hi-hat figure and then supplementing the hi-hat figure with variations that scored "most satisfying" on the audience survey. In order to work, such an optimizing power must inhibit the making of music in which all aspects of swing time are allowed to vary freely: optimization always requires that at least one aspect be fixed while other aspects vary freely—the fixed aspect in this instance being the hi-hat figure. All this is to say, in other words, that optimization inhibits free improvisation in order to prevent there being any ambiguity between what is controlled and what is allowed to vary.

To further illustrate the workings of power over time, let us examine the makings of a Gregorian calendar year.

The stereotypical 365-day year that appears on the Gregorian calendar is part and parcel of the exercise of a disciplinary power over the rhythm and tempo of our lives. In nature, no year has ever been 365 days long, but every Gregorian calendar year is supposed to conform to the stereotypical 365-day measure, with the exception of leap years which are supposed to conform to the 366-day measure. Technically, the "mean solar year" is approximately 365 days, 5 hours, 48 minutes, 45 seconds. But the mean solar year is, itself, only a statistical average which will vary depending on how many years and which years are taken into account in one's survey. Given the right survey sample, the mean solar year may very well be calculated at 365 days, 5 hours, 48 minutes, and 44 seconds rather that 43 seconds. This is to say, in other words, that the mean solar year is also a product of power, but a normalizing power rather than a disciplinary power.

Going further, we must also note that the prioritization of the solar year by the Gregorian calendar is, itself, the result of ruling powers that have determined that the solar year ought to take priority over the lunar year. No doubt, there have been and still are alternative ruling powers that would prioritize the lunar year over the solar year, and there are normalizing powers that would calculate the mean lunar year, consisting of twelve lunar cycles, to be approximately 354 days, 8 hours, 48 minutes, 34 seconds, 11 to 12 days shorter than the solar year. What's more, there are disciplinary powers that would make the lunar year conform to a stereotypical 354 days and 355 days.

Going further still, we can imagine alternatives to the solar and lunar years. For instance, we can imagine a culture in which the first day of the new year is determined by an event in a plant's life cycle: e.g., the day that a certain tree drops its last leaf. Or we can imagine a culture in which the first day of the new year is determined by an event in an animal's life cycle: the day that a sacred animal goes into hibernation or returns from their migration. Or we can imagine a culture in which the first day of the new year is determined by an event in an elemental cycle: e.g., the first day that a certain lake freezes over every year. Each of these cultures, if they were burdened with normalizing powers, would have different "mean years" of different lengths.

We have yet to speak of optimizing powers with respect to the calendar year because, luckily for us, optimizing powers have not taken to determining the length of our calendar years. Indulge me, if you will, and imagine an optimizing power having determined that the first day of the new year will be the mean day on which a select species of tree drops its last leaf. Such an optimizing power would generate controls and devices to intervene in the life cycle of the select species of tree in order to optimize the "mean tree year". These devices might work to ensure, for instance, that the mean tree year is never shorter than the mean lunar year and never longer than the mean solar year but, rather, always within a range between the mean lunar and the mean solar year that has been determined to be "optimal".

The makings of statements, implements, and environments are the makings of worlds. The making of a Gregorian calendar year is the making of a statement that serves both to rule and to discipline the passage of time, serving alongside corresponding implements (e.g., clocks and watches that display and function according to the dates of the Gregorian calendar) and serving alongside corresponding environments (e.g., city squares and workplaces that are built around features, like clock towers, that display and function according to the dates of the Gregorian calendar). This is to say, in other words, that the Gregorian calendar is a statement that can, with the aid of corresponding implements and environments, make for a world in which (i) the solar year reigns supreme and (ii) the solar year is made to conform to the 365-day base year and the 366-day leap year.

A primary world-making task of the (De-/Re-)Constructing Worlds project is the task of countering the ruling and disciplinary powers facilitated by the statements that we make with our calendars. Posed as a question, the project asks, "How can we work with each other to deconstruct our calendars and to (re-)construct alternative statements regarding the passage of time so that we may free time from the powers that work administer and supervise time?"

For a start, I propose that we should never take it for granted that the transition from one year to the next takes place the moment that a clock strikes midnight on a given day.

Instead, I propose that the transition from one year to the next always takes place over a greater or lesser interval of time, often spanning several days, and that this interval roughly traverses a decisive set of pivotal events pertaining to the cycle of the sun (e.g., the solstice that initiates the waxing of the days), the cycle of the moon (e.g., the first new moon following the solstice), the cycles of plant life (e.g., the complete shedding of leaves by a certain species of tree), the cycles of animal life (e.g., the arrival or departure of a migratory bird), the cycles of fungal life (e.g., the sprouting of the mushroom of a certain species of fungus), and the cycles of the elements (e.g., the freezing over of a lake).

In other words, the transition from one year to the next need not be determined by any single pivotal event but, instead, the transition could be said to begin with the occurrence of any one pivotal event belonging to a decisive set of pivotal events, and the transition could be said to end after a critical mass of pivotal events belonging to that decisive set have come to pass.

The problem, then, is how to (re-)construct meaningful statements that (i) articulate a decisive set of pivotal events that initiate and further the transition to a new year and (ii) articulate the critical mass of events needed to complete the transition to a new year. The significant difficulty in this regard is that the decisive set of pivotal events can and should differ in different ecoregions. The same or similar pivotal events in the cycles of the sun and the moon will be decisive in just about every ecoregion, yes, but a wildly differing variety of pivotal events in the cycles of flora, fauna, fungi, and the elements will be decisive in different ecoregions. Indeed, even within the same ecoregion, different pivotal events in the cycles of flora, fauna, fungi and the elements can and should be decisive for the different peoples of the ecoregion.

The question, then, is how do we (re-)construct alternative statements regarding the passage of time — fuzzy, indeterminate, and topological statements — that are open to so many differences? With the follow up question being, how do we (re-)construct implements and environments that correspond with these alternative statements regarding the passage of time?

Blackness and Primitiveness

Powers form themselves by making clear and unambiguous distinctions —
(i) a ruling power forms itself by making clear and unambiguous distinctions
between one group and another, (ii) a disciplinary power forms itself by making
clear and unambiguous distinctions between the stereotypical members of a given
group and the atypical members, (iii) a normalizing power forms itself by making
clear and unambiguous distinctions between those members of a given group that
fit the normal distribution and those that are outliers, and (iv) an optimizing power
forms itself by making clear and unambiguous distinctions between those members
of a given group that are the subjects of varying interventions and those that are
control subjects.

Counterpowers, by contrast, form themselves by undermining the making
of clear and unambiguous distinctions. To riff off the title of a book by
Fred Moten on the black radical tradition — whereas powers aim to enlighten and
discriminate, counterpowers aim to *black and blur*.

In his writings on the black radical tradition, Moten stresses, again and again, that
the black radical tradition is not the tradition of a crisply defined set of peoples that
can be said to fall under the designation "Black". Rather, the black radical tradition
is the tradition of a blur of peoples, a fuzzy and indeterminate set, perpetually
engaged in the process of troubling the designation "Black" that has been imposed
upon them and staying with the trouble. This is to say, in other words, that the
black radical tradition is a counter-cultural tradition: it is a tradition dedicated to
countering the imposing power formations of dominant cultures.

The black radical tradition was formed in response to Western capitalist modernity's imposition of the designation "Negro" and, concomitantly, the designation "Black" on the descendants of dark-skinned peoples form Sub-Saharan Africa.

As R.A. Judy writes in the book *Sentient Flesh*, the imposed designation "Black/Negro" has had two distinct senses. On the one hand, the imposed designation has a political economic sense: "the word Negro, along with all its cognates, entails an anthropological categorization, whereby those so designated belong to a physically distinct type of not fully human hominid, which is what makes them legitimately available as prospective commodity assets." On the other hand, the imposed designation carries an ethnographic sense, "the term [Negro] connotes not only the slave formed in capitalism but also the populations of people who may be enslaved, and who remain Negro after slavery's abolition." Considering these two distinct senses of the term "Negro" together, Judy observes, "While it is indeed the case that in every instance of its expression, Negro connotes the formations of political economy in the Atlantic World in modernity, it also has historical usage as an ethnographic designation for a specific population of people, 'the Negro.' [...] Yet even though that ethnographic sense of Negro contradicts the commercial Negro by recognizing the full humanity of the designated population, it is still within the ambit of the same anthropological categorization."

In sum, only those dark-complexioned Sub-Saharan African peoples who have been made into slaves are Black/Negro in the political economic sense, yes, but all those who are susceptible to becoming Black/Negro in the political economic sense are considered Black/Negro in the ethnographic sense. The political economic sense of the designation Black/Negro is thus the definitive sense: the ethnographic Black/Negro being nothing other than the being susceptible to becoming Black/Negro in the political economic sense. Using myself as an example here, being a child of dark complexioned persons from Sub-Saharan Africa, I am Black/Negro in the ethnographic sense, which is to say, in other words, that I am a person susceptible to receiving the political economic designation Black/Negro under the power formation of racialized slavery. That the power formation of racialized slavery is no longer operative today does not put an end to my being Black/Negro in the ethnographic sense: I continue to be ethnographically Black/Negro because the power formation of racialized slavery did effectively operate for a period time and the remnants of its effective operation have been maintained and repurposed by the power formations that have succeeded it.

My parents migrated from Sub-Saharan Africa to Europe and then to America during the postcolonial period. As a result of this, my being designated Black/Negro has not rendered all my ethnographic designations prior to that of Black/Negro illegible for me. This is, of course, because colonialism in Sub-Saharan Africa made use of such prior ethnographic designations to administer and supervise its subjects. Racialized slavery in the Americas, by contrast, endeavored to obliterate all ethnographic designations prior to the designation Black/Negro. The peoples who were forced to cross the Atlantic and made into slaves in the Americas were the victims of ethnocide: they were forced to put any and all designations prior to that of Black/Negro under such intense erasure that all prior designations became illegible for them and for their descendants. The fact that designations prior to that of Black/Negro have been subjected to erasure remains partially discernible, yes, but these prior designations themselves, though partially discernible, have been rendered more or less indecipherable. The prior ethnicities of the Black/Negro slave have been worn down by racialized slavery to such an extreme degree that, although the slave and their descendants know that they have prior ethnicities, the slave and their descendants cannot know with any certainty what these prior ethnicities are. The prior ethnicities of the Black/Negro slave are like worn silver coins known to have been struck as currency of a certain provenance and value but that have been worn down to such a degree that it cannot be known for certain what provenance and value they were struck with.

The beauty of the black radical tradition is to be found in the manner in which it has embraced peoples without any certain knowledge of their prior ethnicities. In affirming blackness, the black radical tradition neither affirms the ethnicity that racialized slavery imposed upon the Black/Negro nor does it affirm a newly self-constructed ethnicity for those who have become Black/Negro. To the contrary, the black radical tradition affirms blackness as the act of living with uncertainty about one's prior ethnicity. The black radical tradition may be contrasted with the many black reactionary traditions that have sought to make the Black/Negro into a defining ethnic identity, thereby conceding victory to the racist powers that first endeavored to eradicate prior ethnic identities in order to create the Black/Negro as a defining ethnic identity. By contrast, the black radical tradition troubles all black reactionary traditions by affirming blackness as the act of living with uncertainty regarding one's prior ethnicity while also affirming the discernible remnants of prior ethnicities in spite of their erasure.

In line with and in furtherance of the black radical tradition's affirmation of blackness, I have been endeavoring to affirm "primitiveness" not as a definite anthropological rubric but, instead, as the act of living with uncertainty regarding anthropological rubrics. To give you a sense of what this endeavor entails, allow me to quote another passage from R.A. Judy's *Sentient Flesh* on the different senses of the term "primitive".

[I]interpolation into capitalism's terms of order [...] results in the dissolution of long-enduring formations of human community, engendering cosmic disorder by throwing disparate cosmogonies together under the anthropological rubric *primitive*. This term has a rather broad connotation, comprehending both an original inhabitant, an aboriginal, and a person belonging to a preliterate nonindustrial society, but also ancestral early man, or anything else that is archaic. It has been inclusively applied to a wide array of types of natives—also a conceptual category—engendered along the way in capitalism's global expansion and colonial rule. Not all colonial natives are designated primitive, however; there are those who belong to age-old civilizations, the effects of which, according to the narrative of *translatio*, transferred westward to feed the foundations of capitalism—outstanding examples of which are China, India, and most of the Muslim world. The distinction of having been civilizationally long-in-the-tooth does not mitigate the disordering effects of capitalist expansion, however. On the contrary, being construed as archaic civilizational formations surpassed by Western capitalist modernity is another sense of primitive and tends to exacerbate the disordering effects with an aura of civilizational degradation and loss of authenticity. Terminologically, primitive and Negro share the same semantic space to the point of synonymy. Those populations designated Negro, however, are seemingly always primitive, this attributed state playing a role, almost as a neo-Aristotelian afterthought, in legitimating their designation: the absurdly Hegelian argument that the primitive, enslaved and made Negro, enters into civilization and thus benefits from the transformation.

Just as all peoples that were susceptible to racialized slavery were thrown under the ethnographic designation Black/Negro, we find that all peoples who were susceptible to colonization by Western capitalist powers were thrown under the anthropological rubric primitive. What's more, just as all those who endured racialized slavery were forced to put all prior ethnicities under erasure in being designated Black/Negro, we find that all those who endured colonization were forced to put all prior anthropological rubrics under erasure in being designated primitive.

Not all of those who have been designated primitive have been designated Black/Negro, but all who have been designated Black/Negro have also been designated primitive. This means that all peoples who have been designated Black/Negro have had prior anthropologies put under erasure alongside prior ethnicities. It follows from this that the black radical tradition has always also been a radical primitivist tradition insofar as it has affirmed the act of living with uncertainty regarding anthropological rubrics alongside the act of living with uncertainty regarding ethnic identities. What's more, it is as a radical primitivist tradition that the black radical tradition has concurred with and made common cause with the many radical anti-colonial traditions.

Multiplying Confluences

One.

Power formations are assemblages of filters and channels through which matters flow. Power formations first filter out differing elements from the flows that pass through them and then they channel these differing elements apart from one another for a greater or lesser duration of time.

Ruling *powers* filter out differing varieties of elements and channel the differing varieties apart from one another: for instance, a racist ruling power might filter and channel white peoples apart from black peoples.

Disciplinary *powers* filter and channel the stereotypical specimens of a given element apart from the atypical specimens of the same: for instance, a racist ruling power might filter and channel stereotypical black people apart from atypical black people.

Normalizing *powers* filter and channel those specimens of a given element that fit the normal distribution apart from those specimens that are outliers: for instance, a racist normalizing power might filter and channel blacks that fit the normal distribution apart from blacks that are outliers.

Optimizing *powers* filter and channel those specimens of a given element that are subjected to varying interventions apart from those specimens that are control subjects: for instance, an optimizing ruling power might filter and channel blacks that have been subjected to varying interventions apart from those that have not been subjected to any interventions.

Two.

Power formations generate determinate elements from what is otherwise indeterminate stuff: the determinate elements that are filtered and channeled from a given flow by a power formation do not exist as determinate elements until after a given flow has been filtered and channeled by a power formation.

For instance, neither blacks nor whites are determined as such prior to the formation of racist ruling powers. Racially determined individuals only ever come into being after racist ruling powers filter and channel what is otherwise racially indeterminate. Which is to say, in other words, that the existence of individuals of determinate races, whites and blacks, is an effect of racist ruling powers. Similarly, we find that racist disciplinary powers are responsible for the existence of stereotypical blacks and atypical blacks; we find that racist normalizing powers are responsible for the existence of the normal distribution of blacks and black outliers; and we find that racist optimizing powers are responsible for the existence of blacks who have been proven to benefit from an intervention and blacks who have been proven to suffer from a lack of intervention.

Three.

Stable power formations (or, alternatively, "pipelines") are power formations that stratify their subjects. —Stratification occurs when the duration of a determinate element's separation from other elements is extended beyond a critical point so as to degrade the determinate element's fluent connection to the indeterminate stuff from which it was parted.

Let us return again to the example of racist powers.

- A racist ruling power is stabilized when differing races, e.g., whites and blacks, are channeled apart from one another for an increasingly extended duration so that it becomes increasingly burdensome and unappealing for either one to commune fluently with the other.
- A racist disciplinary power is stabilized when the stereotypical and atypical members of a race, e.g., stereotypical and atypical blacks, are channeled apart from one another for an increasingly extended duration so that it becomes increasingly burdensome and unappealing for either one to commune fluently with the other.
- A racist normalizing power is stabilized when members that fit the normal distribution for their race and members that are outliers are channeled apart from one another for an increasingly extended duration so that it becomes increasingly burdensome and unappealing for either one to commune fluently with the other.
- A racist optimizing power is stabilized when members of a given race that are proven to benefit from an intervention and members proven to suffer from a lack of intervention are channeled apart from one another for an increasingly extended duration so that it becomes increasingly burdensome and unappealing for either one to commune fluently with the other, and it becomes more practical and appealing for one to dominate or eliminate the other.

Note that I have used the term "commune" above in order to indicate that a stable power formation will not only inhibit fluent communication amongst differing elements but, more profoundly, it will also inhibit differing elements from fluently working *with* one another in accord with the communistic principle "from each according to their ability, to each according to their need".

Four.

Rather than working to prevent the formation of powers, counterpowers (or, alternatively, "leaky designs") work to prevent the stabilization of power formations. Which is to say, in other words, that counterpowers destabilize power formations and, in so doing, they destratify the subjects of powers.

Counterpowers make it increasingly easy and appealing for differing elements to confluently commune with one another. The more confluences that are enabled by counterpowers, the less determinate confluent elements become: which is not to say that confluent elements come to differ less from one another but, rather, is to say that confluent elements come to defer more to one another in spite of differing.

Another way of putting all of this would be to say that counterpowers multiply confluences by deconstructing power formations, making their filters less exclusive and their channels less extensive.

Five.

The makings of worlds are coterminous with the makings of powers and counterpowers.

Meaningful statements, useful implements, and built environments are the filters and channels that both constitute powers and determine the stability the powers they constitute. Whereas statements, implements, and environments that constitute stable powers make for deathly worlds, those that constitute unstable powers make for living worlds. This is because the "strong foci" that I have written about as the defining features of living worlds are themselves, in turn, defined by the multiple confluences that both bound them and connect them to other foci. Counterpowers are formed of and by statements, implements, and environments that feature strong foci bounded by multiple confluences; stable powers are formed of and by statements, implements, and environments that feature "weak foci" that are disconnected from others because they are not bound by multiple confluences.

In sum, weaker foci make for stable power formations and for deadlier worlds, stronger foci make for unstable power formations and for livelier worlds, and the liveliest worlds are those that feature the least stable power formations.

Of the four processes that are most pivotal to the creation of living worlds, it is the process of NOT-SEPARATENESS that is the most pivotal all, for it is itself the very process of countering power, of destabilizing power formations, of multiplying confluences.

For bell hooks

The recent passing of bell hooks has inspired me to reconsider the clinical expression that she often used to name the deathly world of suffering that prevails over us, "imperialist white-supremacist capitalist patriarchy".

Just as the clinical expression "upper respiratory tract infection" says more about the nature of our suffering than the vernacular expression "a cold", I find that the clinical expression "imperialist white-supremacist capitalist patriarchy" says more about the nature of our suffering than a vernacular expression like "the Man", "the White Man", "the West", and "Western civilization". But don't get it twisted: this is no argument for clinical expression as opposed to vernacular expression, as the two are not truly opposites. As I see it, clinical-and-vernacular expressions are not only possible, they are most desirable.

To mark the passing of bell hooks, this dispatch (re-)defines her clinical expression "imperialist white-supremacist capitalist patriarchy" by drawing upon the notions of power and counterpower that I have been developing in some of my most recent dispatches: "Countering Power", "Blackness and Primitiveness" and "Multiplying Confluences". Indeed, this dispatch can be treated as the fourth and final part of a series dispatches searching for clinical expressions to name the deathly world of suffering that prevails over us and to name the processes working to deconstruct this deathly world of suffering and working to (re-)construct living worlds.

"Imperialism"

An imperialism is an endeavor to construct a stable power formation. Stable power formations are power formations that stratify social groups; they filter and channel different social groups apart from one another so as to make it increasingly burdensome and unappealing for different social groups to commune fluently with one another and, what's more, so as to make it more practical and more appealing for some social groups to dominate and eliminate others.

Insofar as all counterpowers endeavor to destabilize power formations and to destratify social groups, all endeavors that promote counterpowers are anti-imperialist endeavors. Counterpowers make it increasingly practical and appealing for social groups to commune fluently, or "to confluence", with one another. The more confluences that are enabled by counterpowers, the less determinate the social groups involved in such confluences will become: it is not the case that confluent social groups become more alike and differ less from one another but, rather, it is the case that confluent social groups come to defer to one another more and more despite differing from one another. This is to say, in other words, that counterpowers generate DEEP INTERLOCKS AND AMBIGUITIES (or, alternatively, "entanglements and indeterminacies") amongst different social groups.

"Imperialist White Supremacy"

An imperialist white supremacy endeavors to stabilize racist ruling powers that enable those who are white to dominate and eliminate others of different races, especially blacks. These racist ruling powers are stabilized when differing races, especially whites and blacks, are filtered and channeled apart from one another so that it becomes increasingly burdensome and unappealing for them to commune fluently with one another and, what's more, so that it becomes more practical and more appealing for whites to dominate and eliminate all others of different races.

The forms of domination and elimination that whites are able to employ against non-whites may be quite subtle: they do not necessarily involve the threat of simple murder as such. To quote Michel Foucault on the matter, in lieu of or in addition to involving the threat of simple murder as such, they may involve threatening "form[s] of indirect murder: the fact of exposing someone to death, increasing the risk of death for some people, or quite simply, political death, expulsion, rejection, and so on." The most subtle way in which whites dominate and eliminate non-whites is, of course, by causing burnout: by exposing non-whites to chronic stresses that either induce or greatly increase their risk of developing deadly and debilitating illnesses (e.g., the imposition on blacks to maintain constant vigilance against being unduly perceived by whites as being angry, hostile, or threatening).

The racist ruling powers that enable white supremacy are supplemented by disciplinary, normalizing and optimizing powers that further enable whites to dominate others of different races. These disciplinary, normalizing and optimizing powers are put to work on all racial groups. This is to say that, like all other races, whites are subjected to concatenations of routine examinations, biased surveys, and variable controls that subordinate and eliminate those sub-populations that threaten the continued maintenance of white supremacy and that elevate those sub-populations that promote the continued maintenance of white supremacy. In other words, whites can themselves suffer from white supremacy.

Creolizing processes are those processes that counter white supremacy. Creolizing processes make it increasingly more practical and appealing for persons of differing races to fluently commune with one another, such that distinctions between races increasingly come to black and blur. A creolizing process does not make it so that persons of different races become more alike and differ less from one another but, rather, it makes it so that persons of races come to defer to one another more and more despite their differences.

"Imperialist Patriarchy"

An imperialist patriarchy endeavors to stabilize sexist ruling powers that enable cisgender heterosexual men to dominate and eliminate others of different genders, sexes, and sexual orientations, especially any and all kinds of women. These sexist ruling powers are stabilized when persons with different genders, sexes, and sexual orientations are filtered and channeled apart from one another so that it becomes increasingly burdensome and unappealing for them to commune fluently with one another and, what's more, so that it becomes more practical and more appealing for cisgender heterosexual men to dominate and eliminate all others of different genders, sexes, and sexual orientations in subtle and not so subtle ways. The most subtle way in which cisgender heterosexual men dominate and eliminate others of different genders, sexes, and sexual orientations is, again, by causing burnout: by exposing others to chronic stresses that either induce or greatly increase their risk of developing deadly and debilitating illnesses (e.g., the imposition on women to maintain constant vigilance against the threat of sexual assault and rape).

The sexist ruling powers that enable patriarchy are supplemented by disciplinary, normalizing and optimizing powers that further enable cisgender heterosexual men to dominate and eliminate all others of different genders, sexes, and sexual orientations. These disciplinary, normalizing and optimizing powers are put to work on everyone, regardless of gender, sex, and sexual orientation. This is to say that, like others of different genders, sexes, and sexual orientations, cisgender heterosexual men are subjected to concatenations of routine examinations, biased surveys, and variable controls that subordinate and eliminate those sub-populations that threaten the continued maintenance of patriarchy and that elevate those sub-populations that promote the continued maintenance of patriarchy. In other words, cisgender heterosexual men can themselves suffer from patriarchy.

Queering processes are those processes that counters patriarchy. Queering processes make it increasingly more practical and appealing for persons of differing genders, sexes, and sexual orientations to fluently commune with one another, such that distinctions between genders, sexes, and sexual orientations increasingly come to black and blur. A queering process does not make it so that persons of different genders, sexes, and sexual orientations become more alike and differ less from one another but, rather, it makes it so that persons of different genders, sexes, and sexual orientations come to defer to one another more and more despite their differences.

"Imperialist Capitalism"

An imperialist capitalism endeavors to stabilize economic ruling powers that enable relations of production that facilitate capital accumulation (i.e., relations that prioritize the exchange values of goods and services) to dominate and eliminate all alternative relations of production, especially those relations of production that facilitate social subsistence (i.e., relations that prioritize of the use values of goods and services). These economic ruling powers are stabilized when different relations of production are filtered and channeled apart from one another so that it becomes increasingly burdensome and unappealing for them to commune fluently with one another and, what's more, so that it becomes more practical and more appealing for capitalist relations of production to dominate and eliminate all alternative relations of production in subtle and not so subtle ways. The most subtle way in which capitalist relations of production dominate and eliminate alternative relations of production is, once again, by causing burnout: by exposing persons engaged in alternative relations of production to chronic stresses that either induce or greatly increase their risk of developing deadly and debilitating illnesses (e.g., the imposition of compounding taxes, rents, debt servicing costs, and healthcare costs on smallholding subsistence farmers).

The economic ruling powers that enable capitalism are supplemented by disciplinary, normalizing and optimizing powers that further enable capitalist relations of production to dominate and eliminate all alternative relations of production. These disciplinary, normalizing and optimizing powers are put to work on all relations of production. This is to say, in other words, that behaviors that facilitate capital accumulation also endure routine examinations, biased surveys, and variable controls in order to perpetuate capitalism. This is to say that, like all other relations of production, capitalist relations of production are subjected to concatenations of routine examinations, biased surveys, and variable controls that subordinate and eliminate the sub-populations of relations that threaten the continued maintenance of capitalism and that elevate the sub-populations of relations that promote the continued maintenance of capitalism. In other words, capitalist relations of productions can themselves suffer from capitalism.

Communizing processes are those that counter capitalism. Communizing processes make it increasingly more practical and appealing for differing relations of production to fluently commune with one another so that distinctions between differing relations of production increasingly come to black and blur. A communizing process does not make it so that all relations of production become more alike and differ less from one another but, rather, it makes it so that different relations of production come to defer to one another more and more despite their differences.

"Imperialist White-Supremacist Capitalist Patriarchy"

An imperialist white-supremacist capitalist patriarchy endeavors to stabilize a concatenation of racist, sexist, and economic powers that enable white men profitably engaged in capitalist relations of production to dominate and eliminate others, especially black, brown, and indigenous women who are engaged in relations that provide for social subsistence.

A confluence of creolizing, queering, and communizing processes is required to counter white-supremacist capitalist patriarchy. Neither creolizing processes nor queering processes nor communizing processes can counter white-supremacist capitalist patriarchy on their own without the aid of the other two. Fully aware of this fact, white-supremacist capitalist patriarchy tirelessly works to filter and channel apart creolizing agents from queering agents from communizing agents, making it increasingly burdensome and unappealing for the three to commune fluently with each other. This it to say, in other words, that white-supremacist capitalist patriarchy is defined by a concatenation of ruling, disciplinary, normalizing, and optimizing powers that work to inhibit confluences of creolizing, queering, and communizing agents.

To counter white-supremacist capitalist patriarchy is to make it increasingly more practical and appealing for creolizing, queering, and communizing agents to fluently commune with one another, such that distinctions between them increasingly come to black and blur.

Black Mythologies

I have been thinking a great deal about an essay by Jacques Derrida titled "White Mythology: Metaphor in the Text of Philosophy". In this essay, Derrida speaks of a coin so old that the images stamped on its heads and tails have worn away. This coin still has some currency, but its provenance is uncertain and, as a result, its value is considered increasingly suspect by those who give it and take it in turns. Derrida holds that philosophical concepts that do not bear any mark of their cultural provenance or any mark of the facticity of their issuers are similar to such coins: such concepts may have currency but their value is rather suspect.

Derrida goes on to chide White European philosophers for believing the opposite. White European philosophers have tended to believe that a concept that bears no mark of its provenance is better than a concept that does bear such marks, and Derrida holds that White European philosophers have worked hard to obscure the provenance of their concepts. Actually, they have done far worse: White European philosophers have held that the concept that bears no mark of its provenance and no mark of its issuer's facticity is one that has "universal currency", and White European philosophers have worked to erase all marks of provenance and facticity from their concepts so as to deal in universals. Derrida tells us that these White European philosophers are like money dealers who maintain that coins whose faces have been worn away are coins of "universal currency" and, thus, these money dealers work to erase the faces from all of the coins in their possession, believing that this will enable their coins circulate anywhere and everywhere they go.

Derrida's wager is, and here is the rub, that the primary marks of a concept's provenance are the metaphors that precede, exceed, and succeed the concept's articulation. The White European philosopher who disdains "mere metaphors" is disdainful of the matter from which concepts are made. Creating a concept without having respect for metaphors, is like knitting a wool sweater without having any respect for wool.

I have imagined myself writing a response or sequel to Derrida's essay titled "Black Mythologies: Grasping for Metaphors as a Subtext for Black Study".

In a previous dispatch, "Blackness and Primitiveness", I wrote about how the "fabrication of the Negro" — "and by extension the fabrication of whiteness and all the policing of racial boundaries that came with it" — is a fabrication effected by and though the erasure of the marks of cultural provenance and facticity of those who are made Negro. This is to say, in other words, that the Negro is fabricated in the very same manner that the White European philosopher fabricates their philosophical concepts: the Negro was made by erasing the provenance and facticity of persons. Indeed, taking a page from Nahum Dimitri Chandler's book, X—*The Problem of the Negro as a Problem for Thought*, the making of the Negro is, in many ways, the making of the most exemplary of all White European philosophical concepts: the concept of a people whose cultural provenance and facticity are of no concern, being without historical significance.

In affirming that which is Negro or Black, the thinkers of the black radical tradition have not in any way affirmed the defaced concept of the Negro that the White European philosopher has scoured of metaphor. Rather, the thinkers of the black radical tradition have affirmed the metaphor from which the concept of the Negro was made, the metaphor which the White European philosopher wants erased. Etymologically, the Negro comes from Spanish or Portuguese negro "black," from Latin *nigrum* "black, dark, sable, dusky" (applied to the night sky, a storm, the complexion), which is perhaps from Proto-Indo-European *nekw-t- "night." The Negro, metaphorically speaking, could be thought of as people(s) who, surviving in spite of the ethnocidal machinations of Imperialist White-Supremacist Capitalist Patriarchy, must grasp for metaphors in the dark if they are comprehend their own cultural provenance and facticity.

To grasp for metaphors in the dark is to engage in what Fred Moten calls "black study" or what RA Judy calls "thinking-in-disorder". Black study assembles and dissembles the hard-learned lessons that have enabled people(s) to become adept not only at finding metaphors in the dark but also at finding movements and musics in the dark. Movements and musics mark our provenance and our facticity just as much as metaphors do, and White European philosophy subject the movements and musics that condition concepts to erasure alongside metaphors that condition concepts. In this ways black study and thinking-in-disorder — which embraces black dance, black music, and black poetry — are practices in and through which we may learn to search for movements, musics, and metaphors in the dark, so that we may comprehend our cultural provenance and our facticity in spite of the ethnocidal machinations of Imperialist White-Supremacist Capitalist Patriarchy.

Convivial Statements

When I use the term "statement" in the context of this project, I am invoking Michel Foucault's usage of the term. This is to say, in other words, that I do not use the term "statement" to simply refer to sentences like this one. This is an important point for me, as it was for Foucault. Indeed, knowing that I cannot mark the distinction between statement and sentence any better than Foucault, I shall quote Foucault at length on the matter:

> When one finds in a Latin grammar a series of words arranged in a column: *amo, amas, amat*, one is dealing not with a sentence, but with the statement of the different personal inflexions of the present indicative of the verb *amare*. One may find this example debatable; one may say that it is a mere artifice of presentation, that this statement is an elliptical, abbreviated sentence, spatialized in a relatively unusual mode, that should be read as the sentence 'The present indicative of the verb *amare* is *amo* for the first person', etc. Other examples, in any case, are less ambiguous: a classificatory table of the botanical species is made up of statements, not sentences (Linnaeus's *Genera Plantaruma* is a whole book of statements, in which one can recognize only a small number of sentences); a genealogical tree, an accounts book, the calculations of a trade balance are statements; where are the sentences? One can go further: an equation of the nth degree, or the algebraic formula of the law of refraction must be regarded as statements: and although they possess a highly rigorous grammaticality (since they are made up of symbols whose meaning is determined by rules of usage, and whose succession is governed by laws of construction), this grammaticality cannot be judged by the same criteria that, in a natural language (*langue*), make it possible to define an acceptable, or interpretable sentence. Lastly, a graph, a growth curve, an age pyramid, a distribution cloud are all statements : any sentences that may accompany them are merely interpretation or commentary; they are in no way an equivalent: this is proved by the fact that, in a great many cases, only an infinite number of sentences could equal all the elements that are explicitly formulated in this sort of statement. It would not appear to be possible, therefore, to define a statement by the grammatical characteristics of the sentence.

So, if it is not a sentence, what is a statement? Again, unable to do him one better, I shall quote Michel Foucault at length on the matter:

> [T]he statement is not the same kind of unit as the sentence, the proposition, or the speech act; it cannot be referred therefore to the same criteria; but neither is it the same kind of unit as a material object, with its limits and independence. In its way of being unique (neither entirely linguistic, nor exclusively material), it is indispensable if we want to say whether or not there is a sentence, proposition, or speech act; and whether the sentence is correct (or acceptable, or interpretable), whether the proposition is legitimate and well constructed, whether the speech act fulfills its requirements, and was in fact carried out. We must not seek in the statement a unit that is either long or short, strongly and weakly structured, but one that is caught up, like the others, in a logical, grammatical, locutory nexus. It is not so much one element among others, a division that can be located at a certain level of analysis, as a function that operates vertically in relation to these various units, and which enables one to say of a series of signs whether or not they are present in it. The statement is not therefore a structure (that is, a group of relations between variable elements, thus authorizing a possibly infinite number of concrete models); it is a function of existence that properly belongs to signs and on the basis of which one may then decide, through analysis or intuition, whether or not they 'make sense', according to what rule they follow one another or are juxtaposed, of what they are the sign, and what sort of act is carried out by their formulation (oral or written).

To get at both Foucault's point and a point of my own in one and the same gesture, I would like to write about two kinds of statements, domineering statements and convivial statements, and I would like to relate these two kinds of statements to the two kinds of communication that they respectively serve to enable, violent communication and nonviolent communication.

Domineering statements are those statements that contribute to the stability of power formations: they are the means by which forms of violent communication come to make sense, to take precedence, to have reference, and to set things in motion. Domineering statements are, in other words, the conditions of possibility for the effectiveness of violent communication.

Convivial statements are those that counter power by contributing to the instability of power formations: they are the means by which forms of nonviolent communication come to make sense, to take precedence, to have reference, and to set things in motion. Convivial statements are, in other words, the conditions of possibility for the effectiveness nonviolent communication.

Nonviolent communication is the compassionate, honest, and mutual way that people are able to communicate their abilities and their needs to one another. Nonviolent communication enables people to work with one another and to work in accord with the communistic principle, "from each according to their abilities, to each according to their needs."

Violent communication, by contrast, is the way in which people in positions of power (or seeking such positions) communicate demands and give orders to those who they compel to work for them. Violent communication disables non-violent communication: it disables the compassionate, honest, and mutual communication of abilities and needs amongst people; it enables those in positions of power to disregard others' needs and to demand that others perform more work than they are able. Violent communication is, in other words, the way in which people in positions of power inspire feelings of impoverishment and ineptitude in those who are compelled to work for them.

Let us consider a specific instance of violent communication: a teacher says to one of their pupils, "You are a poor student." This particular instance of violent communication obscures the needs and abilities of the pupil at whom it is directed while inspiring feelings of ineptitude in that pupil. If you were to ask the teacher, why would you say such a thing, the teacher might say, "It is the truth. Just look at the student's academic transcript."

The student's academic transcript is not a group of sentences, nor is it a group of propositions, nor is it a speech act — the student's academic transcript is a statement. As a statement, the student's academic enables us to discern whether certain sentences (e.g., "You are a poor student.") are correct, whether certain propositions (e.g., "A poor student is one who has a grade point average below 2.5.") are legitimate, and whether certain speech acts (e.g., "You are hereby expelled for poor academic performance.") fulfill their requirements.

Now, let us consider a specific instance of nonviolent communication: the pupil in question responds to their teacher, as I wish I'd have done as child, "I got bad grades because I failed all of my homework assignments, and I failed all of my homework assignments because I do not feel safe at home. I am not able to concentrate and do my homework unless I feel safe at home. My parents fight at home, and I feel scared when they fight. At home, I am always wondering what I might do to make them stop." This instance of non-violent communication enables us to discover a few of the needs and abilities that were obscured by the teacher's violent remark. But, alas, this instance of nonviolent communication will have little effect as long as the academic transcript is the statement that defines the teacher-pupil relation.

The academic transcript is a domineering statement that primarily serves to enable the teacher to make demands of the pupil, "Do your homework, or else you will fail and be expelled from this school." The academic transcript is not a statement that enables the teacher to meet their students' needs and discover the full extent of their students' abilities. Rather, the academic transcript exists to enable the teacher to filter and channel students who "achieve" as ordered and in a "timely" manner apart from students who "fail to achieve", without respecting their student's differing needs and abilities.

The question that follows from all of this is, "How might we deconstruct the domineering statement that is the academic transcript, which primarily enables the demand that pupils perform work for their teachers, and how might we (re-) construct convivial statements that enable teachers to work with their pupils by and through communicating their needs and abilities to one another?"

The academic transcript is but one of the many domineering statements that I am interested in deconstructing in and through this project. To cite other such statements, I am also interested in deconstructing those statements that contribute most to the constitution of capitalist powers — the many different accounting statements that define our economic relations. These include bank statements, credit statements, billing statements, and invoice statements, of course, but they also include statements like our credit reports or credit histories, which are aggregate many different accounting statements in order to determine their normal distributions and optimize their trends. These many different account statements, like the student's report card, obscure our needs and abilities: they primarily serve to filter and channel apart people who regularly make required deposits and payments in a timely manner from people who are irregular and untimely with their deposits and payments, without respect for whether and how being irregular and untimely can make sense.

We will never have communistic economic relations if domineering accounting statements define our economic relations. So, my question in this regard is, "How do we (re-)construct convivial statements that enable different economic actors to express their needs and abilities to one another, especially when they have needs that make them untimely?"

Entrapment

Detective fiction has been my favorite genre of fiction since I was a young boy. I have read and reread the books, and I have watched and rewatched the films in which the exploits of the great fictional detectives are dramatized — the greatest of these, in my opinion, being the books and films of the exploits of Auguste Dupin, Sherlock Holmes, and Hercule Poirot.

The great fictional detective solves a whodunnit by discovering who had the motive, the means, and the opportunity to commit the crime under investigation. While all three of the great fictional detectives excel at discerning all three of these factors, Poirot is the greatest when it comes to discerning motives, Holmes is the greatest when it comes to discerning means, and Dupin is the greatest when it comes to discerning opportunities.

To have motive to commit a crime is to have "the right reasons"; and to discern motives is to attend to the statements that have enabled a crime to occur. Hercule Poirot's great mysteries are defined by his close regard for statements that bear witness to crimes. To cite one of his most masterful performances: in *Cards on the Table*, Hercule Poirot uses the score sheets of different players from a bridge game as statements to discern who committed a murder.

To have the means to commit a crime is to have "the right tools"; and to discern means is to attend to the implements that have enabled a crime to occur. Sherlock Holmes's great mysteries are defined by the manner in which Holmes closely regards implements. To cite one of his most masterful performances: in the opening chapter of *The Sign of the Four*, titled "The Science of Deduction", Holmes describes the character and life circumstances of Watson's elder brother after examining an old watch that once belonged to him, demonstrating to Dr. Watson that "it is difficult for a man to have any object in daily use without leaving the impress of his individuality upon it in such a way that a trained observer might read it."

To have opportunity to commit a crime is to be "in the right place at the right time"; and to discern opportunities is to attend to the environments that have enabled a crime to occur. Auguste Dupin's great mysteries are each defined by their environments: "The Murders in the Rue Morgue" is about finding the opportunity to commit a crime in warren of city streets; "The Mystery of Marie Rogêt" in the great outdoors; and "The Purloined Letter" in an enclosed private space.

While it is certainly fun to attend to how the great detective discovers the criminal by deducing motives, means, and opportunities from statements, implements, and environments, I find that the detective work is never the most interesting part of a detective story for me. As I see it, before the criminal can be discovered by the detective, the crime and the criminal must themselves be produced by the power formations that constitute the world in which the detective novel is set. What I love to do when considering detective fiction is to read between the lines and consider how it is that power formations have produced the criminal that the great detective will discover.

A power formation manufactures a criminal by manufacturing motives, means, and opportunities for criminals to commit crimes. When an individual or group is discovered to have intentionally manufactured motives, means, and opportunities for criminals to commit crimes, we call it entrapment. But when pre-individual processes and supra-individual structures manufacture such motives, means, and opportunities, it is taboo to call it entrapment, although that is precisely what it is. If we do not call it entrapment when pre-individual processes and supra-individual structures are at work, it is because we do not want to acknowledge the fact that the world that we have made for ourselves is responsible for most crimes, not the criminal. Indeed, I wager that most criminals are made such by their worlds: they are not "true criminals" in and of themselves. I hold that the only "true criminal" is the one who has self-consciously made themself into a criminal: who has self-consciously manufactured motives, means, and opportunities for themselves in order to enable themselves to commit crimes.

Now, what I would like to do here is generalize the concept of entrapment further and to argue that entrapment is, in essence, the modus operandi of all stable power formations. Most people who dominate others by way of ruling, disciplinary, normalizing, and optimizing powers have been entrapped: they are the victims of pre-individual processes and supra-individual structures that have furnished them with motives, means, and opportunities to dominate others.

We who would counter power must, like the great detectives, attend to the statements, implements, and environments that provide motives, means, and opportunities for domination and exploitation. However, unlike the great detectives, we are not interested in simply apprehending who is dominating and exploiting whom at any given time. Rather, we are interested in preventing domination and exploitation from taking place: we aim to deconstruct the statements, implements, and environments that enable domination and exploitation and to (re-)construct statements, implements, and environments that enable people(s) to commune with one another.

Imagine, if you will, a great detective who did not concern themselves with being able to identify and apprehend murderers or thieves. Imagine that this detective chose to concern themselves with providing people with motives, means, and opportunities to live otherwise than becoming murderers and thieves. Instead of taking a world of murderers and thieves for granted, such a detective would be someone who endeavors to make a world in which fewer people might become murderers and thieves

In and through the (De-/Re-)Constructing Worlds project, I am advocating for a similar approach to dealing with power and its addicts. Instead of identifying and condemning people for being power addicts, hooked on the potent power-cocktail that is imperialist white-supremacist capitalist patriarchy, I am concerned with furnishing persons who are vulnerable to becoming power addicts with motives, means, and opportunities to live otherwise than becoming power addicts. Instead of taking a world of power addicts for granted, I would endeavor to make a world in which fewer people might become power addicts.

Ethnocide and Ecocide

Genocide is the extermination of one or more determinate ancestries effected by and through the eradication of individuals belonging to the given ancestries. The fact that genocide primarily targets individuals, depriving individuals of their liberties and their lives, makes genocide easy for the liberal minded to recognize and decry as an atrocity. What makes it difficult for the liberal minded to recognize and decry ethnocide and ecocide is the fact that the targets of ethnocide and ecocide are not individuals but pre-individual processes and supra-individual structures.

Ethnocide is the extermination of one or more determinate cultures effected by and through the inhibition of the pre-individual processes and the destruction of the supra-individual structures that together constitute the given cultures. Ethnocide and genocide do not necessarily imply one another insofar as a given ancestry can survive the extermination of its culture and a given culture can survive the extermination of some of its ancestries. This is the case because a person of a given ancestry may not be initiated into the culture of their ancestors, and because a person may be initiated into a given culture without having any ancestral ties to the culture. Regard, for instance, how the ethnocide of Indigenous American peoples occasionally involved genocide but was also effected by other many other means including displacement, re-education, and criminalization. Alternatively, regard how the enslavement of Black peoples in the Americas was ethnocidal without always being genocidal: ancestry needed to be maintained as part and parcel of being Black and being a slave, but being Black and being a slave meant being continually deprived of ties to an ancestral culture. And as final example, regard how White American and European eugenicists conducted a genocide without ethnocide when they endeavored to eradicate the "degenerate" ancestries of the mentally and physically "disabled" from White American and European cultures.

Ecocide is the extermination of one or more determinate habitats effected by the inhibition of the pre-individual processes and the destruction of the supra-individual structures that together constitute the habitats. Ecocide does not necessarily mean genocide for all ancestries with ties to threatened habitats: individuals of a given ancestry may survive the extermination of the habitat that nurtured their ancestors. Neither does ecocide necessarily mean ethnocide for cultures with ties to threatened habitats: a pastoral nomadic culture, for instance, may survive the extermination of one of the different habitats that they occasionally pass through.

Cultures threatened by ethnocide and habitats threatened by ecocide are to be found wherever and whenever you find that imperialist white-supremacist capitalist patriarchy has spread, and it has spread very far and very wide. Indeed, imperialist white-supremacist capitalist patriarchy has spread so far and wide that (i) any and every culture that does not yield to the advance of capitalist relations of production is now threatened with ethnocide, and (ii) any and every habitat on our planet that has yet to be exploited in the service of advancing capitalist relations of production is now threatened with ecocide.

The evidence of ecocide is mounting everyday. A radio news broadcast informs us, "Human activities have caused the world's wildlife populations to plummet by more than two-thirds in the last 50 years, according to a new report from the World Wildlife Fund." And keen observers tell us the crisis is much more than an extinction crisis, "The numerical robustness, the plenitude within nature, has dwindled. Many species continue to exist but in greatly diminished numbers, which means that the species itself has a far more tenuous hold on existence. As species crash and vanish, the world loses diversity, but the loss of abundance is even more startling." Yet when liberals in positions of power speak of promoting sustainability and conserving wildlife, I find that they are not earnestly speaking of confronting ecocide and promoting robust natural diversity. To the contrary, they are speaking of adopting a more deliberate and controlled approach to ecocide, an approach that destroys even more habitats but leads to even fewer outright extinctions.

The evidence of ethnocide is also mounting everyday. A newspaper article informs us, "Of the estimated 7,000 languages spoken in the world today, linguists say, nearly half are in danger of extinction and are likely to disappear in this century. In fact, they are now falling out of use at a rate of about one every two weeks." But when liberals in positions of power speak of promoting diversity, equity, and inclusion, I find that they are not earnestly speaking of confronting ethnocide and promoting robust cultural diversity. To the contrary, I find that they are speaking of enlisting more and more individuals of diverse ancestries as proxies in the ethnocidal and ecocidal endeavors of imperialist white-supremacist capitalist patriarchy.

Though it is taboo for those in positions of power acknowledge it explicitly, ethnocide and ecocide are the great scourges of our time. There is no need, however, for us to identify and round up all those who are, have been, or may become complicit in ethnocide and ecocide. Instead, let us work to deconstruct the statements, implements, and environments that furnish people with motives, means, and opportunities to become complicit in ethnocide and ecocide; and let us work to (re-)construct alternative statements, implements, and environments, so as to furnish persons who are vulnerable to becoming complicit in ethnocide and ecocide with motives, means, and opportunities to live otherwise than becoming complicit in these atrocities.

A Case In Point

During the Late Victorian period three waves of drought and famine killed no less than 30 million people in tropical Africa, Asia, and South America between 1870-1914, "at the precise moment ... when [the] labor and products [of tropical humanity] were being dynamically conscripted into a London-centered world economy." As Mike Davis writes in *Late Victorian Holocausts*, "Millions died, not outside the 'modern world system,' but in the very process of being forcibly incorporated into its economic and political structures."

Karl Polanyi, writing about the devastation that took place in India in particular during the Late Victorian period, keenly observed that "Indian masses in the second half of the nineteenth century did not die of hunger because they were exploited by Lancashire; they perished in large numbers because the Indian village community had been demolished."

Over the course of centuries, Indian village communities had become attuned to their ecologies and were fully aware that drought and famine could occur when one least expected it. They had developed a variety of different cultural practices around the conservation and sharing of grain and other foodstuffs in order to prevent mass deaths by malnutrition and starvation. Millions died during the Late Victorian period because these cultural practices had been suppressed by British colonists so that excess grain went to industrial cities like Lancashire instead of being conserved in granaries in India for use by Indian villages the event of drought and famine. Deprived of these cultural practices, Indian village communities had become defenseless against mass deaths by malnutrition and starvation during droughts and famines. This is to say, in other words, that British colonists had ensured that mass deaths were the inevitable result of drought and famine—as one keen British observer remarked at the time, they had devised "a brilliant way to organize famine."

What happened in India happened all over tropical Africa, Asia, and South America between 1870-1914. White European colonial powers integrated colonized peoples into the "modern world system" by suppressing cultural practices that had, prior to colonization, served to ward off mass deaths by malnutrition and starvation during droughts and famines. Deprived of these cultural practices, colonized peoples all over Africa, Asia, and South America had become defenseless against malnutrition and starvation during droughts and famines.

The Late Victorian Holocausts that Mike Davis chronicles were not the inevitable result of the droughts and famines. Rather, they were the inevitable result of the ethnocides that had preceded the droughts and famines. Ethnocide, you will recall, is the extermination of one or more determinate cultures effected by and through the inhibition of the pre-individual processes and the destruction of the supra-individual structures that together constitute the given cultures. The Late Victorian Holocausts that Mike Davis chronicles occurred because White European colonial powers had effectively exterminated cultures that had previously enabled non-White and non-European peoples to collectively endure drought and famine by conserving, sharing, and redistributing resources.

The Late Victorian Holocausts that Mike Davis chronicles are limited to the 30 to 60 million deaths linked to the post-ethnocide El Niño droughts and famines of 1876–1878, 1896–1897, and 1899–1902. These 30 to 60 million deaths are only a portion of the after-effects of ethnocide on the peoples of the colonized world since 1492. Ay, and all these millions of deaths only hint at the many millions more who have suffered and who continue to suffer transgenerational traumas as a result of colonization, ethnocide, mass murder, and mass death by exposure. All of this put together constitutes the makings of the "Third World" which are, concomitantly, the makings of the "First World". Alternatively, to use the terms currently preferred by Davos Man and his ilk, all of this constitutes the makings of the "developing world" which are, concomitantly, the makings of the "developed world". The deathly El Niño famines chronicled by Mike Davis only mark an inflection point for all this carnage. The horrors encountered in the apocalyptic and post-apocalyptic scenarios of popular science fiction are pale after-images of the experiences of peoples, White and non-White, who suffered the creation of the developed and developing worlds.

When I write about the need for artful reparations in my Four Essays on Reparations, I am writing about reparations for ethnocide and all of its aftereffects, which cannot be limited to the profits that were made from the exploitation of the developing world. Artful reparations, as I conceive of them, must enable peoples who have suffered ethnocide (i) to grieve the cultures they have lost as a result of ethnocide, (ii) to recover what remains of the cultures they have lost, and (iii) to artfully repair (and/or repurpose) what remains of their lost cultures. Imperialist white-supremacist capitalist patriarchy refuses to let us grieve the loss of our cultures and, instead, demands that we celebrate the "progress" occasioned by the extermination of our cultures. Then, to rub salt into the wound, imperialist white-supremacist capitalist patriarchy proceeds to employ us to recover those fragments of our lost cultures that are sought after as raw materials for the academic knowledge industry, the cultural tourism industry, and the commercial culture industry. Ay, and it employs us in this regard while frustrating our efforts to recover those fragments that are not sought after raw materials for industry and that might sustain us apart from industry.

Going further, to make sense of what I mean by artful reparations, it is important that I stress the fact that ethnocide is the extermination of *determinate* cultures. I stress this fact in order to point out that ethnocide begins by making otherwise indeterminate cultures into determinate cultures. In making this point, I am expanding upon the point made in Edward Said's *Orientalism*. Said teaches us that determinate "Oriental" cultures did not pre-exist the ethnocidal machinations of White European colonial powers. White European colonial powers bent on ethnocide were initially faced with otherwise indeterminate landscapes composed of many confluent and dynamic cultures that could neither be disentangled from each other nor from Western cultures. White European colonial powers bent on ethnocide had to transform this otherwise indeterminate landscape into a determinate landscape, one composed of fewer segregated and stagnant "Oriental" cultures that could be more easily disentangled from each other and from Western cultures. It was only after segregating groups of different "Oriental" cultures apart from each other and from Western cultures that White European colonial powers could endeavor to exterminate different groups of "Oriental" cultures separately, apart from one another. Similar ethnocidal operations were carried out by Western European colonial powers in Africa, Asia, and the Americas. Indeed, the national borders that we see on world maps today are evidence of so many effective ethnocidal operations of this sort, including many such operations carried out by some Europeans against other Europeans.

Artful reparations for ethnocide can only be made by and through the recreation of otherwise indeterminate landscapes composed of many confluent and dynamic cultures, and this re-creation is the aim of the (De-/Re-)Constructing Worlds project. The project asks the following questions:

· How can we identify and deconstruct the statements, implements, and environments that have furnished motives, means, and opportunities for ethnocide?

· How can we (re-)construct alternative statements, implements, and environments that will furnish us with motives, means, and opportunities to (i) grieve cultures devastated by ethnocide, (ii) recover what remains of these devastated cultures, and (iii) artfully repair (and/or repurpose) what remains of these cultures so as to recreate otherwise indeterminate landscapes composed of confluent and dynamic cultures?

Returning to the devastation that took place in India during the Late Victoria period, we could begin by examining the environments that furnished British colonists with the opportunity to perpetrate the ethnocides that resulted in mass deaths during the droughts and famines of the period.

In this regard, it is worth quoting a little bit from the book *Saffron, White, and Green* by Subhadra Sen Gupta:

> India had been invaded many times, and after the Greeks, Afghans, Mongols
> and Persians, the English were the last in the line. However, there was one big
> difference between the British and other conquerors like the Mughals. The earlier
> invaders remained in India and gradually merged with the people; the British
> never made India their home. They lived in segregated, gated communities, did
> not mix socially with Indians and would all go back to England with their fortunes
> and generous pensions. Often there was mutual respect and at times great
> kindness, but the distances between the ruler and the ruled were always carefully
> maintained.

The mass deaths that occurred during the droughts and famines of the Late
Victorian period in India were opportuned in part by the *segregated environments*,
the gated communities, in which the British colonial agents lived their protected
lives, relatively untouched by drought and famine, keeping the starving Indian
masses at a distance. Previous conquerors were never eager to destroy Indian
cultural practices that protected against drought and famine because they never
segregated themselves apart from Indian peoples in the scrupulous manner that
was characteristic of the British colonists. Indeed, as Gupta notes in the passage
above, previous conquering cultures became increasingly confluent with conquered
Indian cultures and conquered Indian cultures became increasingly confluent with
conquering cultures. Indeed, the progressive development of increasingly devious,
scrupulous, and subtle operations for segregating populations is one of the hallmarks
of imperialist white-supremacist capitalist patriarchy.

Another hallmark of imperialist white-supremacist capitalist patriarchy is its
claim that such segregation is necessary in order to protect defenseless White
women against the seductive and/or rapacious behavior of non-White peoples.
One of the primary justifications that the British claimed for building more and
more segregated communities in India was their need to protect White women
from being exposed to and contaminated by Indian culture and by Indian men.
Segregated communities of colonists increasingly became the norm in India
as more and more White women arrived in India, some accompanying their
husbands, parents and siblings but others seeking to escape Europe to make a new
life for themselves. A whole host of domineering, *paternalistic statements* regarding
the susceptibility of White women to seduction and rape by non-White men
had motivated White European acquiescence to mass deaths in India during the
droughts and famines of the Late Victorian period. These statements, which
included pornography exoticizing the bodies and sexual practices of non-White
peoples, were doubly pernicious because they often simultaneously furnished
White men with motives to perpetrate acts of sexual exploitation and violence
against non-White others.

197

Let us discuss one last hallmark of imperialist white-supremacist capitalist patriarchy: the construction of means of transport that enable people to go from one place to another without having to care for the places existing between the one and the other.

Mike Davis writes in Late Victorian Holocausts that we need to "weigh smug claims about the life-saving benefits of steam transportation and modern grain markets [against the fact that] so many millions, especially in British India, died alongside railroad tracks [and] on the steps of grain depots". In doing so, one will quickly recognize that the railways in India were not built to enable the equitable distribution of shared resources amongst grain-producing Indian villages in the event of drought and famine. Rather, they were built to get grain from large grain depots to ports from which they could be shipped to the imperial metropole and lucrative grain markets.

This is to say, in other words, that the *exploitative implementation* of railway services in India provided the means for White Europeans to acquiesce to the mass deaths in India that occurred during the droughts and famines of the Late Victorian period.

If I was living in India during the El Niño droughts and famines of the Late Victorian period, I would be asking you the following questions:

- How might we deconstruct the environments that are segregating British colonists apart from starving Indians? And how might we (re-)construct environments that would integrate the British and the Indians?

- How might we deconstruct the statements that are motivating this segregation, including statements that enable British colonists to cite the susceptibility of White women to seduction and/or rape by non-White men? And how might we (re-)construct statements that would motivate integration, including statements enabling us to cite the potential for intimate, caring, and loving relationships amongst peoples of different cultures and races?

- How might we deconstruct the implementation of rail services that has enabled the transport of grain from India to the imperial metropole and lucrative grain markets while so many Indians are starving? And how might we (re-)construct railway services so as to implement the sharing of resources amongst dispersed Indian farming villages in the event of drought and famine?

For better or for worse, I am not living in India during the El Niño droughts and famines of the Late Victorian period. I am living in the United States of America during what could be called the Late Davosian period — named after the town, Davos, that hosts the annual World Economic Forum.

Living in America during the Late Davosian period, I am confronted by a cascade of economic, ecological, and public health crises that are devastating all the peoples, cultures, and habitats across the globe that have not yet yielded to the advance of imperialist white-supremacist capitalist patriarchy. Confronted with Late Davosian Holocausts fueled by so many climate catastrophes, what questions might I be asking you?

Another Black Man In America

By the time I was ten years old, the imperative had been drummed into my ears, beamed into my eyes, and even beaten into my flesh: excel intellectually, maintain good manners, be well-spoken, and, by all means, never let your appearance, bearing, and conduct slacken when you are under the Gaze of the White Man (or his proxies), lest you be taken for an uncultured, uncouth, and uncivilized Negro.

Whenever I failed in this regard — whenever I performed poorly at school, whenever I spoke and acted out of turn, whenever my appearance, bearing, and conduct was wild and unruly — I would be punished by my parents, and my punishment would inevitably be accompanied by the refrain, "Keep this up and you'll become just another Black man in America."

My parents knew that I knew that being "just another Black man in America" was something dreadful, even though the reasons why this was the case had never been explicitly stated to me by them or by anyone else. There was, of course, no need for them to state the obvious to me, was there? All that they had to teach me explicitly was the imperative that I save myself from the dreadful fate of becoming "just another Black man in America" by and through becoming a "Black man of distinction".

Now, I must state the obvious here, lest any reader play innocent. To be taken for "just another Black man in America" is to be subject to murder as an unintended consequence of routine disciplinary action, or as normal(ized) accident, or as the collateral damage of society's pursuit of progressive optimization. My murder requires little extra formal justification if I am taken for "just another Black man in America", but it requires detailed formal justification if I am taken for a Black man of distinction and not "just another Black man". Intellectual achievement, good manners, proper diction, a sophisticated appearance, bearing, and code of conduct — all of this signals to the world at large that I may be a Black man of distinction and that my murder may require detailed formal justification.

Knowing that my life was in real danger otherwise, my parents quite literally beat the imperative to signal distinction into me as a child, from the age of six up until the age of twelve. I am not alone in this regard: too many Black boys have been and are still being taught the imperative to signal distinction by and through injury and insult, acts of corporeal and communicative violence inflicted upon their bodies and psyches by people known to them as family, friends, mentors, and teachers. This sort of violence is but one of the many scourges of racism.

"What is racism?" Michel Foucault asked at the end of his 1975-1976 lectures at the Collège de France, titled "Society Must Be Defended". Foucault's answer to this question has stuck with me. In part, this is because being able to cite the sophisticated conjectures of erudite and esoteric Frenchmen is a mark of distinction for a Black man in America, but it is also because the sophistication of Foucault's conjecture is actually rather profound. Foucault's answer runs as follows:

[Racism] is primarily a way of introducing a break into the domain of life that is under power's control: the break between what must live and what must die. [...] In a normalizing society, race or racism is the precondition that makes killing acceptable. When you have a normalizing society, you have a power which is, at least superficially, in the first instance or in the first line a biopower, and racism is the indispensable condition that allows someone to be killed, that allows others to be killed. Once the state functions in the biopower mode, racism alone can justify the murderous function of the state. [...] If the power of normalization wished to exercise the old sovereign right to kill, it must become racist. And if, conversely, a power of sovereignty, or in other words a power that has the right of life and death, wishes to work with the instruments, mechanisms, and technology of normalization, it too must become racist. When I say "killing," I obviously do not mean simply murder as such, but also every form of indirect murder: the fact of exposing someone to death, increasing the risk of death for some people, or quite simply, political death, expulsion, rejection, and so on.

So, what is profound about Foucault's definition of racism? Well, as Foucault himself puts it, his definition holds that "[t]he specificity of modern racism, or what gives it its specificity, is not bound up with mentalities, ideologies, or the lies of power. It is bound up with the technique of power, with the technology of power." To be rather more specific, modern racism is bound up with techniques and technologies of normalizing power: normalizing statements, normalizing implements, and normalizing environments. Going a step beyond Foucault, insofar as optimizing powers are variable controllers and modulators of normalizing powers, I hold that prevailing techniques and technologies of optimizing power give rise to modular racisms or "postmodern racisms" that are more "liberal" and "progressive" than the modern racisms engendered when techniques and technologies of normalizing power prevail.

Techniques and technologies of normalizing power operate in rather obvious ways but, at the same time, they make it easy for some individuals to disavow their rather obvious operations, to mis-attribute their effects, to blame "isolated bad actors", "being at the wrong place at the wrong time", and "accidents of birth". Those who say that the police murder of another Black man in America is just a "normal accident" are disavowing the obvious fact that techniques and technologies of power have effectively normalized the "accidental" murder of Black men by police in America. Of course, those who find it easy to disavow this obvious fact are those for whom "accidental" murder by police has not been so normalized. By contrast, those for whom "accidental" murder by police has been normalized must perform remarkable mental gymnastics if they are to disavow this obvious fact and, what's more, they risk being murdered if they act in accord with such a disavowal.

Techniques and technologies of optimizing power are more subtle and insidious. Taking it for granted that the murder of another Black man in America is a "normal accident", optimizing powers aim to find ways to decrease the occurrence of "normal accidents" by subjecting Black men to increased administration and supervision. In other words, an optimizing power asks itself, "How can we better administer and supervise the lives of Black men so as to lower their normal murder-rate?" Optimizing powers tell us that Black males must not be left to their own devices: they "prove" to us that Black males are less likely to be murdered if they are placed into special after-school detention programs as young children, placed into special summer employment programs as young adults, and live their entire lives in neighborhoods patrolled by squadrons of police officers equipped with body-mounted surveillance cameras.

Optimizing powers teach us that Black male populations are "at risk populations" or "populations in crisis" that really ought to be set apart from other populations and put under special administration and supervision. To teach us this, optimizing powers will invariably cite the "fact" that Black male populations are unusually vulnerable to the "normal accident" that is murder, conveniently forgetting that this "fact" is artificially induced, the result of the effective operation of normalizing powers. Next, optimizing powers will "prove" the virtues of special administration and supervision by running more or less "controlled" experiments: they will demonstrate that sub-populations of Black men that submit to special administration and supervision are less likely to murdered than sub-populations that are left to their own devices. What needs to be understood here, however, is the fact that optimizing powers effectively work to maintain and increase murder-rates in sub-populations left to their own devices relative those that receive special administration and supervision. In effect, this means that optimizing powers confront Black males with a deathly ultimatum, "If you want to reduce your chances of being murdered, you must submit to some form of special administration and supervision; there is no alternative".

THE WAR ON TERRA & THE NEW UNDERGROUND RAILROAD

Optimizing powers, in other words, constitute a protection racket that compels its victims to surrender their autonomy instead of (or in addition to) their money. To recognize this is to recognize that incarceration as form of socio-political death in the US is only the most obvious part of the New Jim Crow power formation. To get a fuller picture of the New Jim Crow, I suggest you pay closer attention to the organs of the white savior industrial complex that operate within the US: they pass for social services and charitable organizations but they effectively compel Black people to surrender their autonomy, to submit to special administration and supervision, in order to receive protection from physical and socio-political death.

The Black man who signals to the world that they are a "Black man of distinction" is signaling to the world that they are ready, willing, and able to submit to special administration and supervision at all times. The Black man who signals to the world that they are "just another Black man" is signaling to the world that they will resist special administration and supervision. Black parents, fearing for the lives of their Black boys, endeavor to ensure that their boys are always ready, willing, and able to receive special administration and supervision. Indeed, returning to my own example, my parents wanted to ensure that I was ready, willing, and able to submit to extra-curricular administration and supervision but, between the ages of six and twelve at least, I actively resisted submitting to the most basic curriculum of administration and supervision — I was a truant and an underachiever. Knowing that my failure to submit to administration and supervision might very well result in my being murdered, my parents employed injury and insult, corporeal and communicative violence, to teach me a lesson and to compel me to submit. This is to say, in other words, that my parents thought that it was reasonable to employ corporeal and communicative violence against their child if doing so effectively meant keeping their child from being murdered. Raising me up in New York City and Pittsburgh during 1990s, the heyday of the Black boy as superpredator myth, my parents were by no means alone in this regard.

I need to reiterate that, throughout this text, I have not been referring to "simply murder as such" but "also every form of indirect murder: the fact of exposing someone to death, increasing the risk of death for some people, or quite simply, political death, expulsion, rejection, and so on."

In other words, rather than "simply murder as such", I have been referring murder as unintended consequence of routine disciplinary action, to murder as normal(ized) accident, and to murder as the collateral damage of society's pursuit of progressive optimization. To clarify this point, please allow me to interpolate a text by Friedrich Engels:

> When one individual inflicts bodily injury upon another such that death results, we call his deed murder. But when society places hundreds [...] in such a position that they inevitably meet a too early and an unnatural death, one which is quite as much a death by violence as that by the sword or bullet; when it deprives thousands of the necessaries of life, places them under conditions in which they cannot live — forces them, through the strong arm of the law, to remain in such conditions until that death ensues which is the inevitable consequence — knows that these thousands of victims must perish, and yet permits these conditions to remain, its deed is murder just as surely as the deed of the single individual; disguised, malicious murder, murder against which none can defend himself, which does not seem what it is, because no man sees the murderer, because the death of the victim seems a natural one, since the offence is more one of omission than of commission. But murder it remains.

Indeed, recognizing this, one must realize that loving Black parents are furnished with motives to inflict corporeal and communicative violence on their children by the proliferation of statements that enable authorities to treat the murders of their children as no more than the unintended consequences of routine disciplinary action, as normal(ized) accidents, and as the collateral damage of society's pursuit of progressive optimization. It is the prevalence of such domineering statements that enables the Black parent to legitimately think and say to a child as they beat and/or berate them, "I am teaching you a lesson that will save your life."

Looking beyond racism, I find that the sexist powers of patriarchy operate much like the racist powers of white-supremacy. Normalizing powers have made suffering sexual assault into a "normal accident" for women, and optimizing powers have compelled women to seek out special administration and supervision in order to reduce their chances of being sexually assaulted. The forms of special administration and supervision sought after include, but are not limited to, being chaperoned, obeying implicit or explicit dress codes, accepting ubiquitous surveillance, and allowing inquisitors and tribunals to scrutinize other women's sexual histories in order to "evaluate" their claims of sexual assault (but only so as to punish the most obvious and offensive perpetrators). Women who resist being subjected to these and other forms of special administration and supervision are slut shamed, told that they "are asking for it", "should know better", and "will get what they deserve". Too many parents with daughters feel that it is their duty to teach their daughters distinguish themselves from "other women" by willingly submitting to special administration and supervision whenever possible. They preemptively slut shame their own daughters in order to teach them this lesson at home before the harsh world outside teaches it to them. Too many parents overlook the fact that normalizing and optimizing powers are working together, in tandem, to ensure that women who resist submitting to special administration and supervision face an increased risk of being sexually assaulted relative those who willingly submit. In other words, the woman who resists administration and supervision becomes "just another woman" and is subject to sexual assault as unintended consequence of routine disciplinary action, as normal(ized) accident, and as the collateral damage of society's pursuit of progressive optimization. Ay, and it is most important that, when you read "sexual assault" here, you remind yourself that sexual assault comes in many different forms, physical and mental, direct and indirect, fatal and nonfatal.

The economic powers of capitalism also operate likewise. Normalizing powers ensure that compounding indebtedness, homelessness, and hunger are "normal accidents" for those who are unemployed; and optimizing powers compel the unemployed to seek special administration and supervision in order to reduce their chances of enduring compounding indebtedness, homelessness, and hunger. Those unemployed persons who resist being subjected to special administration and supervision are told they have "chosen" a life of compounding indebtedness, homelessness, and hunger: their sufferings are construed to be their own fault. Paternalistic public policies are then designed to make life harder for unemployed persons who resist special administration and supervision, with public servants making the paternalistic claim that such policies will "teach people to make smarter choices." In other words, the jobless person who resists administration and supervision becomes "just another one of the unemployed" and is subject to compounding indebtedness, homelessness, and hunger as unintended consequence of routine disciplinary action, as normal(ized) accident, and as the collateral damage of society's pursuit of progressive optimization.

205

Putting this all together, there is no worse fate today than being (mis)taken for "just another unemployed black, brown, or indigenous woman" by prevailing white-supremacist capitalist patriarchal powers. To be so (mis)taken is to be subject to murder, to sexual assault, to compounding indebtedness, to homelessness, to hunger, and to have all of this framed as the unintended consequence of routine disciplinary action, as normal(ized) accident, and as the collateral damage of society's pursuit of progressive optimization. It follows that those who may be (mis)taken for "just another unemployed black, brown, or indigenous woman" are put under the most pressure to submit to special administration and supervision, and they are judged most harshly when they dare to resist administration and supervision. With all this in mind, I beg you to indulge me and consider the single black mother who might easily be (mis)taken for "just another unemployed black woman" but who still has the courage and autonomy not only to resist administration and supervision herself but also to enable her black children to resist administration and supervision. If, like me, you would consider her to be the embodiment of a "free spirit par excellence", you will have no problem dismissing the Nietzschean pretensions of privileged White male artists and philosophers, as you will be thinking far more of Tupac's "Dear Mama" and far less of *Also sprach Zarathustra*.

Summing matters up, the champions of normalizing and optimizing powers will inevitably say that members of "at risk" population groups ought to submit themselves to special administration and supervision for their own good. By contrast, we who would counter power cannot and will not accept that further administration and supervision is a desirable solution for those who are "at risk", but what alternative solutions might we offer to the "at risk"? Well, it seems to me that whatever alternatives we might offer will almost certainly involve (i) the deconstruction of existing forms of administration and supervision that contribute to the making of separate and distinct "at risk" population groups, and (ii) the (re-) construction of convivial alternatives to administration and supervision that enable different populations to commune, confluence, and share risks with each other. Under this light, we might rephrase the question we just asked as follows: what constitutes a convivial alternative to administration and supervision?

Fugitive Planning

When I first announced the (De-/Re-)Constructing Worlds project, I was insistent that the project would promote "dilettantisms" in order to counter "careerist imperialisms". Taking my initial cues from Ivan Illich's work, I identified the advance of careerist imperialisms with "the mushrooming of professional monopolies over production." Pivoting now from Illich's work to the work of Michel Foucault, I would like to introduce this dispatch by proposing that any imperialism that privileges optimizing powers over ruling, disciplinary, and normalizing powers is, by definition, a careerist imperialism.

Readers will recall that my last dispatch described how optimizing powers prevail over normalizing powers. I wrote that normalizing powers first create "at risk" populations, then optimizing powers compel "at risk" individuals to submit to special administration and supervision by modulating normalizing powers: lowering risks for those individuals who submit to special administration and supervision; heightening risks for those individuals who cannot or will not submit. In other words, I proposed that the formation of optimizing powers always involves the proliferation of special administrative and supervisory organs that serve to modulate normalizing powers. Going further along this line of flight, I would like to propose now that the proliferation of special administrative and supervisory organs always involves the proliferation of specialized professions and specialized knowledges in their service. Ipso facto, any imperialism that privileges optimizing powers must also privilege the proliferation of specialized professions, which is to say, in other words, that any imperialism that privileges optimizing powers is a careerist imperialism. Imperialist white-supremacist capitalist patriarchy, the imperialism of greatest concern to me, has become a careerist imperialism insofar as it has come to privilege optimizing powers in its currently prevailing neoliberal manifestations.

In and through taking up the problem of (re-)constructing convivial alternatives to administration and supervision, the present dispatch is concerned with finding ways to counter careerist imperialisms, in general, and, in particular, with finding ways to counter the currently prevailing careerist manifestations of imperialist white-supremacist capitalist patriarchy.

Convivial (Re-)Construction

Members of "at risk" population groups are compelled by normalizing and optimizing powers to submit to special administration and supervision in order to lower the risks that they face. I left off the dispatch proposing that we who would counter power cannot and will not accept that submitting to special administration and supervision is a desirable solution for those "at risk". But this proposition begged the question, "What alternatives to administration and supervision might we propose to members of 'at risk' population groups?"

Rather than submitting to administration and supervision, I propose that, whenever one finds oneself "at risk", one may endeavor to engage in direct action and to defend direct action with due process, with the caveat being that one ought to prepare, execute, and evaluate every direct action with a mind for further direct action and every defense by due process with a mind for further defense by due process. To be more brief, I propose engaging in forms of direct action and in forms of defense by due process that are guided by forms of fugitive planning.

Many will find this proposal daunting. Most of us feel trapped in circumstances that make taking direct action seem nigh impossible for us. We feel that we have no alternative but to submit to administration and supervision whenever we find ourselves "at risk". This is because we have, in fact, been entrapped. Our present world of suffering furnishes us with numerous motives, means, and opportunities to submit to administration and supervision, but we search this world in vain for motives, means, and opportunities to live otherwise by engaging in forms of direct action, defense by due process, and fugitive planning. Personally, finding that I lack the motives, means, and opportunities to live otherwise, I regularly present myself to others as a Black man who is always ready, willing, and able to submit to administration and supervision. I am too afraid of becoming "just another unemployed Black man in America", being subjected to hunger, homelessness, ruthless indebtedness, and murder, and having all of this framed by authorities as the unintended consequence of routine disciplinary action, as normal(ized) accident, and as the collateral damage of society's pursuit of progressive optimization.

Recognizing the real and frightening difficulties here, I cannot simply propose that those "at risk" should engage in direct action, defense by due process, and fugitive planning. The aim of the (De-/Re-)Constructing Worlds project is (i) to deconstruct some of the domineering statements, implements, and environments that are presently furnishing us with motives, means, and opportunities to submit to administration and supervision and (ii) to (re-)construct convivial statements, implements, and environments that furnish us with motives, means, and opportunities to live otherwise by engaging in forms of direct action, defense by due process, and fugitive planning.

Direct Action

David Graeber defined direct action by marking the difference between direct action and protest.

> [T]he difference between protest and direct action ... [is that] protest, however militant, is an appeal to authorities to behave differently; [by contrast,] direct action is [...] a matter of proceeding as one would if the existing structure of power did not exist. Direct action is, ultimately, the defiant insistence on acting as if one is already free.

Graeber's definition appeals to me a great deal, but I believe that it could be made more precise. To use my own clinical language here, I propose that engaging in direct action is not simply a matter of acting as if existing power formations do not exist but, rather, it is a matter of acting as if existing power formations are unstable and continuously (re-)negotiable as opposed to stable and non-negotiable.

Direct action never assumes that anyone has the power to rule, to discipline, to normalize, or to optimize. Much to the contrary, direct action always assumes that no power can rule, discipline, normalize, or optimize without its subjects' consent, and it further assumes that consent is only ever given provisionally and may be withdrawn at a moments notice without instigating any retaliation from powers' agents in response. It follows from this that a direct action must always involve a continuous consensus process — not a discrete consent form or a discrete polling forum, but a continuous conversation that (re-)negotiates a dissensus in consensus and a consensus in dissensus. Direct action that doesn't make time for conversation as it proceeds is not really direct action, because direct action cannot proceed on the basis of an established command hierarchy. Those engaged in direct action are always engaged in making time for conversation. They know that conversation can never be a waste of time if there is ample time to converse; conversation can only ever be a waste of time when there is scarce time to converse.

With this clinical definition in mind, let us reconsider the difference between protest and direct action. As I read it, Graeber's point is that those who protest are, in effect, insisting that ritualized spectacles, routine examinations, biased surveys, and/or variable controls have gained power over them without their consent. This is to say, in other words, that those who protest are reacting against what they believe to have power over them. Thus, power should be, and often is, flattered more than it is frightened by protest because protest is evidence that power doesn't have to prove itself anymore, it is evidence that people believe that they must appeal to power.

Whereas a protest is a reaction that appeals to powers that may (or may not) be, a direct action is an enaction that exposes the powers that be for what they are. When we engage in direct action we insist that ritualized spectacles, routine examinations, biased surveys, and variable controls must prove that they have power over us. In so doing, we discover to what extent we are already free and precisely what freedoms we are lacking. Power should fear direct action more than protest because people engaged in direct action are demanding proof that power is what it claims to be. A power that has to prove itself is, by definition, a power that might fail to prove itself. Nay, more, a power that has to prove itself is a power that is failing, because a power diminishes itself every time it proves itself.

Protest on its own can only ever interpret the world; direct action challenges and changes the world. Protest is only ever coterminous with direct action when powers fear their own shadows, a situation which is not uncommon, and they endeavor to prohibit and punish protest because of this fear, turning protest into a rather curious form of direct action. In all other instances, protest is an idealist practice, an expression of ideology. Direct action, by contrast, is always an empiricist practice, an experiment in praxis.

Now, this is all very abstract, I know. But this is because each and every direct action must be a reflection of the particular needs and abilities of the actors involved. In lieu of a case study, I implore you to use your imaginations. Imagine, if you will, that you are at risk for hunger and homelessness. Are there forms of direct action that you might engage in with others so as to forage, cultivate, and fabricate your way out of hunger and homelessness? When asking yourself this question, don't think of others in general but, rather, think of particular others with whom you might associate. As I see it, only particular assemblies of people can effectively plan, execute, and evaluate direct actions; general assemblies can effectively engage in protest and establish policies but they cannot effectively engage in direct action.

Defense by Due Process

Let's say that we engage in direct action and that we face retaliation from a power formation: imprisonment, eviction, public censure, police brutality, and/or even murder. If the retaliation is enacted or overseen by a lower administrative and supervisory organ that is subject to review and regulation by higher administrative and supervisory organs, we (or our survivors) may defend our direct action with due process: we may appeal to the higher authority, and we may make the case that the lower authority overstepped in retaliating against us.

The defense by due process practiced by the direct activist is not the same as the defense by due process practiced by the rights activist. This practical difference is of great importance. The rights activist demands that human or civil rights are enshrined by higher authorities and respected by lower authorities, and the rights activist engages in direct action as a means to this end. The rights activist uses direct action to demonstrate that lower forms of administration and supervision are liable to overstep their authority, and then to make the case that higher authorities must be vigilant in reviewing and regulating lower authorities.

The rights activist is not interested in direct action for itself but, rather, they are interested in whether and how direct action might initiate forms of due process that subject lower forms administration and supervision to review and regulation by higher forms of administration and supervision.

The direct activist, by contrast, is interested in direct action for itself. The direct activist holds that the goal of direct action is to defy administration and supervision and to demonstrate that direct action can be desirable and effective. The direct activist holds that direct action is both the means and the end. The direct activist engages in defense by due process if, and only if, they encounter retaliation from a lower administrative and supervisory organ upon engaging in direct action. If the direct activist encounters no such retaliation, they will simply continue to engage in direct action, and that is that.

Going further, when engaging in defense by due process, the direct activist doesn't really care to subject lower forms administration and supervision to higher forms of administration and supervision. Rather, when engaging in defense by due process, the direct activist is endeavoring to put higher and lower forms of administration and supervision into conflict with one another in such a way that they short circuit and cancel one another out.

In other words, the direct activist is not appealing to higher forms of administration and supervision in order to restrain lower forms but, rather, they are engaging higher forms in order to sabotage lower forms and they are engaging lower forms in order to sabotage higher forms. According to the direct activist, the end result of defense by due process ought to be that neither higher forms nor lower forms of authority can effectively administer and supervise anyone any longer without their freely and continuously given consent.

I am taking my cues from Gilles Deleuze in this regard. Deleuze, in an interview with Claire Parnet, went so far as to identify jurisprudence with the defense of direct action, chiding those who concerned themselves exclusively with the defense of rights.

> I mean, we say "human rights", but in the end, that's a party line for intellectuals, and for odious intellectuals, and for intellectuals without any ideas of their own. Right off the bat, I've noticed that these declarations of human rights are never done by way of the people that are primarily concerned.

> [...] All of the abominations through which humans have suffered are cases. They're not denials of abstract rights; they're abominable cases. One can say that these cases resemble each other, have something in common, but they are situations for jurisprudence.

> [...] [T]hose who are content to remind us of human rights, and recite lists of human rights — they are idiots. It's not a question of applying human rights. It is one of inventing jurisprudences where, in each case, this or that [abomination] will no longer be possible. And that's something quite different.

Those engaged in defining and defending rights often refuse to recognize due process in defense of direct action as a legitimate form of due process. Indeed, those who "manage" our existing assemblies for due process, our so-called justice systems, tend to believe that rights activism is the only kind of activism that can be defended by due process, and they decry due process in defense of direct action as a form corruption. Ivan Illich remarks upon this fact in *Tools for Conviviality*:

> The use of [due process] for the purpose of hampering, stopping, and inverting [processes of administration and supervision] will appear to its managers and addicts as a misuse of the law and as subversion of the only order which they recognize. The use of [due process] to [defend direct action] appears corrupt and criminal to the bureaucrat, even one who calls himself a judge.

The rights activist is acceptable to the powers that be because the rights activist believes in the rule of law. The direct activist is unacceptable because the direct activist doesn't believe in the rule of law but in direct action. To explain this, you may recall that direct action assumes that there can be no power to rule, discipline, normalize, or optimize without consent, and it further assumes that all consent is given provisionally and may be withdrawn at a moments notice.

It follows from this that direct action assumes that there can be no rule of law without consent and that consent to the rule of law is only ever provisional and may be withdrawn at a moments notice; thus, to believe in direct action is not to believe in the sanctity of the rule of law but to believe in the need for a continuous consensus process.

Again, imagine that you are at risk for hunger and homelessness. Are there forms of direct action that you might engage in with others so as to forage, cultivate, and fabricate your way out of hunger and homelessness? Are these forms of direct actions prohibited and/or punishable? What forms of due process might enable you to skirt prohibitions and ward off punishments when engaging in direct action?

Fugitive Planning

Fugitive planning, as I understand it, is the way in which direct activists make sense of direct action and due process in defense of direct action.

In brief, fugitive planning means three things to me:

- Fugitive planning means planning to defend direct action with due process whenever possible, because there is no sense in engaging in a direct action if we have yet to consider whether and how we might have recourse to defense by due process.

- Fugitive planning means planning to follow every direct action with further direct action, because there is no sense in a direct action that doesn't enable further direct action.

- Fugitive planning means planning to follow every defense by due process with further defense by due process, because there is no sense in a defense by due process that doesn't enable further defense by due process.

Imagine, once again, that you are at risk for hunger and homelessness. Are there forms of direct action that you might engage in with others so as to forage, cultivate, and fabricate your way out of hunger and homelessness? Which of these forms of direct action might enable further direct action? Are these enabling forms of direct actions prohibited and punishable? If so, are there any forms of defense by due process that might enable you to skirt prohibitions and ward off punishments while engaging in enabling forms of direct action? Which of these forms of defense by due process might enable further defense by due process?

Asking and answering the series of questions above constitutes an exemplary instance of fugitive planning.

213

Every instance of fugitive planning (and every fugitive planner) maintains that world-making ought to precede, exceed, and succeed any and all direct actions and defenses by due process. Indeed, another way to define fugitive planning would be to say that fugitive planning is a practice that aims to ensure that every direct action and every defense by due process somehow contributes to the making of worlds, to the making of statements, implements, and environments, that furnish us with motives, means, and opportunities for further direct actions and defenses by due process.

Earlier on, I had to distinguish direct action from protest and to distinguish due process in defense of direct action from due process in defense of rights. In a similar vein, I now have to distinguish fugitive planning from public policy. To this end, please allow me to cite a rather difficult passage from *The Undercommons* by Fred Moten and Stefano Harney.

> Planning is self-sufficiency at the social level, and it reproduces in its experiment not just what it needs, life, but what it wants, life in difference [...] Planning starts from the solidity, the continuity, and the rest of this social self-sufficiency, though it does not end there [...] Planning begins [...] with what we might call a militant preservation. And these are its means. Policy deputises those willing to, those who come to want to, break up these means as a way of controlling them, as once it was necessary to de-skill a worker in a factory by breaking up his means of production. And it does this by diagnosing the planners. Policy says that those who plan have something wrong with them, something deeply – ontologically – wrong with them. This is the first thrust of policy as dispersed, deputised command. What's wrong with them? They won't change. They won't embrace change. They've lost hope. So say the policy deputies. They need to be given hope. They need to see that change is the only option. By change what the policy deputies mean is contingency, risk, flexibility, and adaptability to the groundless ground of the hollow capitalist subject, in the realm of automatic subjection that is capital. Policy is thus arrayed in the exclusive and exclusionary uniform/ity of contingency as imposed consensus, which both denies and at the very same time seeks to destroy the ongoing plans, the fugitive initiations, the black operations, of the multitude.

> As resistance from above, policy is a new class phenomenon because the act of making policy for others, of pronouncing others as incorrect, is at the same time an audition for a post-fordist economy that deputies believe rewards those who embrace change but which, in reality, arrests them in contingency, flexibility, and [...] administered precarity.

What are Moten and Harney getting at with all of this? Well, as I read them, they are pointing out that public policy endeavors to placate protesters and to facilitate due process in defense of rights. Fugitive planning, by contrast, endeavors to nurture direct activists and to facilitate due process in defense of direct action. Public policy, working against fugitive planning, aims to encourage members of "at risk" populations to engage in protest and rights activism and to discourage them from engaging in direct activism and fugitive planning. To this end, public policy pathologizes direct activists and fugitive planners for lacking faith in the rule of law and in the power of protest to shape public policy. For their part, self-conscious fugitive planners respond to this pathologization, "You want to oblige us to govern, to become complicit in our own subordination and extermination, to help you optimize ethnocide and ecocide. We won't yield to that pressure."

I write this recalling years as protester behind me, recalling my first ever protest as a teenager during the run up to the Iraq War. I write this with a hand bearing the scar of an encounter with a police baton received at the last protest that I ever attended, a march in Chicago against mass incarceration and for the rights of victims of police brutality from whom confessions had been extracted by torture. I write this with a heartfelt appreciation for the ways in which protest and rights activism can bring people together and ease their sufferings by shaping public policy. Yet I know from experience that, unless protests can gather a critical mass, the powers that be usually get to determine the pace and the terms that enable protests and rights activism to work, and I know that the powers that be always set the pace and the terms to effect optimal burnout in "at risk" populations. Indeed, I write this recalling the experience of burnout: I had to learn the hard way that more tends to be suffered than gained whenever one protests in support of a cause that lacks mass appeal and, even worse, whenever one dresses up one's cause in the latest fashion in a bid for mass appeal. Ay, and I write in favor of direct action, defense by due process, and fugitive planning because these practices enable people to continuously and convivially (re-)negotiate the pace and the terms for their coming together and for the easing of their sufferings.

Planning to Flee From Schooling

Why do we live in a deathly world of suffering in which schooling is considered to be more important than learning?

It is well understood that schooling is but one of many different forms of learning. What's more, it is well known that schooling has never been proven the best form of learning. Nevertheless, schooling is undoubtedly the most privileged form of learning in our deathly world of suffering; all other forms of learning are considered suspect and those who learn otherwise than being schooled are prejudiced against.

Given that the benefits of schooling for learning are unproven, I would hazard a guess that privileges and prejudices favoring schooling and the schooled are part and parcel of the power formations prevailing over our deathly world of suffering — imperialist white-supremacist capitalist patriarchy being the most prevalent but by no means the only power formation that privileges schooling and the schooled.

Lest I be woefully misunderstood, let me definitively state for the record that I am not at all against learning (this should be obvious), nor am I always necessarily against schooling as a particular form of learning. I am chiefly against privileges and prejudices that favor schooling and the schooled.

Modern schooling is a highly administered and supervised form of learning. The primary purpose of subjecting individuals to compulsory schooling during their formative years is to get individuals into the unconscious habit of submitting to administration and supervision. Our deathly world of suffering privileges schooling over all other forms of learning for this very reason. The prevailing power formations that filter and channel those who are more schooled apart from those who are less schooled are, in other words, power formations that effectively filter and channel those who have proven themselves more often ready, willing, and able to submit to high levels of administration and supervision apart from those who have proven themselves more often unready, unwilling, and/or unable.

Many readers will recognize that I am, once again, taking my cues from Ivan Illich here. Indeed, because I feel I cannot do him one better on this point, I will quote at length from Illich, some bits and pieces sutured together from the books *Deschooling Society* and *Tools for Conviviality*.

Neither learning nor justice is promoted by schooling because educators insist on packaging instruction with certification. Learning and the assignment of social roles are melted into schooling. Yet to learn means to acquire a new skill or insight, while promotion depends on an opinion which others have formed. Learning frequently is the result of instruction, but selection for a role or category in the job market increasingly depends on mere length of attendance.

Age-specific, compulsory competition on an unending ladder for lifelong privileges cannot increase equality but must favor those who start earlier, or who are healthier, or who are better equipped outside the classroom. Inevitably, it organizes society into many layers of failure, with each layer inhabited by dropouts schooled to believe that those who have consumed more [schooling] deserve more privilege because they are more valuable assets to society as a whole. [...] High consumers of education get postdoctoral grants, while dropouts learn that they have failed [...] [T]hey are schooled to [...] rationalize their growing frustration outside school by accepting their rejection from scholastic grace. [...] As Max Weber traced the social effects of the belief that salvation belonged to those who accumulated wealth, we can now observe that grace is reserved for those who accumulate years in school.

Schools select for each successive level those who have, at earlier stages of the game, proven themselves good risks for the established order. Having a monopoly on both the resources for learning and the investiture of social roles, the university coopts the discoverer and the potential dissenter. A degree always leaves an indelible price tag on the curriculum of it's consumer. Certified college graduates fit only into a world that puts a price tag on their heads, thereby giving them the power to define the level of expectations in their society. In each country the amount of consumption by the college graduate sets the standard for all others; if they would be civilized people on or off the job, they will aspire to the style of life of college graduates.

There is no question that at present the university offers a unique combination of circumstances which allows some of its members to criticize the whole of society. It provides time, mobility, access to peers and information, and a certain impunity — privileges not equally available to other segments of the population. But the university provides this freedom only to those who have already been deeply initiated into the consumer society and into the need for some kind of obligatory public schooling.

The American university has become the final stage of the most all encompassing initiation rite the world has ever known. No society in history has been able to survive without ritual or myth, but ours is the first which has needed such a full, protracted, destructive, and expensive initiation into its myth. The contemporary civilization is also the first one which has found it necessary to rationalize it's fundamental initiation ritual in the name of education.

School is not only the New World Religion. It is also the fastest growing labor market. [...] If we add those engaged in full-time teaching to those in full-time attendance, we realize that this so-called superstructure has become society's major employer. [...] The New World Church is the knowledge industry, both purveyor of opium and workbench during an increasing number of years of an individual's life. Deschooling is, therefore, at the root of any movement for human liberation.

217

In our deathly world of suffering, those who do not go to school find themselves "at risk" of never learning what they need to learn in order to realize their abilities. This is not because schooling is the only way for them to learn but, rather, it is because schools have a monopoly over access to most of the intellectual and material resources required for learning. In other words, "public policy" has made it so that going to school is the only accessible and affordable way for most people to learn what they need in order to realize their abilities.

Recognizing this, let us engage in some fugitive planning. To recap, we who refuse to go to school find ourselves "at risk" of never learning what we need to learn in order to realize our abilities and, given the many privileges and prejudices favoring the schooled, we also find ourselves "at risk" of unemployment and all that comes with it: homelessness, hunger, ruthless indebtedness. However, rather than submitting to administration and supervision, by way of schooling or otherwise, let us ask ourselves the following questions:

- What forms of direct action might we engage in with others so that we may forage, cultivate, and fabricate what we need in order to live and learn otherwise than being schooled?

- Which of these forms of direct action might enable further direct action?

- Are these enabling forms of direct actions prohibited and punishable?

- Are there any forms of defense by due process that might enable us to skirt prohibitions and ward off punishments while engaging in enabling forms of direct action?

- Which of these forms of defense by due process might enable further defense by due process?

Those to whom I spoke and wrote of the (De-/Re-)Constructing Worlds project before it launched will, no doubt, find these five questions somewhat familiar. This is because the project initially arose from my own planning to flee from schooling, and these questions outline the very practical problems that I have been seeking solutions for in and through this project.

Schooling and the privileging of the schooled do not make any sense without reference to statements, implements, and environments that furnish individuals with motives, means, and opportunities to submit to schooling and the privileging of the schooled. Recognizing this, any and all planning to flee schooling must involve (i) the deconstruction of the domineering statements, implements, and environments that privilege schooling and the schooled and (ii) the (re-)construction of convivial statements, implements, and environments that serve to (re)create confluences of different forms of learning and of people who learn differently.

In a previous dispatch on "convivial statements", I began deconstructing the academic transcript insofar as it is a statement that motivates submission to schooling and the privileging of the schooled. I argued that, rather than regarding an academic transcript as measure of a student's ability to learn, the academic transcript should be considered a measure of whether and how schooling has oppressed the student: it is the school system, rather than the student, that is to be evaluated by way of academic transcripts. Indeed, as I see it, the student with poor grades suffers from having been degraded by schooling, and they are owed artful reparations for suffering such degradation. The artful reparations owed to the student should take the form of access to resources that enable the student conduct their own experiments in learning otherwise than being schooled. To facilitate such artful reparations, I wonder how we might deconstruct transcripts that document students' academic failures and use what remains to (re-)construct alternative statements that would enable students to conduct and log their own experiments in learning otherwise than being schooled.

Planning to Flee From Financing

"If it don't make money, it don't make sense." — That is gist of the domineering statements, implements, and environments that form the capitalist powers that prevail over our deathly world of suffering.

Capitalist power formations are bent on filtering and channeling what makes money apart from what doesn't make money, privileging the former over the later. The end result of this filtering and channeling: what makes money comes to make the most sense, and everything else either comes to make less sense or becomes nonsensical.

You will never find a job doing philosophy that way.

You won't make any money with that style of art.

Nobody is going to fund that line of scientific research.

If the lines above make sense to you, it is because you are familiar with the financial statements implied by these lines: bank statements, credit statements, billing statements, and invoice statements, of course, but also statements like credit reports, which aggregate the earlier mentioned statements in order to facilitate the normalization and optimization of their distributions and trends.

The existence and prevalence of such financial statements are what allow us make sense of so many propositions which take it for granted that practicing philosophy, art, and science must either be (i) a way to turn our time into money, (ii) a way to spend what extra money we might have when we have time to waste, or (iii) a senseless waste of time and money that we cannot spare.

The domineering financial statements discussed above often work in tandem with the domineering educational statements that I discussed in my previous dispatch. Working in tandem, these statements privilege the well-schooled and the well-financed; they tell us, "If you ain't been schooled, you ain't really learned nuthin'. But school learnin' ain't all that! Those who ain't bein' schooled to make money are bein' schooled in nonsense."

To drive home this point a little bit, let us regard how it is that concatenations of financing and schooling powers stratify our societies. In first place, the well-schooled moneymakers, the Masters of the Universe, live the highlife. In last place, the poorly schooled scroungers, the Wretched of the Earth, live the lowlife. Jostling and mingling to make a life for themselves somewhere betwixt and between the highlife and the lowlife, we find the poorly schooled moneymakers, the Horatios, on the one hand, and, on the other hand, we find the well-schooled scroungers, the Rogers. The Horatios endeavor to use their hard won economic capital as leverage to gain a higher social status; the Rogers, by contrast, endeavor to use their cleverly won cultural capital as leverage to the same end.

The Masters of the Universe play Horatios and Rogers against each other and against the Wretched of the Earth by extending honorary Master of the Universe status to the Horatios who can make the most money and to the Rogers who can secure the most rarefied educational and cultural credentials. The ruse is, of course, that the Horatios and the Rogers have to grapple amongst themselves and trample over the Wretched of the Earth in order to win honorary Master of the Universe status.

Masters of the Universe (n.): Tom Wolfe (1930-2018) coined the term "Masters of the Universe" in his novel *The Bonfire of the Vanities* (1987) to describe Wall Street types — specifically white males working in the FIRE industries (i.e., finance, insurance, and real estate) who thought they could do whatever they wanted without answering to anyone. Thirty-five years hence, the Big Tech-Bros (i.e., the surveillance capitalists) have joined the FIRE-men in forming the upper echelons of the Masters of the Universe.

Rogers (n.): 16th century thieves' slang for begging vagabonds who pretend to be poor scholars from Oxford or Cambridge.

Horatios (n.): persons resembling characters from the fiction of Horatio Alger (1832-1899) who rise from humble beginnings to achieve success through self-reliance and hard work.

Wretched of the Earth (n.): Frantz Fanon (1925-1961) coined the term "Wretched of the Earth" in his treatise of the same name (1961) to describe the oppressed masses of peoples — primarily black, brown, and indigenous peoples — whose lives had been rendered superfluous and expendable by the advance of imperialist white-supremacist capitalist patriarchy.

I have a dream. It is (i) to be able live and learn otherwise than being schooled, (ii) to be able to make sense of my life and my learning otherwise than making money, and (iii) to be able to do all the above without being counted amongst the Wretched of the Earth and subjected to murder as the unintended consequence of routine disciplinary action, or as normal(ized) accident, or as the collateral damage of society's pursuit of progressive optimization.

How, I wonder, might I deconstruct the domineering statements, implements, and environments that have furnished me with motives, means, and opportunities to dismiss my dream as a mere fantasy? And, going further, how might I (re-)construct convivial statements, implements, and environments so as to furnish myself with motives, means, and opportunities to make my dream a reality?

These are my problems. What are my solutions?

Recapping the conclusion of my previous dispatch, rather than regarding a student's wretched transcript as an evaluation of a student's ability to learn, I propose regarding their wretched transcript as an evaluation of the performance of the schooling system, and I propose using the wretched transcript not to reform the school system but, instead, to determine what artful reparations are owed to the student for having been failed by the school system. What's more, I propose that artful reparations in this regard should come in the form of time and resources to conduct experiments in living and learning otherwise than being schooled. With respect to schooling, then, I would deconstruct wretched transcripts that document students' academic failures and use what remains of them to (re-) construct alternative statements that would enable students to conduct and log their own experiments in living and learning otherwise than being schooled.

I would proceed in a similar manner when it comes to financing. Rather than regarding an individual's wretched credit report as an evaluation of an individual's ability to earn, I propose regarding the wretched credit report as an evaluation of the performance of the financial system, and I propose using the wretched credit report not to reform the financial system but, instead, to determine what artful reparations are owed to the individual for having been failed by the financial system. What's more, I propose that artful reparations in this regard should come in the form of time and resources to conduct experiments in making sense of life and learning otherwise than making money. With respect to financing, then, I would deconstruct wretched credit reports that document individuals' economic failures and use what remains of them to (re-)construct alternative statements that would enable individuals to conduct and log experiments in making sense of life and learning otherwise than making money.

Planning to Flee From Calendaring and Clocking

Indulge me, if you will, and allow me begin this dispatch by citing two etymologies that you may already be familiar with.

calendar (n.) — c. 1200, "the year as divided systematically into days and months;" mid-14c. as table showing divisions of the year;" from Old French *calendier* "list, register," from Latin *calendarium* "account book," from *calendae/ kalendae* "the calends" the first day of the Roman month, when debts fell due and accounts were reckoned.

clock (n.) — "machine to measure and indicate time mechanically" (since late 1940s also electronically), late 14c., *clokke*, originally "clock with bells," probably from Middle Dutch *clocke* (Dutch *klok*) "a clock," from Old North French *cloque* (Old French cloke, Modern French *cloche* "a bell"), from Medieval Latin *clocca* "bell," which probably is from Celtic (compare Old Irish *clocc*, Welsh *cloch*, Manx *clagg* "a bell") and spread by Irish missionaries (unless the Celtic words are from Latin).

I cite these etymologies because I feel the need to be precise from the outset about what I mean when I use the terms "calendar" and "clock" and when I write that I am "planning to flee from calendaring and clocking".

To be brief, taking into account the etymologies above, I use the term "calendar" to refer to the tabular division of concrete sunrises and sunsets, new moons and full moons, equinoxes and solstices, and seasonal life cycles into abstract days, months, and years; and I use the term "clock" to refer to machinic measures of time. In turn, "planning to flee from calendaring and clocking" means (i) planning to live in accord with concrete turns of sunrises and sunsets, new moons and full moons, equinoxes and solstices, and seasonal life cycles (as opposed to abstract tabulations of days, months, and years), and (ii) it means planning to live in accord with metabolic measures of time, seasonally varying circadian rhythms (as opposed to machinic measures of time).

If my desire to flee from calendaring and clocking seems fanciful, it is only because we have become accustomed living in a deathly world of suffering that unduly privileges machinic measures of and abstract tabulations of days, months, and years. This begs the question: how and why have we become unduly prejudiced against metabolic measures of time and the concrete turns of sunrises and sunsets, new moons and full moons, equinoxes and solstices, and seasonal life cycles?

The etymology of the term "calendar" is suggestive: "from Latin *calendarium* 'account book,' from *calendae/kialendae* 'the calends' the first day of the Roman month, when debts fell due and accounts were reckoned." With this etymology in mind, my wager is that the privileging of calendaring and clocking has a great deal to do with the prevalence of domineering capitalist financial statements that take abstract seconds, minutes, hours, days, months, and years for granted when determining schedules of fees and payments.

When I first introduced the notion of fleeing from calendaring in my dispatch on freeing time, I proposed that calendaring and clocking were appealing to any and every sort of power formation, and not just capitalist power formations. If calendars and clocks are becoming ever more prevalent and pervasive, it is a sign that we are living in a world in which power in general is becoming ever more prevalent and pervasive. That being said, however, a defining feature of capitalist power formations in particular is that they can only sustain themselves by becoming ever more prevalent and pervasive (there will be more on this in later dispatch). Ipso facto, calendars and clocks have become such prevalent and pervasive features of our lives today because of the prevalence and pervasiveness of capitalist power formations that are forever bent on becoming ever more prevalent and pervasive.

As such, it should be no wonder that my planning to flee from calendaring and clocking is integral to my planning to flee from schooling and from financing. So, if you will, allow me to recap the points of my previous dispatches on fleeing from schooling and financing so as to better articulate the point of this dispatch on fleeing from calendaring and clocking.

- Planning to flee from schooling means planning to engage in direct action in order to live and learn otherwise than being schooled.

- Planning to flee from financing means planning to engage in direct action in order to make sense of one's life and learning otherwise than making money.

- Planning to flee from calendaring and clocking means planning to engage in direct action in order to measure the rhythm and tempo of one's life, learning, and sense-making otherwise than calendaring and clocking one's time.

Thinking of these three projects in fugitive planning as separate and distinct projects is a mistake because these projects mutually condition one another. The failures of the poorly schooled and poorly financed are, almost by definition, failures to manage time and keep pace. The poorly schooled are "slow learners": their academic failures are failures to learn and to turn in their assignments in a timely manner. The poorly financed are "slow earners": their economic failures are failures to earn and make their payments in a timely manner.

All this is to say, in other words, that powers determining what is and isn't timely are part and parcel of the powers that privilege the well-financed and the well-schooled. The well-financed and the well-schooled are those able to live, learn, and make sense according rhythms and tempos set by today's prevailing power formations. The poorly financed and poorly schooled are untimely for not keeping to the rhythms and tempos given by prevailing power formations but, instead, making their own rhythms (i.e., living, learning, and making sense idiorrythmically) and making their own tempos (i.e., living, learning, and making sense in *rubato*).

idiorhythmic (adj.): Meaning "according to one's own rhythm", from Greek *idios* "particular to oneself" + *rhythmos* "measured flow or movement, rhythm; proportion, symmetry; arrangement, order; form, shape, wise, manner; soul, disposition". In his 1976-1977 seminar at the Collège de France, titled "How to Live Together", Roland Barthes investigated idiorrhythmic ways of living — collective ways of living wherein, whereby, and wherefore "each subject lives according to his own rhythm". Barthes writes:

> [Idiorrhythmy] has to do with subtle forms of way of life: moods, unstable configurations, phases of depression or elation; in short the exact opposite of an inflexible, implacably regular cadence.

rubato (adj.): Meaning "free in presentation", short for *tempo rubato*, literally "robbed time". The Oxford English dictionary defines rubato as follows: "Of a piece of music: played, or directed to be played, with a temporary disregard for strict tempo to allow an expressive quickening or slowing, typically without altering the overall pace."

My deconstruction of statements in support of calendaring and clocking shall proceed in and through my deconstructions of financial and educational statements.

Rather than regarding wretched marks for untimeliness in a credit report or academic transcript as marks against an individual's ability to earn or learn, I propose regarding wretched marks for untimeliness as marks against calendaring and clocking systems, and I propose using wretched marks for untimeliness not to reform calendaring and clocking systems but, instead, to determine what artful reparations are owed to individuals for having been failed by calendaring and clocking systems. What's more, I propose that artful reparations in this regard should come in the form of time and resources to conduct experiments in measuring rhythms and tempos of life, learning, and sense-making otherwise than calendaring and clocking time.

With respect to calendaring and clocking, then, I would deconstruct the wretched marks for untimeliness that characterize individuals' academic and economic failures and then use what remains to (re-)construct alternative statements that would enable individuals to conduct experiments in measuring rhythms and tempos of life, learning, and sense-making otherwise than calendaring and clocking time.

Planning to Flee From Profiling

A nationally representative 2017 survey of American adults found that about 39 percent of heterosexual couples reported meeting their partner using an internet dating service, making internet dating services the most popular way for heterosexual couples to meet in the US.

Internet dating services are automated and networked profiling services, which is to say, in other words, that they are services that work by and through employing the administrative technique known as profiling. Individuals seeking romantic and sexual partners via such services are required to compile and upload information about themselves into *profiles* — (data) structures used to capture certain characteristics of the individual. These profiles are then fed into automated and networked systems that record, sort, filter, and, most importantly, match profiles. The increasing prevalence of internet dating services in the US points to the remarkable prevalence and pervasiveness of profiling techniques and technologies in today's world, as it it can now be said that profiling techniques and technologies are among the most common initiators of intimate social relations in the richest and most heavily armed nation in the world.

Profiling is evermore rapidly becoming part and parcel of every aspect of individuals' lives in today's world. Once upon a time it was the paid administrator's task to profile subjects under administration. In today's deathly world of suffering, subjects under administration are tasked with profiling themselves without pay. We are all becoming unpaid administrators, engaged in compiling and reviewing profiles about ourselves and others, and desperately trying to find ways to advantage ourselves in administrative rat races by exploiting the (mal)functioning of automated and networked systems that record, sort, filter, and match profiles. You are made into an unpaid administrator when you fill in a dating profile on OkCupid, when you search for products and make purchases on Amazon, when you perform searches on Google, when you like posts on Facebook, when you heart songs on Spotify, when you rate films thumbs up or thumbs down on Netflix, etc.

The so-called "Big Tech" firms (Google, Meta, Amazon, etc.) are in the business of cajoling people into profiling themselves for the purposes of submitting to and receiving the "benefits" of greater administration and supervision. These firms engineer and maintain automated and networked systems for recording, sorting, filtering, and matching profiles, and they design lures that make it appealing and easy for people to compile profiles on themselves and to feed their profiles into the firms' automated and networked recording, sorting, filtering and matching systems. Amazon was built to facilitate the recording, sorting, filtering, and matching of people's shopping profiles. Google was built to facilitate the recording, sorting, filtering, and matching of people's internet search profiles. Facebook was built to facilitate the recording, sorting, filtering, and matching of people's social network profiles. Spotify was built the facilitate recording, sorting, filtering, and matching of people's music listening profiles. Netflix was built to facilitate the recording, sorting, filtering, and matching of people's film and television viewing profiles. OkCupid was built to facilitate the recording, sorting, filtering, and matching people's dating profiles. LinkedIn was built to facilitate recording, sorting, filtering, and matching people's career profiles. The list goes on...

An individual's profile is never properly their own; rather, it is only ever the profile that they happen to fit according to the (mal)functioning of systems that record, sort, filter, and match profiles. One doesn't ever really compile a profile that is unique to oneself as a concrete individual; rather, one compiles one's life, learning, and sense-making in a (mis)representative manner so as to fit oneself to an abstract profile that many other individuals may also fit themselves to. One does so to fit a given profile in order to benefit from a given system that dispenses access to resources by recording, sorting, filtering, and matching profiles.

The individual who doesn't fit any dating profile will get poor dating placements from an internet dating service. The individual who doesn't fit any internet search profile will get poor search results from an internet search provider. The individual who doesn't fit any shopping profile will get poor product placements from an e-commerce provider. The individual who doesn't fit any viewing profile will get poor viewing recommendations from a streaming film and television provider. The individual who doesn't fit any listening profile will get poor listening recommendations from a streaming audio provider.

The work of compiling a profile is the hard work of making oneself fit a given profile so that one can derive some "benefit" from administration and supervision, and fitting a given profile means diminishing one's idiosyncrasies so as to facilitate the easy and rapid recording, sorting, filtering, and matching of profiles. Indeed, the proper aim of profiling powers is to make subjects diminish their idiosyncrasies so that they can be more easily and rapidly recorded, sorted, filtered, and matched with the resources that they "deserve".

Leaving aside "Big Tech", I would like to return to my previous dispatches on planning to flee from schooling and planning to flee from financing. As I see it, these dispatches were very much also about planning to flee from profiling. For what is an individual's academic transcript if it isn't an educational profile? And what is the individual's credit report if it isn't a financial profile? The aim of the maintenance of academic transcripts as educational profiles is to diminish the idiosyncratic needs and abilities of learners so that it becomes easier to administer and supervise their learning; and the aim of the maintenance of credit reports as financial profiles is to diminish the idiosyncratic needs and abilities of earners so that it becomes easier to administer and supervise their earnings.

In my previous dispatch on "planning to flee from calendaring and clocking", I proposed that clocking and calendaring have become ever more prevalent and pervasive parts of life, learning, and sense-making because capitalist power formations have become evermore prevalent and pervasive. In this dispatch, I want to propose the very same thing with respect to profiling. All power formations engage in profiling of some sort or another and the increasing pervasiveness and prevalence of profiling is part and parcel of the increasing pervasiveness and prevalence of power formations in general.

That being said, however, capitalist power formations are uniquely defined by the fact that they cannot maintain themselves without becoming evermore pervasive and prevalent, and the ever increasing profiling that we are subject to has a great deal to do with capitalist power formations becoming evermore pervasive and prevalent. If we have only recently begun talking about surveillance capitalism, this is not because ever increasing profiling is a new feature of capitalism; rather, this is because capitalism now infiltrates almost every part of our lives and, as a result, every part of our lives is now profiled.

To recap, being profiled means having one's life, learning, and sense-making compiled in a (mis)representative manner so as to be more easily and rapidly recorded, sorted, filtered, and matched with resources. In every instance, being profiled involves the diminishment of the idiosyncrasies of the profiled subject's life, learning, and sense-making for the sake of easing and speeding the administration and supervision of access to resources. It follows that, to be otherwise than profiled means accentuating one's idiosyncrasies by compiling one's life, learning, and sense-making in a non-representative manner. Or, in other words, being otherwise than profiled means making one's own life, learning, and sense-making increasingly more difficult to record, sort, filter, and match so as to defy administration and supervision.

So, let's say we plan to flee from profiling after deconstructing both the academic transcript as a statement of one's educational profile and the credit report as a statement of one's financial profile. This would mean (re-)constructing alternative statements that enable individuals to conduct and log experiments in living, learning, and sense-making otherwise than being schooled and making money, yes... But this would also mean that whatever alternative statements we (re-) construct must enable individuals to log their experiments otherwise than being profiled. This is the great challenge and difficulty...

All of the above demands further elaboration, and this will come in (un)due time. However, lest you be left believing the challenge and difficulty is too great, I will leave you with a quotation from a piece by John Berger on the work of Jean-Michel Basquiat that suggests a way forward.

> [Basquiat's] painting *Boy and Dog in a Johnnypump* (1982) is a screen of splashes spelling out the excitement, the fury, the fun of a boy and dog on a stifling summer day in Brooklyn dousing themselves with jets of cold water from a fire hydrant. But neither dog nor boy can be identified. They have very strong and precise features, but none of these features can be accommodated on an identity card. And all the features demanded by IDs have been scratched out or painted over. This doesn't mean that the dog and the boy are being evasive; it simply means they are free.

Ecoregionalism

When I announced the (De-/Re-)Constructing Worlds project, I claimed that the project was an anti-imperialist project.

To make this claim meaningful, I cited Ivan Illich from *Tools for Conviviality* on the three prevailing modes of imperialism, each successive mode being more insidious and intractable than the last. First, Illich described a nationalist imperialism characterized by "the pernicious spread of one nation beyond its boundaries." Second, Illich described a capitalist imperialism characterized by "the omnipresent influence of multinational corporations." Third, and finally, Illich described a careerist imperialism, the most insidious and intractable of the three, characterized by "the mushrooming of professional monopolies over production."

After citing Illich, I wrote that, as have come to see it, the antidote to a nationalist imperialism is a ecoregionalism, the antidote to a capitalist imperialism is a communism, and the antidote to a careerist imperialism is a dilettantism. In turn, I wrote that the (De-/Re-)Constructing Worlds project would be an exercise in dilettantism, supplemented by exercises in ecoregionalism and communism, that would serve to generate antidotes to careerist imperialisms. Thus far, I have written a good deal about dilettantism as an antidote to careerist imperialisms and about communism as an antidote to capitalist imperialisms, but I have yet to write much about ecoregionalism as an antidote to nationalist imperialisms.

This week, the nation of Russia attacked the nation of Ukraine in what is widely and rightly being regarded as a brazen act of nationalist imperialism. The liberal news media in the West has tended to criticize Russia's actions in the name of the sovereignty of the nation of Ukraine, taking the inviolability of sovereign national territories for granted. Reading and watching all of this as it unfolds, I have been thinking that more is lost than gained when we take the inviolability of sovereign national territories for granted.

In this dispatch, I propose that we criticize acts of nationalist imperialism otherwise than affirming the inviolability of sovereign national territories. In brief, I propose that we criticize acts of nationalist imperialism by affirming nations' shared concern for ecoregions and by affirming more or less permeable ecoregional boundaries.

What do I mean when I use the term "nation", "nationalism", and "nationalist imperialism"?

To answer this question, I will need to quote an extended passage from my previous dispatch on ethnocide and ecocide, marking the distinctions between genocide, ethnocide, and ecocide.

Genocide is the extermination of one or more determinate ancestries effected by and through the eradication of individuals belonging to the given ancestries. The fact that genocide primarily targets individuals, depriving individuals of their liberties and their lives, makes genocide easy for the liberal minded to recognize and decry as an atrocity. What makes it difficult for the liberal minded to recognize and decry ethnocide and ecocide is the fact that the targets of ethnocide and ecocide are not individuals but pre-individual processes and supra-individual structures.

Ethnocide is the extermination of one or more determinate cultures effected by and through the inhibition of the pre-individual processes and the destruction of the supra-individual structures that together constitute the given cultures. Ethnocide and genocide do not necessarily imply one another insofar as a given ancestry can survive the extermination of its culture and a given culture can survive the extermination of some of its ancestries. This is the case because a person of a given ancestry may not be initiated into the culture of their ancestors, and because a person may be initiated into a given culture without having any ancestral ties to the culture. Regard, for instance, how the ethnocide of Indigenous American peoples occasionally involved genocide but was also effected by other many other means including displacement, re-education, and criminalization. Alternatively, regard how the enslavement of Black peoples in the Americas was ethnocidal without always being genocidal: ancestry needed to be maintained as part and parcel of being Black and being a slave, but being Black and being a slave meant being continually deprived of ties to an ancestral culture. And as final example, regard how White American and European eugenicists conducted a genocide without ethnocide when they endeavored to eradicate the "degenerate" ancestries of the mentally and physically "disabled" from White American and European cultures.

Ecocide is the extermination of one or more determinate habitats effected by the inhibition of the pre-individual processes and the destruction of the supra-individual structures that together constitute the habitats. Ecocide does not necessarily mean genocide for all ancestries with ties to threatened habitats: individuals of a given ancestry may very well survive the extermination of the habitat that nurtured their ancestors. Neither does ecocide necessarily mean ethnocide for cultures with ties to threatened habitats: a nomadic culture, for instance, may very well survive the extermination of one of the different habitats that they occasionally pass through.

I cite the passage above because we often (con)fuse two terms that I have distinguished above when we talk of "nations": we use the term "nation" to simultaneously refer to a people with a given ancestry and to a people with a given culture. For the purposes of this dispatch, I would like to separate these two subjects of the term "nation", recognizing full well that these two subjects always defer to one another despite differing from one another.

What I want to propose here is that there is no nation without a national culture, however artificial and superficial that national culture may be. Indeed, I use the term "nation" simply to refer to a population with a more or less determinate culture and, as such, I hold that all nations are ethno-nations and all nationalisms are ethno-nationalisms. That being said, however, to the extent that some determinate cultures will only initiate and integrate individuals into their folds when individuals belong to certain ancestries, it could be said that some nations are geno-nations in addition to being ethno-nations and, concomitantly, some nationalisms are geno-nationalisms in addition to being ethno-nationalisms. For instance, today's white-supremacist nationalisms are geno-nationalisms in addition to being ethno-nationalisms: individuals who overtly demand respect and, as a historical consequence, reparations for their Black Sub-Saharan African ancestors (or any other oppressed non-White ancestors) are, for that very reason, denied full initiation and integration into the national cultures championed by white-supremacist nationalists.

A given habitat becomes the "territory" of a given nation when the members of a given nation secure privileged access to a given habitat for themselves. In other words, a given habitat becomes the territory of a given nation when more or less stable and non-negotiable power formations provide the members of a given nation privileged access to a given habitat — this feat is achieved via the subordination and/or extermination of all others who occupy a given habitat.

Not all nations possess territories and, what's more, it cannot even be said that all nations want to possess territories. There are, of course, nomadic nations that make no claims to possessing any of the territories that they pass through, but there are also sedentary nations that do not maintain stable and non-negotiable power formations and, thus, do not turn the habitats that they care for and call home into their own privileged territories. Just consider, for instance, the indigenous nations of North America that initially accommodated the European settlers who took up residence on lands that the indigenous nations could have claimed as their own privileged territory and exclusive property. Later some of these indigenous nations would accommodate and become confluent with settlements of maroons who had fled slavery and formed their own nations without privileged territories.

Nations that neither possess nor want to possess their own privileged territories are "nations-without-nationalisms" — for all nationalisms are claims that nations should possess their own privileged territories. Nations-without-nationalisms are neither rare nor even uncommon, but history tends to overlook them. History tends to be nationalistic, written as the history of territorial and would-be territorial nations. Only territorial nations and would-be territorial nations are said to make "real" history; nations-without-nationalisms, or "non-territorial nations" for short, have been (mis)represented as anthropological curiosities that do not make "real" history apart from resisting or yielding to the offenses of territorial nations.

As I see it, any and every act by and through which a nation makes, maintains, and conquers territories for themselves is an act of nationalist imperialism. This is to say, in other words, that all territorial nations are perpetually engaged in acts of nationalist imperialism insofar as they are perpetually engaged in making and maintaining their own privileged territories against others. The maintenance of a balance of power amongst territorial nations is just as much an act of nationalist imperialism as the upsetting of a balance of power by a territorial nation with hegemonic aspirations. Indeed, riffing on the work of Antonio Negri and Michael Hardt, the making and maintenance of a balance of power amongst territorial nations is what I call the making and maintenance of Empire with a capital "E"; and the making and maintenance of an expansionary territorial nation is what I call the making and maintenance of an empire with a lower case "e". The ongoing crisis in Ukraine is, in these terms, a conflict between empire and Empire — Russia has attacked Ukraine in order to expand its own (little "e") empire but, in so doing, it is threatening the stability of (capital "E") Empire.

My anti-imperialist position runs counter to both the (little "e") empires of particular territorial nations and the (capital "E") Empire that maintains a balance of power amongst territorial nations. Against both empire and Empire, my anti-imperialist position advances a non-territorial nationhood, a nationhood-without-nationalism, a nationhood that eschews possessing privileged territories. Indeed, opposed to securing separate territories for different nations, my anti-imperialist position favors caring for habitats in such a way that many different nations may share them. I call my anti-imperialist position an ecoregionalism because my position is that the sharing of a habitat or, more broadly, the sharing of an ecoregion formed of contiguous and comparable habitats ought to be the criteria for political kinship — this as opposed to the sharing of a nationality. In other words, my position holds that all nations that share an ecoregion should, by and through sharing an ecoregion, become politically confluent with one another and deferential to one another's differences. From an ecoregionalist point of view, then, Russia's attack on Ukraine is not to be criticized as a transgression of Ukraine's sovereign territory but, rather, it is to be criticized as the advance of a Russian imperialism that would subordinate and/or eliminate the non-Russian peoples (Ukrainians, Belarusians, Moldovans, Crimean Tatars, Bulgarians, etc.) that share in and care for the habitats currently claimed by the nation of Ukraine as privileged national territories.

When I first introduced the notion of ecoregionalism as part of this project, I quoted an excerpt from A *Pattern Language* by Christopher Alexander, Sara Ishikawa and Murray Silverstein. I will quote it again here.

> [Territorial nations] have grown mightily and their governments hold power over tens of millions, sometimes hundreds of millions of people. But these huge powers cannot claim to have a natural size. They cannot claim to have struck the balance between the needs of towns and communities, and the needs of the world community as a whole. Indeed, their tendency has been to override local needs and repress local culture, and at the same time aggrandize themselves to the point where they are out of reach, their power barely conceivable to the average citizen.

> [...] Unless regions have the power to be self-governing, they will not be able to solve their own environmental problems. The arbitrary lines of [territorial nations], which often cut across natural regional boundaries, make it all but impossible for people to solve regional problems in a direct and humanly efficient way.

> [...] [Furthermore,] unless the present-day great nations have their power greatly decentralized, the beautiful and differentiated languages, cultures, customs, and ways of life of the earth's people, vital to the health of the planet, will vanish.

Alexander, Ishikawa, and Silverstein strike me as having padded their language quite a bit to soften the landing of their claims. Allow me to remove some of their cushioning in order to land with impact. The "great nations" of our day are powerful engines of ethnocide and ecocide, and all those who wish for cultural and natural diversity to flourish must endeavor to dismantle these "great nations". This means dismantling both the (little "e") empires of particular territorial nations and the (capital "E") Empire that maintains a balance of power amongst territorial nations. While we might occasionally play Empire against empires, let us not deceive ourselves: Empire does not aim to save cultural and natural diversity from empires. To the contrary, Empire aims to optimize ethnocide and ecocide, to make ethnocide and ecocide evermore tolerable by checking the most brazen excesses of empires.

Empire (with a capital "E") will allow empires (with a little "e") to pursue their ethnocidal and ecocidal projects unimpeded provided (i) that empires do not step on each other's toes too often as they go about their business and (ii) that empires do not stomp on the necks of conquered peoples in an "uncivilized" manner that egregiously offends Empire's prevailing sensibilities. Given that Empire's prevailing sensibilities are, at present, white-supremacist sensibilities, empires are presently allowed much more liberty to stomp harshly on the necks of non-White peoples and much less liberty to stomp harshly on the necks of White peoples.

A White-on-White offense, Russia's attack on Ukraine is a test of Empire's power to check the excesses of empires. Many worry that Empire, led by the US and its European allies, will fail to check the expansion of the Russian empire and then, by extension, the Chinese empire, and that this will spell the end for Empire as we know it. No one knows what will happen next, but anti-imperialists do know for certain that Empire and empires must both fail to achieve their aims if anti-imperialists are to succeed in achieving theirs. Yet the failure of both Empire and empires does not necessarily spell success for anti-imperialists insofar as anti-imperialists are ecoregionalists. More would be lost than gained if Empire and empires were to decimate cultural and natural diversity in the process of frustrating each other's aims — this is to say, in other words, that anti-imperialists will only gain if Empire and empires frustrate each other's aims without harming cultural and natural diversity. Given this, anti-imperialists have little chance of gaining anything from the current crisis in Ukraine, which only serves to test Empire's wherewithal to check empires.

So, my fellow anti-imperialists, let us engage in some fugitive planning so that we may flee from participation in past, present, and future imperial contests.

- What forms of direct action might we engage in with others in order to destabilize and (re-)negotiate relations amongst nations otherwise than making, maintaining, and securing privileged national territories?

- Which of these forms of direct action might enable further direct action?

- Are these enabling forms of direct actions prohibited and punishable?

- Are there any forms of defense by due process that might enable us to skirt prohibitions and ward off punishments while engaging in enabling forms of direct action?

- Which of these forms of defense by due process might enable further defense by due process?

Late Davosian Holocausts

I have taken to calling the era in which we are living the "Late Davosian" era — named for the town, Davos, that hosts the World Economic Forum, an annual festival celebrating imperialist white-supremacist capitalist patriarchy and the good deeds that it supports via the white savior industrial complex.

The Late Davosian era that we are living through is an era defined by a cascade of economic, ecological, and public health crises fueled by climate catastrophes that are devastating peoples, cultures, and habitats across the globe — especially those peoples, cultures, and habitats that have yet to yield to the advance of imperialist white-supremacist capitalist patriarchy and to submit themselves to administration and supervision by the various organs of the white savior industrial complex.

I have taken to calling the devastating crises of our era the "Late Davosian Holocausts" because they echo the devastating crises that Mike Davis named the "Late Victorian Holocausts", which took place between 1870-1914. I want to write to you about the manner in which the ongoing Late Davosian Holocausts echo the Late Victorian Holocausts.

I will begin by quoting at length from a previous dispatch, titled "A Case in Point", in which I performed a reading of Mike Davis's text on the *Late Victorian Holocausts*.

During the Late Victorian period, three waves of drought and famine killed no less than 30 million people in tropical Africa, Asia, and South America between 1870-1914, "at the precise moment ... when [the] labor and products [of tropical humanity] were being dynamically conscripted into a London-centered world economy." As Mike Davis writes, "Millions died, not outside the 'modern world system,' but in the very process of being forcibly incorporated into its economic and political structures."

[...] [All over tropical Africa, Asia, and South America between 1870-1914,] White European colonial powers integrated colonized peoples into the "modern world system" by suppressing cultural practices that had, prior to colonization, served to ward off mass deaths by malnutrition and starvation during droughts and famines. Deprived of these cultural practices, colonized peoples all over Africa, Asia, and South America had become defenseless against malnutrition and starvation during droughts and famines.

[...] [T]he Late Victorian Holocausts that Mike Davis chronicles were not the inevitable result of the droughts and famines of the time. Rather, they were the inevitable result of the ethnocides that had preceded the droughts and famines. Ethnocide, you will recall, is the extermination of one or more determinate cultures effected by and through the inhibition of the pre-individual processes and the destruction of the supra-individual structures that together constitute the given cultures. The Late Victorian Holocausts that Mike Davis chronicles occurred because White European colonial powers had effectively exterminated cultures that had previously enabled non-White and non-European peoples to collectively endure drought and famine by conserving, sharing, and redistributing resources.

Consider that the Late Victorian Holocausts that Mike Davis chronicles are limited to the 30 to 60 million deaths linked to the post-ethnocide El Niño droughts and famines of 1876–1878, 1896–1897, and 1899–1902. These 30 to 60 million deaths are only a portion of the deaths that can be attributed to the after-effects of ethnocide on the peoples of the colonized world since 1492. Ay, and all these millions of deaths only hint at the many millions more who have suffered and who continue to suffer transgenerational traumas as a result of colonization, ethnocide, mass murder, and mass death by exposure. All of this put together constitutes the makings of the "Third World" which are, concomitantly, the makings of the "First World". Alternatively, to use the terms currently preferred by Davos Man and his ilk, all of this constitutes the makings of the "developing world" which are, concomitantly, the makings of the "developed world". The deathly El Niño famines chronicled by Mike Davis only mark an inflection point for all this carnage. The horrors encountered in the apocalyptic and post-apocalyptic scenarios of popular science fiction are pale after-images of the experiences of peoples, White and non-White, who suffered the creation of the developed and developing worlds.

Considering the above, I want to propose the following: the Late Davosian Holocausts are poised to do by way of neocolonialism what the Late Victorian Holocausts did by way of colonialism, marking a new inflection point in the history of the havoc wreaked by imperialist white-supremacist capitalist patriarchy. This proposition, of course, begs the question, 'What is neocolonialism?''

Think of it this it this way... During the colonial era, Western colonizers conducted ethnocides on the peoples of Africa, Asia, and the Americas, decimating the different cultures of these regions by attacking the different customs and structures by and through which these different cultures conserved, shared, and (re-)distributed resources. Western colonists then proceeded to institute colonial administrations in Africa, Asia, and the Americas that were designed to extract resources (people, know-how, and materials) from the regions, to enrich colonial administrators in the process, and to leave behind the dregs of the extraction process for colonized peoples to survive on.

As the colonized peoples of Africa, Asia, and the Americas managed to rise up and turnout their colonizers, the "leaders" of these anti-colonial movements inherited the administrations of their former colonizers and, given this, they quickly became the new self-enriching administrators of the extraction of resources (people, know-how, and materials) from the newly created postcolonial territorial nations. They did not become so out of simple greed and negligence, but out of perverse necessity: the techniques and technologies of administration that they inherited had been organized around resource extraction and the enrichment of administrators, and the peoples of the new postcolonial nations would suffer increasingly more dire poverty and starvation if resource extraction and the enrichment of administrators were to immediately cease. Thus, colonial techniques and technologies of administration did not leave Africa, Asia, and the Americas with Western colonists. Rather, the techniques and technologies were turned over to the peoples of Africa, Asia, and the Americas to use on themselves: the corrupt government administrators of the postcolonial territorial nation are the direct descendants of the corrupt Western administrators of the colony.

As I see it, artful reparations for the ravages of colonialism demand that Western nations give the peoples of Africa, Asia, and the Americas time and resources to experiment in (re-)constructing alternative cultural practices for the convivial conservation, sharing, and (re-)distribution of critical cultural and natural resources. Artful reparations have yet to be made. Instead, Western nations have used their financial and military advantages to ensure that the peoples of Africa, Asia, and the Americas have neither the time nor resources to conduct experiments in conviviality. Indeed, Western nations have ceaselessly pressured the peoples of Africa, Asia, and the Americas to maintain and advance the colonial techniques and technologies of administration that Western colonists left behind. Ay, and this is precisely what I call neocolonialism: the use of financial and military advantages to compel postcolonial territorial nations to maintain and advance colonial techniques and technologies of administration.

Footnote: Haiti was the first postcolonial nation to be subjected to neocolonial domination, and the story of Haiti is worth examining as an exemplary informative anecdote in order to understand the genesis of neocolonialism. That being said, however, the genesis of neocolonialism is one thing and the characteristic structures of neocolonialism are another. The exemplary informative anecdotes that are worth examining in order to understand the characteristic structures of neocolonialism are the stories of the most extreme and totally encompassing regimes of neocolonial domination; these stories include, but are not limited to, (i) the stories of the Indian Reserves dominated by the United States and Canada; (ii) the stories of the Bantustans dominated by Apartheid-era White South Africa; and (iii) the stories of the Palestinian territories dominated by Israel. The stories of Haiti, the Indian Reserves, the Bantustans, and the Palestinian territories are worthy of attention not only because they can teach us a great deal about the genesis and structure of neocolonialism, but because they can also teach us a great deal about the insistence, persistence, and consistency of those who have been resisting neocolonialism since its inception.

The ethnocides that began under colonialism have continued under neocolonialism but with three major differences. One major difference is that these ethnocides are now administered by the "sovereign" governments of postcolonial territorial nations rather than by Western colonial governments. Another major difference is that these ethnocides are now perpetrated in the name of "development" — which is the prevailing euphemism for the extermination of cultural practices that are obstacles to the maintenance and advancement of imperialist white-supremacist capitalist patriarchy. A third major difference is that the white savior industrial complex now serves to provide postcolonial nations with "development aid" in order to optimize the number of deaths by conflict, disease, malnutrition, and starvation that take place during events like droughts and famines. Cultural practices that revolve around receiving "development aid" from developed nations have been taken up by developing nations as compensation for the manner in which "development" suppresses alternative cultural practices that would otherwise ward off mass deaths but that are considered obstacles to the maintenance and advancement of imperialist white supremacist capitalist patriarchy. "Receiving development aid" is only the prevailing euphemism for submitting to administration and supervision by organs of the white savior industrial complex in order to minimize the casualties of development

The Late Davosian Holocausts are the inevitable result of colonialism yielding to neocolonialism instead of yielding to the making of artful reparations. Developing nations have been denied motives, means, opportunities to (re-)construct alternative cultural practices for the convivial conservation, sharing, and (re-)distribution of critical cultural and natural resources. Developing nations have, instead, been furnished with motives, means, and opportunities to pursue development and to become dependent on development aid. The problem now is that developing nations are facing a cascade of economic, ecological, and public health crises fueled by climate catastrophes, and they are rapidly discovering that sufficient development aid will never arrive in sufficient time to ward off mass deaths by conflict, disease, malnutrition, and starvation as a result of climate catastrophes.

Indeed, this is precisely what the latest report from the Intergovernmental Panel on Climate Change says: sufficient development aid does not seem to be arriving in sufficient time to ward off mass deaths by conflict, disease, malnutrition, and starvation as a result of climate catastrophes. Responding to this report, progressive liberal policymakers are calling for the construction of more robust development aid programs to mitigate climate catastrophes. In so doing, progressive liberal policymakers are not calling for artful reparations to be made with respect to postcolonial nations. To the contrary, they are calling for the expansion of the white savior industrial complex, and they are demanding that developing nations submit to greater administration and supervision by new organs of the white savior industrial complex that are dedicated to mitigating climate catastrophes.

It remains to be seen whether such an expansion of the white savior industrial complex is achievable, but I hold that such an expansion of the white savior industrial complex is undesirable — such an expansion would only serve to further the insane ethnocidal and ecocidal machinations of imperialist white supremacist capitalist patriarchy. Reading the summary of the latest IPCC report and the progressive liberal policy responses to the report, I was constantly reminded of a passage from the book *To Our Friends* by the Invisible Committee. It is a passage in which the writers comment upon the manner in which the "objective disaster" of the anthropocene differs and defers to a "subjective disaster".

At the apex of his insanity, Man [read here: the "White Man" or, to be more precise, the "Imperialist White-Supremacist Capitalist Patriarch"] has even proclaimed himself a "geological force," going so far as to give the name of his species to a phase of the life of the planet: he's taken to speaking of an "anthropocene." For the last time, he assigns himself the main role, even if it's to accuse himself of having trashed everything — the seas and the skies, the ground and what's underground — even if it's to confess his guilt for the unprecedented extinction of plant and animal species. But what's remarkable is that he continues relating in the same disastrous manner to the disaster produced by his own disastrous relationship with the world. He calculates the rate at which the ice pack is disappearing. He measures the extermination of the non-human forms of life. As to climate change, he doesn't talk about it based on his sensible experience — a bird that doesn't return in the same period of the year, an insect whose sounds aren't heard anymore, a plant that no longer flowers at the same time as some other one. He talks about it scientifically with numbers and averages. He thinks he's saying something when he establishes that the temperature will rise so many degrees and the precipitation will decrease by so many inches or millimeters. He even speaks of "biodiversity." He observes the rarefaction of life on earth from space. He has the hubris to claim, paternally, to be "protecting the environment," which certainly never asked for anything of the sort. All this has the look of a last bold move in a game that can't be won.

The objective disaster serves mainly to mask another disaster, this one more obvious still and more massive. The exhaustion of natural resources is probably less advanced than the exhaustion of subjective resources, of vital resources, that is afflicting our contemporaries. If so much satisfaction is derived from surveying the devastation of the environment it's largely because this veils the shocking destruction of interiorities. Every oil spill, every sterile plain, every species extinction is an image of our souls in shreds, a reflection of our absence from the world, of our personal inability to inhabit it. Fukushima offers the spectacle of this complete failure of man and his mastery, which only produces ruins — and those Japanese plains, intact in appearance but where no one can live for decades. A never-ending decomposition that is finishing the job of making the world uninhabitable: the West will have ended up borrowing its mode of existence from what it fears the most — radioactive waste.

Those who continue to champion the expansion of the white savior industrial complex either cannot or will not admit to themselves that the objective disaster of the anthropocene was initially precipitated and is presently being perpetuated by the subjective disaster of the anthropocene.

Preceding and exceeding the objective disaster, the subjective disaster is two-fold. On the one hand, there is the ongoing destruction of motives, means, opportunities for the making of artful reparations. On the other hand, there is the continued proliferation of motives, means, and opportunities for yielding to the advance of imperialist white-supremacist capitalist patriarchy (or an equally ethnocidal and ecocidal would-be successor) and subjecting all life on earth to ever increasing administration and supervision.

Proxies and Redeemers

One.

Imperialist white-supremacist capitalist patriarchy is an ethnocidal and ecocidal concatenation of racist, sexist, and economic power formations that have enabled white men who are profitably engaged in capitalist relations of production to subordinate and exterminate others, especially black, brown, and indigenous women engaged in relations of production that provide for social subsistence.

Two.

Imperialist white-supremacist capitalist patriarchy maintains itself by exercising ruling, disciplinary, normalizing, and optimizing powers that prevent confluences of creolizing, queering, and communizing processes from occurring.

Creolizing, queering, and communizing processes are processes wherein and whereby racial, sexual, and economic differences come to defer to one another so as to become *black and blurred*. Confluences of creolizing, queering, and communizing processes prevent racial, sexual, and economic differences from being used to characterize and maintain social stratification.

Three.

The aim of the (De-/Re-)Constructing Worlds project is two-fold. On the one hand, the project aims to deconstruct the statements, implements, and environments that furnish people with motives, means, and opportunities to become complicit in the ethnocidal and ecocidal projects of imperialist white-supremacist capitalist patriarchy. On the other hand, the project aims to (re-)construct statements, implements, and environments that constitute living worlds, furnishing people with motives, means, and opportunities to become confluent with creolizing, queering, and communizing agents.

Four.

White men profitably engaged in capitalist relations of production are the principal beneficiaries of imperialist white-supremacist capitalist patriarchy, but there are too few of them to maintain its power formations on their own — they are always in need of proxies. This is to say, in other words, that white-supremacist capitalist patriarchs must enlist non-whites, non-men, and the unprofitable as proxies in their efforts to maintain their privileges.

Five.

Why do those belonging to the oppressed mass — non-whites, non-men, and the unprofitable — become proxies for white-supremacist capitalist patriarchs? Activist and journalist Chris Hedges suggests the following:

> [Imperialist white-supremacist capitalist patriarchy] forces the vast majority into the mass, but it allows a selected few, willing to do its dirty work, to rise above the multitude. These privileged few are given the license and authority to carry out the acts of sadism that have become the primary forms of social control. These enforcers do this work vigorously, for their greatest fear is being pushed back into the mass. The more these foot soldiers for the elite insult, persecute, torture, humiliate and kill, the more they seem to magically widen the divide between themselves and their victims. This is why Black police and corrections officers can be as cruel, and sometimes crueler, than their white counterparts. [...] [Their] sadism eradicates, at least momentarily, [their] feelings of worthlessness, vulnerability and susceptibility to pain and death. It imparts feelings of omnipotence. It is pleasurable.
>
> [...] [The most banal and, simultaneously, the most cruel among these sadists are] the colorless bureaucrats and technocrats churned out of business schools, law schools, management programs and elite universities. [...] These systems managers carry out the incremental tasks that make vast, complicated systems of exploitation and death work. They collect, store, and manipulate our personal data for digital monopolies and the security and surveillance state. They grease the wheels for ExxonMobil, BP and Goldman Sachs. They write the laws passed by the bought-and-paid-for political class. They pilot the aerial drones that terrorize the poor in Afghanistan, Iraq, Syria, and Pakistan. They profit from the endless wars. They are the corporate advertisers, public relations specialists and television pundits that flood the airwaves with lies. They run the banks. They oversee the prisons. They issue the forms. They process the papers. They deny food stamps and medical coverage to some and unemployment benefits to others. They carry out the evictions. They enforce the laws and the regulations. They do not ask questions. They live in an intellectual vacuum, a world of stultifying minutia.

Six.

The recruitment of proxies for white-supremacist capitalist patriarchs is carried out by way disciplinary, normalizing, and optimizing powers that engage in profiling. Of all the powers that serve this purpose, the powers that engage in educational and financial profiling are of paramount importance. These powers serve to filter out the atypical and outlying members of oppressed races, genders, sexes, and classes who are best suited to serve as effective proxies. These powers work by offering distinctions to individuals who serve as proxies — often in the form of educational, financial, and professional credits and credentials. They incrementally elevate some members of oppressed groups to the status of honorary white-supremacist capitalist patriarchs in order to encourage them to serve as proxies.

Seven.

But the very same disciplinary, normalizing, and optimizing powers also serve to filter out the members of oppressed groups who are liable to become atypical and outlying "dangers" — that is to say, in other words, they filter out those most liable to become confluent with creolizing, queering, and communizing agents. These "dangerous" individuals filtered out from the mass are subjected to deprivation and to communicative and corporeal violence, insult and injury, and this subjection takes place in such a manner that these "dangerous" individuals come to serve as examples. The mass learns from these examples that becoming confluent with creolizing, queering, and communizing agents means subjecting oneself to higher than usual risks of deprivation and violence framed as the unintended consequences of disciplinary action, or as normal(ized) accidents, or as the collateral damage of society's pursuit of progressive optimization.

Eight.

The members of oppressed races, genders, sexes, and classes who are best suited to act as effective proxies often turn out to be the very same individuals who are most liable to become "dangers". When power makes one suffer early and often, one is taught early and often how power works and how power might serve one better if one were to serve power. As a result, one is often faced with a stark choice in life: either (i) become a proxy and subject others to deprivation and violence, or (ii) endure deprivation and violence oneself. Alternatively, to riff on Hedges by way of the existential dilemma that Jean-Paul Sartre wrote of in Being and Nothingness, the stark choice is this: sadism or masochism?

Nine.

Returning to the main point of this dispatch, we have seen that white-supremacist capitalist patriarchs are too few to be the only ones complicit in the perpetuation of imperialist white-supremacist capitalist patriarchy: many non-whites, non-men, and the unprofitable must also be complicit. Members of these oppressed groups often loathe the prospect of being (mis)taken for "just another member of an oppressed group", and they seize upon motives, means, and opportunities to serve as proxies and to incrementally become honorary white-supremacist capitalist patriarchs. It has almost become a cliche observation that poor white men who find themselves unable to profitably engage in capitalist relations of production will gladly serve as proxies for white-supremacist capitalist patriarchs in spite of the fact that capitalism has done them more harm than good. It is perhaps less of a cliche but still widely observed that the "talented tenth" culture of "respectable" Black meritocrats and the "lean in" culture of women climbing the corporate ladder have both lent themselves to the sadism of proxy-hood and complicity in the ethnocidal and ecocidal projects of imperialist white-supremacist capitalist patriarchy.

Ten.

White-supremacist capitalist patriarchs and their proxies call themselves "conservatives" (or, alternatively, "traditionalists") when they seek to minimize diversity, equity, and inclusion in the recruitment of new proxies. There are racist conservatives who believe that non-whites should be discriminated against by the powers that recruit proxies. Then there are sexist conservatives who believe that non-men should be discriminated against by the powers that recruit proxies. Finally, there are fiscal conservatives who believe that the unprofitable should be discriminated against by the powers that recruit proxies.

White-supremacist capitalist patriarchs and their proxies call themselves "liberals" when they seek to maximize diversity, equity, and inclusion in the recruitment of new proxies. This is to say, in other words, that liberals are those who believe that non-whites, non-men, and the unprofitable should all be given equal motives, means, and opportunities to serve as proxies for white-supremacist capitalist patriarchs.

Riffing on Hedges and Sartre again, to choose between liberalism and conservatism is to choose between a softcore sadism and a hardcore sadism, respectively.

Eleven.

There is no point in naming and shaming people for choosing proxy-hood and sadism over and against masochism and persecution. Instead, let us name and shame our deathly world of suffering and the ways in which our world compels people to choose between proxy-hood and persecution, to choose between sadism and masochism. Let us not only deconstruct those statements, implements, and environments that furnish us with motives, means, and opportunities to engage in sadistic power-plays, but let us also deconstruct those statements, implements, and environments that furnish us with motives, means, and opportunities to engage in masochistic passion-plays. Let us undermine both choices, robbing sadistic power-plays of their glorified pleasures and robbing masochistic passion-plays of their glorified sufferings.

Twelve.

Having already said enough about the glorified pleasures of sadism, let us turn to the glorified sufferings of masochism. For me, this means attending to those curious organs of imperialist white supremacist capitalist patriarchy that, following Teju Cole, I call the white-savior industrial complex.

One of the primary activities of the white-savior industrial complex is to coordinate the great spectacles known as the "Suffering Olympics". In the "Suffering Olympics", those who choose persecution over proxy-hood, who choose masochism over sadism, are compelled compete against one another for the title of "redeemer". A "redeemer" is a person who, by and through enduring and overcoming persecution, is said to "redeem" the "sins" of imperialist white supremacist capitalist patriarchy. The title of "redeemer" is awarded to those suffering masochists who have mass appeal and who are ripe for co-option and patronage by white-supremacist capitalist patriarchs and their proxies. "Redeemers" are celebrated during the major festivals of imperialist white-supremacist capitalist patriarchy, like the annual World Economic Forum in Davos.

Thirteen.

We mustn't be too hasty in criticizing those suffering masochists who accept the title of "redeemer" when sadists offer it to them. For one, we must recognize that many of these "redeemers" have suffered for profound causes in a manner that has made a significant difference in people's lives. Going further, however, we must also recognize that those suffering masochists who reject the title of "redeemer" when it is offered to them are effectively claiming a higher title for themselves: they would be "redeemer of redeemers". By refusing the title of "redeemer" when it is offered to them, these suffering masochists "redeem" the choice of masochism for those who have accepted the title of "redeemer"; in so doing, these suffering masochists make choosing masochism into an end in itself.

Fourteen.

The choice between proxy-hood and persecution, between sadism or masochism, is a bad choice. When asked to choose between them, it is best to reply, Bartleby-like, "I prefer not to."

Let us have done with the choice between proxy-hood and persecution, done with the choice between sadism and masochism.

Instead, let us (re-)create ways of living otherwise than becoming proxies for power, otherwise than becoming redeemers for power, otherwise than becoming redeemers for power's redeemers, otherwise than becoming common victims of power, and otherwise than forming rival powers that can compete for supremacy. In other words, let us engage in fugitive planning so as to flee from sadistic power-plays and masochistic passion-plays and so as to live radically everyday lives.

Design Constraints for the Makings of Statements

In a previous dispatch, titled "Living Words", I examined the fifteen processes (or "structure preserving transformations") that the architect Christopher Alexander found to be pivotal (i) for the deconstruction of deathly worlds composed of domineering statements, implements, and environments and (ii) for the (re-) construction of living worlds composed of convivial alternatives.

In a subsequent dispatch, titled "Pivotal Processes", I proposed that, while all fifteen of Alexander's processes have their place in my project, four of his processes are more pivotal for my project than all of the others. These four pivotal processes are the processes of (i) NOT-SEPARATENESS, (ii) DEEP INTERLOCK AND AMBIGUITY, (iii) ROUGHNESS, and (iv) SIMPLICITY AND INNER CALM.

This dispatch sketches out ways of treating the four aforementioned processes as "design constraints" when (de-/re-)constructing statements, but those of you who have read my *Four Essays on Reparations* will recognize that these "design constraints" are, in fact, the conditions of possibility for "leaky designs".

My informative anecdotes in this dispatch are the statements discussed in my recent dispatches on fugitive planning — (i) planning to flee from schooling, (ii) planning to flee from financing, (iii) planning to flee from calendaring and clocking, and (iv) planning to flee from profiling.

Please note that the repetitiveness of this text is very intentional. The repetitions serve to encourage the reader to attend to the form of the "design constraints" relative to the contents being subjected to them. The reader is advised to take their time and linger over the repetitions and their differences. Readers of modernist novels might read this dispatch as they would read a section of Gertrude Stein's *The Making of Americans*.

All of the quoted passages in this dispatch are from The Phenomenon of Life, the first volume of Christopher Alexander's *The Nature of Order*. In keeping with my previous dispatches, I have interpolated the terms "focus" and "foci" wherever Alexander has used the terms "center" and "centers", respectively.

NOT-SEPARATENESS is "the way the life and strength of a focus depends on the extent to which that focus is merged smoothly — sometimes even indistinguishably — with the foci that form its surroundings."

If we are to flee from profiling, it is imperative that no determinate individual or group be burdened with a profile that can be retrieved, reviewed, and judged separately from the profiles of other neighboring individuals/groups.

With respect to fleeing from schooling, this would mean, for instance, (i) dispensing with academic transcripts that assume the existence of discrete individuals and (ii) dispensing with education statistics that assume the existence of separate interest groups divided by race, sex, and income. Consider, if you will, the present schooling system that assigns each and every individual their own academic transcript. The individual's academic transcript is retrieved, reviewed, and judged by powers that determine whether or not an individual will advance from one grade of schooling to the next. The schooling system is, thus, designed to allow some individuals to advance from grade to grade while others are left behind — profiling some individuals as "deserving educational advancement" and others as "not deserving educational advancement". In this way, the schooling system assumes that each individual is only responsible for their own education; caring for one's neighbor is not built into the school system as a responsibility. Might we reject the deathly individualism built into the schooling system by making it more and more difficult for powers to retrieve, review, and judge individuals' educational profiles separately, one-by-one?

With respect to fleeing from financing, this would mean, for instance, (i) dispensing with credit reports that assume the existence of discrete individuals and (ii) dispensing with economic statistics that assume the existence of separate interest groups divided by race, sex, and income. Consider, if you will, the present financial system that assigns each and every individual their own credit report. The individual's credit report is retrieved, reviewed, and judged by those who determine whether or not an individual will be given access to credit. The financial system is, thus, designed to ease access to credit for some individuals and to deny ease of access to others — profiling some individuals as "creditworthy" and others as "uncreditworthy". In this way, the financial system assumes that each individual is only responsible for their own finances; caring for one's neighbor is not built into the financial system as a responsibility. Might we reject the deathly individualism built into the financial system by making it more and more difficult for powers to retrieve, review, and judge individuals' financial profiles separately, one-by-one?

If we are to flee from calendaring and clocking, it is imperative that no determinate period of time be counted separately from other neighboring periods of time.

With respect to schooling, determinate educational periods should not be counted discretely from other neighboring educational periods. Curricula, conceived of as "planned sequences of instruction", are divided up into classes which run on set days for set periods of time over the course of which students are required to submit a set number of assignments on set dates. These classes are to be taken in a set order over the course of a set series of quarters, trimesters, or semesters, adding up to set number of years of coursework. The purpose of this stepwise periodization is to ensure that powers can identify whether and when a given individual has "fallen behind" — in other words, it is to ensure that powers can "objectively" measure out how "uneducated" the individual who has "fallen behind" is relative to those individuals who manage to keep up or skip ahead in their schooling. In this way, powers are formed that can "objectively" discriminate against those who are "retarded" in their schooling and grant privileges to those who have advanced further and more rapidly in their schooling. In other words, the stepwise periodization of schooling serves to encourage individuals to "out-learn" each other, kicking up dust as they out-pace and leave others behind. Might we reject the encouragement to "out-learn" built into the school system by making it more difficult for powers to count determinate educational periods one-by-one?

With respect to financing, determinate financial periods should not be counted discretely from other neighboring financial periods. As a contract worker or wage-worker, you have to clock in your working hours during every bi-weekly pay period. As a debtor and a renter, you have to make your monthly debt servicing payments and rent payments. To make ends meet, you need to clock in a set minimum number of working hours over the course of a set of bi-weekly pay periods to keep up with your monthly debt servicing payments and rental payments. If you do not clock-in the set minimum working hours and you fall behind on your monthly payments, you will be charged compounding late fees that you will have to pay in addition to paying your standard monthly payments. All of this serves to ensure that powers can identify whether and when you "fall behind" — in other words, all of this serves to ensure that powers can "objectively" measure out how "uncreditworthy" you are relative to those who have managed to keep up with their payments or make their payments ahead of time. In this way, powers are formed that can "objectively" discriminate against those who earn less and earn slowly and grant privileges to those who earn more and earn quickly. In other words, discrete periodizations of credits and debits serve to encourage individuals to "out-earn" each other, kicking up dust as they out-pace and leave others behind. Might we reject the encouragement to "out-earn" built into the financial system by making it more difficult for powers to count determinate financial periods separately, one-by-one?

DEEP INTERLOCK AND AMBIGUITY is "the way in which the intensity of a given focus can be increased when it is [attached to / entangled with] a nearby focus, through a third set of foci that [ambiguously / indeterminately] belong to both."

If we are to flee from profiling, it is imperative that the profile of a determinate individual or group becomes entangled with the profiles of other neighboring individuals/groups via a set of regional profiles that ambiguously belong to both the determinate individual/group and their neighbors.

With respect to schooling, the question is this: how can we make it so that powers can only ever retrieve, review, and judge regional educational profiles as opposed to the educational profiles of determinate individuals/groups? Imagine if we could replace academic transcripts belonging to determinate individuals with regional academic transcripts indeterminately belonging to neighboring individuals. Individualism would be discouraged as a result and, instead, we would be encouraged to find the willingness and the ability to care for our neighbors' learning.

With respect to financing, the question is this: how can we make it so that powers can only ever retrieve, review, and judge regional financial profiles as opposed to the financial profiles of determinate individuals/groups? Imagine if we could replace credit reports belonging to determinate individuals with regional credit reports that indeterminately belong to several neighboring individuals. Individualism would be discouraged as a result and, instead, we would be encouraged to find the willingness and the ability to care for our neighbors' earnings.

If we are to flee from calendaring and clocking, it is imperative that every determinate period of time becomes entangled with other neighboring periods of time via a set of transitional periods of time that indeterminately belong to both the determinate period of time and its neighbors.

With respect to schooling, the question is this: how can we make it so that powers can only ever count transitional educational periods as opposed to determinate educational periods? Imagine that credits towards graduation could not be divided up into separately counted courses with set term lengths and imagine that these separately counted courses could not be divided up into separate assignments with specified due dates — with the result being that powers could no longer pinpoint with certainty whether and when anyone has "fallen behind" in their schooling.

With respect to financing, the question is this: how can we make it so that powers can only ever count transitional financial periods as opposed to determinate financial periods? Imagine that billing cycles, pay periods, and working hours could not be specified and counted separately from one another — with the result being that powers could no longer pinpoint with certainty whether and when anyone has "fallen behind" on their payments.

ROUGHNESS is "the way that the field effect of a given foci draws its strength, necessarily, from irregularities in the scales, forms and arrangements of other nearby foci."

If we are to flee from profiling, it is imperative that irregularities characterize all regional profiles that indeterminately belong to several neighboring individuals or groups. Regional profiles should not enable powers to pinpoint the average profile of a set of neighboring individuals/groups. To the contrary, regional profiles should span the range of the profiles of neighboring individuals/groups without ever enabling powers to pinpoint an average or "central tendency" that characterizes the range.

With respect to schooling, regional educational profiles should not enable powers to pinpoint the average educational profile of a set of neighboring individuals/groups. To the contrary, regional educational profiles should span the range of the educational profiles of neighboring individuals/groups without ever enabling powers to pinpoint an average or "central tendency" that characterizes the range. In this way, powers would not be able count on neighboring individuals/groups having an average educational profile; powers would only be able to count on there being a range of educational profiles amongst neighboring individuals/groups .

With respect to financing, regional financial profiles should not enable powers to pinpoint the average financial profile of a group of neighboring individuals/groups. To the contrary, regional financial profiles should span the range of the financial profiles of neighboring individuals/groups without ever enabling powers to pinpoint an average or "central tendency" that characterizes the range. In this way, powers would not be able count on neighboring individuals/groups having an average financial profile; powers would only be able to count on there being a range of financial profiles amongst neighboring individuals/groups .

If we are to flee from calendaring and clocking, it is imperative that irregularities characterize all transitional periods of time that indeterminately belong to several neighboring periods of time. Transitional periods of time should not enable powers to pinpoint an average period of time. To the contrary, transitional periods of time should span a range of times without ever enabling powers to pinpoint an average or "central tendency" that characterizes the range.

With respect to schooling, transitional educational periods should not enable powers to pinpoint the average time that it takes for a set of neighboring individuals/groups to earn enough credits to graduate from one determinate educational period to the next. To the contrary, transitional educational periods should span the range of times that it takes a set of neighboring individuals/groups to earn enough credits to graduate from one determinate educational period to the next without ever enabling powers to pinpoint an average or "central tendency" that characterizes the range. In this way, powers would not be able count on neighboring educational periods having an average time-to-graduation; powers would only be able to count on there being a range of times-to-graduation amongst neighboring educational periods.

With respect to financing, transitional financial periods should not enable powers to pinpoint the average time that it takes for a set of neighboring individuals/groups to enough credits to make their next payment. To the contrary, transitional financial periods should span the range of times that it takes a set of neighboring individuals/ groups to earn enough credits to make a payment without ever enabling powers to pinpoint an average or "central tendency" that characterizes the range. In this way, powers would not be able count on neighboring financial periods having an average rate-of-payment; powers would only be able to count on there being a range of rates-of-payment amongst neighboring financial periods.

SIMPLICITY AND INNER CALM is "the way the strength of a foci depends on its simplicity — on the process of reducing the number of different foci which exist in it, while increasing the strength of these foci to make them weigh more."

If we are to flee from profiling, it is imperative that we gradually work to expunge those sets of regional profiles that powers can use to reverse engineer the profiles of determinate individuals/groups and the central tendencies amongst them; and it is imperative that we should only maintain those sets of regional profiles that effectively obscure the profiles of determinate individuals/groups and the central tendencies amongst them.

With respect to schooling, the aim is (i) to prevent powers from ever identifying determinate individuals/groups who have outlying educational profiles relative to neighboring individuals/groups and, in so doing, (ii) to prevent powers from subjecting outlying individuals/groups to special administration and supervision. This is to say, in other words, that powers should never be given the ability to identify unusually fast learners and unusually slow learners and to place them in separate special/specialized education programs that privilege fast learners and stigmatize slow learners (or vice versa). Rather, powers should only ever be given the ability to expand access to general education, making it more inclusive and less discriminating.

With respect to financing, the aim here is (i) to prevent powers from ever identifying determinate individuals/groups who have outlying financial profiles relative to neighboring individuals/groups and, in so doing, (ii) to prevent powers from subjecting outlying individuals/groups to special administration and supervision. This is to say, in other words, that powers should never be given the ability to identify unusually fast earners and unusually slow earners and to place them in separate special/specialized financing programs that privilege fast earners and stigmatize slow earners (or vice versa). Rather, powers should only ever be given the ability to expand access to general financing, making it more inclusive and less discriminating.

If we are to flee from calendaring and clocking, it is imperative that we gradually work to expunge those sets of transitional periods of time that powers can use to reverse engineer determinate periods of time and the central tendencies amongst them; and we should maintain only those sets of transitional periods of time that effectively obscure determinate periods of time and the central tendencies amongst them.

With respect to schooling, the aim is (i) to prevent powers from ever identifying educational periods with outlying times-to-graduation relative to neighboring periods and, in so doing, (ii) to prevent powers from subjecting individuals/groups to special administration and supervision during outlying educational periods. This is to say, in other words, that powers should never be given the ability to identify unusually fast learning periods and unusually slow learning periods and to optimize times-to-graduation during these outlying periods by subjecting individuals/groups to special administration and supervision during these periods. Rather, powers should only ever be given the ability to accommodate an ever widening range of times-to-graduation generally, across different educational periods.

With respect to financing, the aim is (i) to prevent powers from ever identifying financial periods with outlying rates-of-payment relative to their neighboring periods and, in so doing, (ii) to prevent powers from subjecting individuals/groups to special administration and supervision during outlying financial periods. This is to say, in other words, that powers should never be given the ability to identify unusually fast earning periods and unusually slow earning periods and to optimize rates-of-payment during these outlying periods by subjecting individuals/groups to special administration and supervision during these periods. Rather, powers should only ever be given the ability to accommodate an ever widening range of rates-of-payment generally, across different financial periods.

Three Freedoms

What do I mean when I use the term "freedom"?

I have been asking myself this question again recently, inspired by the passage below from David Graeber and David Wengrow's *The Dawn of Everything*.

> [W]e are not talking here about 'freedom' as an abstract ideal or formal principle [...] [W]e [are] instead talk[ing] about basic forms of social liberty which one might actually put into practice: (1) the freedom to move away or relocate from one's surroundings; (2) the freedom to ignore or disobey commands issued by others; and (3) the freedom to shape entirely new social realities, or shift back and forth between different ones.

> ... [T]he first two freedoms — to relocate, and to disobey commands — often [act] as a kind of scaffolding for the third, more creative one.

When I have used the term "freedom" in my writings, I have almost exclusively been referring to the third freedom that Graeber and Wengrow identify in the passage above, "the freedom to shape entirely new social realities, or shift back and forth between different ones." My preferred term for Graeber and Wengrow's third freedom is "the freedom to (de-/re-)construct worlds" — this is because what Graeber and Wengrow call a "social reality" is roughly equivalent to what I have been calling a "world".

Now, I must admit that I was a bit taken aback by Graeber and Wengrow's claim that the freedom to migrate and the freedom to disobey often serve to supplement the freedom to (de-/re-)construct worlds. I had always proposed the reverse: the freedom to (de-/re-)construct worlds serves to supplement all other freedoms, including the freedom to relocate and to disobey. Going even further, in keeping with Jacques Derrida's usage of the term "supplement", I had always proposed that the freedom to disobey and to migrate are only ever meaningful when these freedoms both enable and are enabled by the freedom to (de-/re-)construct worlds.

The stories of undocumented refugees and migrants in our present world of suffering bears witness to my proposition. Undocumented refugees and migrants are those who have taken direct action to realize their freedoms by disobeying border laws and migrating to new lands. When they arrive in new lands, however, the powers-that-be in those lands are such that they prevent the undocumented from (de-/re-)constructing worlds in these new lands. The powers-that-be force the undocumented to fit themselves into established roles in a world that is more or less ready-made for them. All those who have undocumented family and friends in the United States, for instance, will know that the undocumented are by no means excluded from social reality here in the United States. Rather, they are included in a subordinate position that precludes them from actively participating in the (de-/re-)construction of social reality here in the United States. To be more pointed, the United States runs on the labor of the undocumented, and subordinate positions in the social reality of the United States are ready-made for the undocumented when they arrive here. The U.S. Immigration and Customs Enforcement service (ICE) does not exist to prevent people from disobeying border laws and from migrating to the United States without proper documentation. Rather, ICE primarily exists to ensure that people who disobey and migrate to the United States without documentation can only ever occupy the places that are ready-made for them in the United States and that they cannot exercise the freedom to (de-/re-)construct worlds while living here in the United States. In so doing, ICE effectively renders the direct exercise of the freedoms to disobey and to migrate meaningless.

Putting the example of the undocumented aside, however, I think that Graeber and Wengrow point out something that I really have been missing all along. They point out that the freedom to (de-/re-)construct worlds is itself meaningless without the freedoms to disobey and to migrate. All three freedoms mutually condition one another: the freedom to (de-/re-)construct worlds is only meaningful when it enables the freedoms to disobey and to migrate; the freedom to disobey is only meaningful when it enables the freedoms to migrate and to (de-/re-)construct worlds; and the freedom to migrate is only meaningful when it enables the freedoms to disobey and to (de-/re-)construct worlds. These three freedoms will be confluent with one another or they will not be. There is no freedom to be had when the (de-/re-)construction of worlds results in the construction of a world in which one can neither disobey nor migrate.

Recognizing that the freedom to (de-/re-)construct worlds is entangled with the freedoms to disobey and to migrate, I am now much better able articulate what imperialism is and how it is that imperialism ought to be countered.

My dispatches have, thus far, mostly focused on one imperialist power formation above all others — that is, imperialist white-supremacist capitalist patriarchy. As I have defined it, imperialist white-supremacist capitalist patriarchy is a power formation that maintains itself by inhibiting confluences of creolizing, communizing, and queering processes. Point for point, I hold that creolizing processes run counter to white-supremacy, that communizing processes run counter to capitalism, and that queering processes run counter to patriarchy. Attentive readers will have noted, however, that I have been leaving one term un-countered, and they will likely have asked themselves, "But, generally speaking, what runs counter to imperialism?"

Thinking with and through Graeber and Wengrow, I would like to propose that an imperialist power formation is one that inhibits peoples' capacities to meaningfully exercise the freedoms to disobey, to migrate, and to (de-/re-)construct worlds. Ay, and that which runs counter to imperialism is that which nurtures and activates peoples' capacities to meaningfully exercise the same three freedoms.

Imperialist white-supremacist capitalist patriarchy happens to be the pre-eminent imperialist power formation on our planet today, but it is only one species of the broader genera of imperialist power formations. Imperialist white-supremacist capitalist patriarchy works to ensure that white men profitably engaged in capitalist enterprise (and those who serve them as proxies and redeemers) are given the greatest leeway to exercise the freedoms to disobey, to migrate, and to (de-/re-) construct worlds. In turn, all others are given far less leeway to exercise the three freedoms, with the least leeway being given to black, brown, and indigenous women who are engaged in providing for social subsistence.

This order of things is not only plainly horrible to me, it is also impossible to justify this order of things when one realizes that black, brown, and indigenous women engaged in providing for social subsistence have been responsible for many, if not most, of the remarkable social and technical inventions that have nurtured life on our planet ever since, well, the "Dawn of Everything". It is worth quoting Graeber and Wengrow as they make this point with respect to the beginnings of agriculture.

Nobody, of course, claims that the beginnings of agriculture were anything quite like, say, the invention of the steam-powered loom or the electric light bulb. We can be fairly certain there was no Neolithic equivalent of Edmund Cartwright or Thomas Edison, who came up with the conceptual breakthrough that set everything in motion. Still, it often seems difficult for contemporary writers to resist the idea that some sort of similarly dramatic break with the past must have occurred. In fact, as we've seen, what actually took place was nothing like that. Instead of some male genius realizing his solitary vision, innovation in Neolithic societies was based on a collective body of knowledge accumulated over centuries, largely by women, in an endless series of apparently humble but in fact enormously significant discoveries. Many of those Neolithic discoveries had the cumulative effect of reshaping everyday life every bit as profoundly as the automatic loom or lightbulb.

Every time we sit down to breakfast, we are likely to be benefiting from a dozen such prehistoric inventions. Who was the first person to figure out that you could make bread rise by the addition of those microorganisms we call yeasts? We have no idea, but we can be almost certain she was a woman and would most likely not be considered 'white' if she tried to immigrate to a European country today; and we definitely know her achievement continues to enrich the lives of billions of people. What we also know is that such discoveries were, again, based on centuries of accumulated knowledge and experimentation — recall how the basic principles of agriculture were known long before anyone applied them systematically — and that the results of such experiments were often preserved and transmitted through ritual, games and forms of play (or even more, perhaps, at the point where ritual, games and play shade into each other).

Today, we are being told that the innovations and inventions that will "save the environment" will emerge from state and corporate bureaucracies formed by the well schooled and the well financed — by "Green Meritocrats" and "Green Entrepreneurs" with eco-modernist pretensions . This is one of the most insidious conceits of imperialist white-supremacist capitalist patriarchy.

First, it needs to be said that being both well-schooled and well-financed very often means being either a rich White businessman, or a proxy for rich White businessmen, or a redeemer of rich White businessmen. Second, it needs to be said that state and corporate bureaucracies formed by the well schooled and the well financed have given us two and a half centuries of unsustainable innovations and inventions: fossil fuel exhausts, un-recyclable plastics, hazardous chemical spills, radioactive wastes, desertified landscapes, expanding dead-zones in our oceans, and stockpiles of weapons of mass destruction. Third, and most importantly, it needs to be said that sustainable innovations and inventions have, since time immemorial, tended to be the handiwork of unschooled women meaningfully exercising the freedoms to disobey, to migrate, and to (de-/re-)construct worlds while being engaged in providing for social subsistence.

How can anyone seriously propose that state and corporate bureaucracies formed by the well schooled and the well financed will "save the environment"? State and corporate bureaucracies formed by the well schooled and the well financed have been complicit in ethnocide and ecocide for at least two and a half centuries now, and it behooves us to compare the ethnocidal and ecocidal track record of these bureaucracies to the track record of unschooled women engaged in subsistence activities — women who have been responsible for many millennia of sustainable inventions and innovations.

Reflecting on how it is that people have come to champion state and corporate bureaucracies as saviors, Arundhati Roy remarks,

> We ought not to speak only about the economics of globalization, but about the psychology of globalization. It's like the psychology of a battered woman being faced with her husband again and being asked to trust him again. That's what is happening. We are being asked by the [states and corporations] that invented nuclear weapons and chemical weapons and apartheid and modern slavery and racism — [states and corporations] that have perfected the gentle art of genocide, that colonized other people for centuries — to trust them when they say that they believe in a level playing field and the equitable distribution of resources and in a better world. It seems comical that we should even consider that they really mean what they say.

Instead of championing bureaucracies formed by the well schooled and the well financed, my suggestion is that we "save the environment" by enabling women engaged in subsistence activities to meaningfully exercise the freedoms to disobey, to migrate, and to (de-/re-)construct worlds — and that we do so without discriminating against any woman because of race, nationality, or schooling.

Many will tell you that my suggestion is preposterous. This is because imperialist patriarchs, their proxies, and their redeemers have successfully endeavored to convince people(s) that women engaged in subsistence activities are of little or no importance to the "advancement of civilization". Imperialist white-supremacist capitalist patriarchy has an ideological history that spans five hundred years, but imperialist patriarchy, minus the white-supremacy and capitalism, has an ideological history that spans five millennia. The basic argument against giving more freedoms to women engaged in subsistence activities runs as follows: the "advantages" of imperialist patriarchies must have some natural correspondence with a reality beyond dispute because imperialist patriarchies have stubbornly persisted in oppressing women engaged in subsistence activities for five millennia.

Let us not forget that women engaged in subsistence activities have been resisting imperialist white-supremacist capitalist patriarchy for the past five hundred years. Let us not forget that women engaged in subsistence activities have been resisting imperialist patriarchy, minus the white-supremacy and capitalism, for the past five millennia. Let us not forget that many people(s) have lived relatively free lives for millennia without submitting to imperialist patriarchies thanks to the efforts of women engaged in subsistence activities. Indeed, let us take some cues here from Graeber and Wengrow in this regard, given that they wrote the Dawn of Everything without forgetting these three things.

> [W]hat happens if we accord significance to the 5,000 years in which cereal domestication did not lead to the emergence of pampered aristocracies, standing armies or debt peonage, rather than just the 5,000 in which it did? What happens if we treat the rejection of urban life, or of slavery, in certain times and places as something just as significant as the emergence of those same phenomena in others? In the process, we often found ourselves surprised. We'd never have guessed, for instance, that slavery was most likely abolished multiple times in history in multiple places; and that very possibly the same is true of war. Obviously, such abolitions are rarely definitive. Still, the periods in which free or relatively free societies existed are hardly insignificant. In fact, if you bracket the Eurasian Iron Age (which is effectively what we have been doing here), they represent the vast majority of human social experience.

> Social theorists have a tendency to write about the past as if everything that happened could have been predicted beforehand. This is somewhat dishonest, since we're all aware that when we actually try to predict the future we almost invariably get it wrong — and this is just as true of social theorists as anybody else. Nonetheless, it's hard to resist the temptation to write and think as if the current state of the world, in the early twenty-first century, is the inevitable outcome of the last 10,000 years of history, while in reality, of course, we have little or no idea what the world will be like even in 2075, let alone 2150.

> Who knows? Perhaps if our species does endure, and we one day look backwards from this as yet unknowable future, aspects of the remote past that now seem like anomalies — say, bureaucracies that work on a community scale; cities governed by neighbourhood councils; systems of government where women hold a preponderance of formal positions; or forms of land management based on care-taking rather than ownership and extraction — will seem like the really significant breakthroughs, and great stone pyramids or statues more like historical curiosities.

With all of the above in mind, I would now like to re-articulate the aims of the (De-/Re-)Constructing Worlds project in more pointed terms.

In and through this project, I am trying to discover what we can do in our time, the present, to (re-)construct a world in which imperialist power formations are historical curiosities and the freedoms to disobey, to migrate, and to (de-/re-)construct worlds are decisive.

Six Theses on Science

Science becomes entangled with art and philosophy whenever science is "put to the test" in an experiment.

The artistry of the experimentalist and experimentalism of the artist can never be neatly distinguished from one another and, what's more, the choice of an experiment by the artist-experimentalist is always a philosophical choice — which means that the artist-experimentalist can never be neatly distinguished from the philosopher.

The artist, the philosopher, and the scientist are only distinguished from one another by how they use their experiments. The artist uses their experiments to make sensations in a given world, the philosopher to make conceptions of a given world, and the scientist to make predictions about a given world.

Art, science, and philosophy are, otherwise, always being (con)fused with one another in and through the making of experiments. They are always becoming something other than what they are supposed to be — something other than simply art, science, and philosophy. They are always becoming practices of "world-making".

When art, science and philosophy are not (con)fused in experimental practices of world-making — when they simply are what they are — we are left with the banal evils of artistic traditions, scientific establishments, and philosophical dogmas that are gracelessly resolved against creative freedom.

The six theses below are directed at scientists. They aim to motivate scientists to take responsibility for the makings of worlds, to do art and philosophy with and through science, and to become otherwise than they are.

One.

A poster that is quite common on lawns and in windows here in Seattle proclaims, "We believe that science is real."

This proclamation disturbs me to no end because science is not itself real. Rather, science is a "virtual reality". This is to say, in other words, that science is a simulation of reality: a good scientific model is a simulation that can predict observable outcomes with a high degree of accuracy.

Two.

Considering the matter further, we must also note that a scientific prediction of an observable outcome is not itself an objectively real phenomena.

To test the accuracy of a scientific prediction is to intervene in an otherwise indeterminate reality, and the outcome of one's intervention is a determinate reality.

This is to say, in other words, that science induces observable outcomes or "actual realities" in order to test the accuracy of its models or "virtual realities".

Three.

To say that "science is real" is to deny that the scientist has agency and responsibility. It is to cast the scientist as a passive observer of outcomes. But the scientist is, in fact, an active participant in the production of observable outcomes.

Rather than saying that "science is real", we ought to say that "science can effectively shape reality." This phrasing would motivate us to hold scientists accountable for how they choose to test the accuracy of their models.

Four.

Scientists who test their models in and through inducing deathly, degrading, and destructive outcomes are not to be celebrated for doing so. Such scientists include the physicists who made the atomic bomb, the medical scientists who induce illnesses in lab animals and human test subjects, and the psychological and social scientists who "passively" study the adverse effects of pollution, poverty, racism, and sexual violence on individuals and societies.

Scientists who test their models in and through inducing lively, creative, and reparative outcomes are to be celebrated: take, for instance, the astrophysicist whose practice revolves around enabling the public to easily contribute to and access data about the cosmos and to participate in making discoveries; or the ecologist who engages with indigenous knowledges in order to learn and disseminate indigenous know-how to care for a cherished habitat; or the psychological or social scientist who experiments with social forms in order to actively promote care and compassion in and for others.

Five.

The notion that a scientist must remain objective and should not be an activist is a mistaken notion because it doesn't take into account the fact that scientists have agency and responsibility when it comes to testing their models. A deathly, degrading, and destructive prediction should not be induced, whether by action or inaction, in order to prove that a model is correct. Instead, attempts to avoid and mitigate predictable death, degradation, and destruction should be taken with the model in mind, and the success or failure these attempts should be the basis for evaluating the model in question.

In light of climate change and other anthropogenic natural disasters, it is particularly important that we re-conceive of the role of the scientist in this way. Rather than testing and refining models by passively watching death, degradation, and destruction unfold, scientists need to test and refine their models by undertaking experiments that aim to avoid deathly, degrading, and destructive outcomes and to induce lively, creative, and reparative outcomes.

For instance, the climate scientist ought to refuse funding to study how increased deforestation hastens climate change and, instead, seek and accept funding to participate in reforestation efforts in order to study how reforestation mitigates climate change. Participating in reforestation in order to further scientific knowledge is an aesthetically and ethically rich endeavor; observing deforestation to further knowledge is an aesthetically and ethically empty endeavor.

Six.

Scientific knowledge imbued with aesthetic and ethical concerns is the only scientific knowledge worth seeking; scientific knowledge devoid of aesthetic and ethical concerns is only worth questioning.

Those scientists who believe that aesthetics and ethics should have nothing to do with the makings of scientific knowledge are those who have been compelled to disavow aesthetics and ethics when doing science. The question is: what sorts of power formations have compelled these scientists to disavow aesthetics and ethics?

The War on Terra

It is one thing to have a theory that describes the (de-/re-)construction of a world, but it is another thing to have a story that narrates the (de-/re-)construction of a world. Though they can and should defer to one another, the theory that describes and the story that narrates will always differ from one another.

Thus far, I have only been articulating theories and describing my approach to the (de-/re-)construction of our deathly world of suffering.

Beginning with this dispatch, I would like to begin telling my story and narrating my approach to the (de-/re-)construction of our deathly world of suffering.

My story goes something like this...

Imperialist patriarchies have been, by turns, a greater or lesser scourge on our planet for five millennia, but a new and more virulent strain of imperialist patriarchy emerged around five centuries ago — one hellbent on conquering the entire Earth, subjecting the vast majority of her peoples to ethnocide and the vast majority of her places to ecocide.

This new scourge: imperialist white-supremacist capitalist patriarchy.

Turbo-charged by racist and capitalist techniques and technologies of power, this modern scourge has proven itself more virulently ethnocidal, more virulently ecocidal, and more virulently expansionary than previous scourges. In the five-centuries between 1492 and 1992, imperialist white-supremacist capitalist patriarchy has managed to spread itself across the globe and establish the (capital "E") Empire — a globalized capitalist system that advances itself by modulating the balance of power amongst the (lowercase "e") empires of the various territorial nations that have staked claims to all of the terrestrial habitats on Earth.

The "War on Terra" is my preferred term for the series of expansionary, ethnocidal, and ecocidal projects that have advanced (and been advanced) by imperialist white-supremacist capitalist patriarchy since 1492 — from the genocides of the indigenous peoples of the Americas, to the Late Victorian Holocausts, to the ongoing Late Davosian Holocausts.

As I conceive of it, the War on Terra is an interminable war of aggression and extermination that imperialist white-supremacist capitalist patriarchs (along with their proxies and redeemers) have waged against "the beautiful and differentiated languages, cultures, customs, and ways of life of the Earth's people[s], [which are] vital to the health of the planet."

No one living on Earth today has not been touched by the War on Terra: everyone living has some sense and understanding of the devastation that it has wrought. That being said, however, prevailing liberal prejudices demand that most of our esteemed commentators and thinkers refuse to acknowledge the War on Terra for what it is. In a previous dispatch on this matter, I wrote:

> The evidence of ecocide is mounting everyday. A radio news broadcast informs us, "Human activities have caused the world's wildlife populations to plummet by more than two-thirds in the last 50 years, according to a new report from the World Wildlife Fund." And keen observers tell us the crisis is much more than an extinction crisis, "The numerical robustness, the plenitude within nature, has dwindled. Many species continue to exist but in greatly diminished numbers, which means that the species itself has a far more tenuous hold on existence. As species crash and vanish, the world loses diversity, but the loss of abundance is even more startling." Yet when liberals in positions of power speak of promoting sustainability and conserving wildlife, I find that they are not earnestly speaking of countering ecocide and promoting robust natural diversity. To the contrary, I find that they are speaking of adopting a more deliberate and controlled approach to ecocide, an approach that destroys more habitats but leads to fewer outright extinctions.
>
> The evidence of ethnocide is also mounting everyday. A newspaper article informs us, "Of the estimated 7,000 languages spoken in the world today, linguists say, nearly half are in danger of extinction and are likely to disappear in this century. In fact, they are now falling out of use at a rate of about one every two weeks." But when liberals in positions of power speak of promoting diversity, equity, and inclusion, I find that they are not earnestly speaking of countering ethnocide and promoting robust cultural diversity. To the contrary, I find that they are speaking of enlisting more and more individuals of diverse ancestries as proxies in the ethnocidal and ecocidal endeavors of imperialist white-supremacist capitalist patriarchy.

To do away with liberal prejudices and to develop a deep sense and understanding for the War on Terra, I suggest that we take our cues from Michel Serres and recognize how, in the decades since the Second World War, "Our peacetime economic relations, working slowly and continuously, [have produced] the same results as would a short global conflict." This means recognizing that the War on Terra does not belong to soldiers alone: "it is [being] prepared and waged with devices [...] used by civilians in research and industry." It is as if becoming a worker and consumer in an industrial capitalist society today means becoming a conscript in the service of the ethnocidal and ecocidal forces of imperialist white-supremacist capitalist patriarchy.

The War on Terra has been raging for five-hundred years but it has only truly come into its own in the decades since the Second World War. Prior the First World War, the War on Terra had wrapped itself in the guise of wars of colonial conquest, domination, and exploitation. It was only after the carnage First and Second World Wars that the War on Terra revealed its true face to the world at large, an sneering face that had only previously been seen by those living in the colonized world. In a remarkable passage from A *Thousand Plateaus*, Gilles Deleuze and Felix Guattari describe how this shift took place.

> The various factors that tended to make war a "total war," most notably the fascist factor, marked the beginning of an inversion. [...] The entire fascist economy became a war economy, but the war economy still needed total war as its object. For this reason, fascist war still fell under Clausewitz's formula, "the continuation of politics by other means," even though those other means had become exclusive. [...]

> It was only after World War II that the automatization, then automation of the war machine had their true effect. The war machine, the new antagonisms traversing it considered, no longer had war as its exclusive object but took in charge and as its object peace, politics, the world order, in short, the aim. This is where the inversion of Clausewitz's formula comes in: it is politics that becomes the continuation of war; it is peace that technologically frees the unlimited material process of total war. [...] In this sense, there was no longer a need for fascism. The Fascists were only child precursors, and the absolute peace of survival succeeded where total war had failed. The Third World War was already upon us. [...] Wars had become a part of peace.

> [...] [The perpetual and total war machine that now threatens to "keep the peace"] is terrifying not as a function of a possible war that it promises us, as by blackmail, but, on the contrary, as a function of the real, very special kind of peace it promotes and has already installed[.]

As a result of their Eurocentric perspective, Deleuze and Guattari overlooked the fact that the inversion of Clausewitz's formula had already taken place outside of Europe in the colonized world long before the Second World War. For at least a century before the rise of fascism in Europe, the "keeping of the peace" in the colonized world had become a perpetual and total war waged by colonial corporations and governments against the subject peoples of the colonized world. That being said, however, Deleuze and Guattari are on point with their assertion that it was only after the Second World War that the situation of the colonized world became the situation of the world at large. Following the Second World War, the "keeping of the peace" all over the world became a perpetual and total war waged by corporations and governments against subject peoples all over the world.

Long before the Westernized peoples at the centers of Empire had a clue, the colonized and enslaved peoples at the peripheries of Empire had developed a deep sense and understanding of the ethnocidal and ecocidal character of the War on Terra. Following the Second World War, however, Westernized peoples discovered that they could no longer keep up the ceremony of ignorance and innocence as scrupulously as they once could. The War on Terra's blood-dimmed tide had been loosed on the European continent, the homeland of the West, and Westernized peoples were finally being forced confront its true character. Ever since the Second World War, Westernized peoples have been hard pressed to acknowledge the true character of the War on Terra and to admit their part in advancing it. But this has not meant that most or even many Westernized peoples have made such acknowledgments and admitted responsibility. To the contrary, many Westernized peoples, if not most of them, have actually sought to keep the ceremony of ignorance and innocence alive in the most unscrupulous of ways.

That being said, however, as the historian Tony Judt has pointed out, "Since 1989 it has become clearer than it was before just how much the stability of post-war Europe rested upon the accomplishments of Josef Stalin and Adolf Hitler. Between them, and assisted by wartime collaborators, the dictators blasted flat the demographic heath upon which the foundations of a new and less complicated continent were then laid." This is to say, in other words, that the West increasingly knows itself to have inflicted traumas upon "internal others" akin to the traumas it has inflicted upon "external others", and it is obvious to every sober observer that all of these traumas put together have conditioned the "democracy, peace, prosperity, and stability" that has prevailed in the West and failed most everywhere else since the Second World War.

For those of us who have developed a deep sense and understanding of the ethnocidal and ecocidal character of the War on Terra, the question is, of course, "What can be done to bring the War on Terra to a peaceful end?"

As I see it, no offensive action against the forces of imperialist white-supremacist capitalist patriarchy will ever bring a peaceful end to the War on Terra. To effectively launch an offensive action against the forces of imperialist white-supremacist capitalist patriarchy is to establish oneself as an even more virulently ethnocidal and ecocidal force. Those readying themselves to wage offensives against the forces of imperialist white-supremacist capitalist patriarchy are, in fact, readying themselves to take over the reins in the War on Terra.

As I see it, the perpetual and total character of the War on Terra is such that the only way to seek its peaceful end is to enable people(s) to desert the forces of ethnocide and ecocide and to defect to the forces that are countering ethnocide and ecocide. A peaceful end to the War on Terra will only follow from a critical mass of desertions and defections.

I use the term "forces of nature" to refer to the various counterforces that are arrayed against the forces of ethnocide and ecocide, against imperialist white-supremacist capitalist patriarchy and its would-be successors. Since there are no effective offenses that the forces of nature can make against the forces of ethnocide and ecocide, the forces of nature are always making defenses. Working to bring the War on Terra to an end, the forces of nature make their defenses by and through furnishing potential deserters and defectors with motives, means, and opportunities to desert the forces of ethnocide and ecocide and to defect to the forces of nature.

To bring all of this on home, allow me to situate myself and this project within this story.

I was born during the summer of 1987 in New York City, the most prominent node in the network of "Global Cities" where the administrative and supervisory organs Empire are headquartered — the home of Wall Street and the United Nations.

Like all born New Yorkers, my survival has been dependent on the consumption of commodities sold on the global market and on the global exploitation of natural and cultural resources. In other words, as Ivan Illich would say, I was born into a life of "modernized poverty [...]combining the lack of power over circumstances with a loss of personal potency". Modernized poverty is the experience of "frustrating affluence" that occurs in persons "mutilated" by their absolute dependence on the "riches" of industrial productivity. While I cannot help but love the glamorous and gritty city where I began my life, I cannot deny the fact that it is "an urban landscape that is unfit for people unless they devour each day their own weight in metals, plastics, and fuels, [...] in which the constant need for protection against the unwanted results of more commodities and more commands has generated new depths of discrimination, impotence, and frustration."

I was born to Black Africans who had legally migrated to the United States of America. The promised land of "freedom an opportunity" for some, the United States is an exceptional nation for having been built on the genocide of indigenous peoples and the enslavement of black peoples and having risen in industrial and military might to serve as Empire's reigning hegemon/henchman. In spite of these exceptionally disturbing realities, my parents still strove to realize the American immigrant fantasy of "freedom and opportunity" for themselves and their children by championing the virtues of "hard work and upwardly mobility". I was taught from early childhood that it was imperative that I work hard to become a "Black man of distinction" — a proxy or a redeemer for imperialist white-supremacist capitalist patriarchy and its Empire — as opposed to "just another Black man in America".

Lacking the financing necessary to secure my future, my parents taught me to value schooling as the surest route to achieving distinction. To cite Ivan Illich once more, I was taught to believe that "grace is reserved for those who accumulate years in school" and to accept the organization of society into "many layers of failure, with each layer inhabited by dropouts schooled to believe that those who have consumed more [schooling] deserve more privilege because they are more valuable assets to society as a whole."

To sum up my childhood and adolescence in a single sentence: I was effectively born and raised to serve the forces of ethnocide and ecocide in the War on Terra.

Fortunately for me, but much to my parents' chagrin, the forces of nature conspired to teach me to value learning more than schooling and, better still, to value learning about the makings of my world above all else. In my pursuit of such learning, I discovered many facts that horrified me, and I became disgusted at the prospects of becoming a proxy or a redeemer for the ethnocidal and ecocidal forces of imperialist white-supremacist capitalist patriarchy. Indeed, I became convinced that I had to desert the forces of ethnocide and ecocide, defect to the forces of nature, and come to the aid others doing the same. My problem, then, became this: I lacked reliable theoretical-and-practical guides to teach me how to desert, how to defect, and how to commune with other deserters and defectors.

The (De-/Re-)Constructing Worlds project is, thus, the log of my own self-guided attempts to desert, defect, and commune with other deserters and defectors; and my hope is that the failures and successes logged here might serve as a theoretical-and-practical resource for others like me.

Five Considerations

[—]

There are five factors to consider when planning a fugitive undertaking. Take care to consider these five factors and you will be well-prepared for the undertaking. Fail to consider these five factors and you will be caught unprepared.

These five factors are:

1. The Way; or, the Narratives You Have About the Undertaking

2. The Weather; or, the Feelings You Have About the Undertaking

3. The Terrain; or, the Facts You Have About the Undertaking

4. The Guides; or, the Theories You Have About the Undertaking

5. The Maneuvers; or, the Handles You Have on the Undertaking

[―]

It is wise to delay a fugitive undertaking until all five of the following conditions have been met.

1. You know the Way; or, in other words, you have compelling Narratives about the Undertaking that inspire you to commit to it and that inspire others to join you in it.

2. You have favorable Weather; or, in other words, there are no Feelings that you need to deny or dismiss because they stand in your Way and undermine your Narratives.

3. You have favorable Terrain; or, in other words, there are no Facts that you need to deny or dismiss because they stand in your Way and undermine your Narratives.

4. You have discerning Guides; or, in other words, the Theories informing your Undertaking are consistent with all the Facts, Feelings, and Narratives that you have.

5. You are skilled in your Maneuvers; or, in other words, you have the competencies and the means to Handle all of the difficulties that your Theories and Narratives suggest that you will encounter.

[三]

One needn't wait and hope for the proper conditions for a fugitive undertaking to arise. With practice, one can make the proper conditions for a fugitive undertaking.

The practices that make the proper conditions are as follows.

1. Story-Telling — the fabulation of a world — is the practice that makes the Way for the Undertaking.

2. Art — the making of sensations in a world — is the practice that makes the Weather for the Undertaking.

3. Science — the making of predictions about a world — is the practice that makes the Terrain for the Undertaking.

4. Philosophy — the making of conceptions of a world — is the practice makes the Guides for the Undertaking.

5. World-Making — the (de-/re-)construction of a world — is the practice that makes the Maneuvers for the Undertaking.

[囚]

With respect to the "War on Terra", the fugitive undertakings that I have in mind are as follows: (i) deserting the forces of ethnocide and ecocide, (ii) defecting to the forces of nature, and (iii) aiding and abetting fellow deserters and defectors.

Deserting the forces of ethnocide and ecocide, as I now conceive of it, means fleeing the four principal impositions of postmodern living — in other words, it means (i) fleeing from schooling, (ii) fleeing from financing, (iii) fleeing from calendaring and clocking, and (iv) fleeing from profiling.

Defecting to the forces of nature, as I now conceive of it, means making artful reparations so as to enable our planet and her peoples may heal from the scourge of imperialist white-supremacist capitalist patriarchy.

Given the above, I am asking myself the following questions:

1. How can I practice Story-Telling so that I can open the Way to flee from degrading impositions and to make artful reparations?

2. How can I practice Art so that I can make favorable Weather for fleeing from degrading impositions and for making artful reparations?

3. How can I practice Science so that I can make favorable Terrain for fleeing from degrading impositions and for making artful reparations?

4. How can I practice Philosophy so that I can make reliable Guides for fleeing from degrading impositions and for making artful reparations?

5. How can I practice World-Making so that I can make effective Manuevers for fleeing from degrading impositions and for making artful reparations?

When planning and practicing for a fugitive undertaking, even if you feel that you are making progress towards your goal, if the planning and practice drag on too long it will sap your energy and blunt your edge.

There are successful fugitive undertakings that are clumsy but swift, but there are no successful undertakings that are skillful but sluggish.

The most important thing when engaging in a fugitive undertaking is the success of the undertaking and not our persistence in planning and practicing to ensure the "perfect" undertaking.

That being said, however, it is also imperative that we recognize that our fugitive undertakings will not come to fruition thanks to our own planning and practice alone. Rather, we can only ensure that a lack of planning and practice does not sink our fugitive undertakings. We must plan and practice, yes, but we must also wait patiently for the forces opposed to our fugitive undertakings to miscalculate and underestimate our planning and practice.

Know the opposing forces and know your own forces and you will never fail in attempting a fugitive undertaking. Know your own forces but not the opposing forces and you will fail half the time and succeed half the time. Know neither the opposing forces nor your own forces and you will always fail. For this reason, it is imperative that you endeavor to gain as much knowledge as you can about both the opposing forces and your own forces as part of planning and practicing for a fugitive undertaking.

To succeed in a fugitive undertaking in a spectacular show of struggle is to have failed to properly plan and practice. People celebrate the courage of those who struggle to succeed in fugitive undertakings, but what they are celebrating is the masochistic spectacle of "the Redeemer's Struggle" rather than the deep truth of planning and practice.

Those who have done their planning and practice will prevail when it is easy to prevail. They will position themselves where they know that they will have the best chance of succeeding in a fugitive undertaking. They will overcome opposing forces without a spectacular show of struggle because they will overcome opposing forces because opposing forces are self-defeating and have already sabotaged themselves.

The Great Derangement

The perpetration of the War on Terra by imperialist white-supremacist capitalist patriarchs, their proxies and redeemers, and their rivals and would be successors is the consequence of what has been called the "Great Derangement" by Amitav Ghosh. In his book titled *The Great Derangement*, Amitav Gosh writes, "[Today] our lives and our choices are enframed in a pattern of [rationalizing and rationalized] history that seems to leave us nowhere to turn but towards our self-annihilation."

Seeking to understand the genesis and structure of our suicidal pattern of rationalizing and rationalized history, I have found myself returning to Sigmund Freud's work on trauma and anxiety.

In a book titled *Inhibitions, Symptoms, and Anxiety*, Freud proposed that our egos produce anxiety in us in order to keep us from spontaneously acting in ways that our egos anticipate will cause us harm. Our egos do this by calling to mind images of past experiences that (dis)simulate anticipated harms before they actually take place. Sometimes the images that our egos call to mind evoke traumatic events from our past. When traumas are evoked, our super-egos enter the mix and censor the images recalled, repressing and distorting these images before they fully come to mind. The effective result is this: on the one hand, our egos recall images that provoke feelings of anxiety in us and keep us from acting spontaneously; on the other hand, our super-egos repress and distort what is recalled so that we cannot properly make sense of what we are anxious about. Unable to make sense of what we are anxious about, we proceed to rationalize our inability to act spontaneously—that is to say, in other words, that we come up with abstract reasons to explain why we shouldn't act spontaneously.

The person who has been traumatized is often, but not always, a person who is unable to spontaneously act in caring ways because they have come to anticipate that caring will cause them harm. Whenever the traumatized person feels the urge to care for themselves or to care for others, their egos call to mind images of experiences that have taught them to associate caring with harm but, at the same time, their super-egos repress and distort the images called to mind. The effective result is this: the traumatized person is apprehensive about spontaneously caring for themself and for others, but they cannot make sense of what has made them apprehensive about caring. In lieu of making sense of their inability to spontaneously care, the traumatized person will come up with abstract reasons to explain why they shouldn't spontaneously care.

Anyone and everyone who uses abstract reasoning to justify denying themselves or others care is a traumatized person engaged in rationalizing their apprehensions. Freudian psychoanalysis teaches us that the only sensible justifications for denying care to oneself or to another are to be found in one's concrete experiences, and not in one's abstract reasoning. Thus, it is imperative (i) that we dismiss the abstract reasoning that we use to justify our inability to care and (ii) that we uncover the concrete experiences that we are simultaneously recollecting and repressing whenever we have inhibitions about caring.

Psychoanalysis tells us that it is foolish to believe that reasoned debate alone can convince a white-supremacist capitalist patriarch that blacks, women, and the unemployed are deserving of care. We shouldn't devote so much time and effort to debunking claims that care is a privilege for the deserving by way of critiques of the Bible, or Spencer's doctrine of "survival of the fittest", or *Guns, Germs, and Steel*. The white-supremacist capitalist patriarch who believes that others are undeserving of care is not the victim of faulty reasoning. Rather, the white-supremacist capitalist patriarch's belief that others are undeserving of care is a rationalization of anxieties that are the effective result of traumatic experiences that the white-supremacist capitalist patriarch is either too afraid or too ashamed to fully acknowledge to himself.

It is trauma, in other words, that has fueled the advance of imperialist white-supremacist capitalist patriarchy and the War on Terra for the past five centuries. Indeed, the production of certain kinds of traumas is both the means and the ends of the War on Terra. We must all be traumatized if we are able to rationalize the routine denial of the most basic forms of care (food, housing, etc.) to black, brown, and indigenous women engaged in providing for social subsistence while, at the same time, we are able to accept care being lavished in gross excess upon those white men who are most profitably engaged in capitalist relations of production. More profoundly still, we must all be traumatized if we are able to rationalize a way of life that allows us to disregard the fact that wildlife populations on Earth have plummeted by more than two-thirds in the past half-century due to ecocide, and to disregard the fact that half of the languages on Earth are likely to disappear over the course of the next century due to ethnocide. Indeed, simply put, the "Great Derangement" is the very fact of all of us being so traumatized, though in profoundly different ways and to extremely varied degrees.

Trauma has become an increasingly popular topic of conversation today, and this marks a profound and propitious shift. People are finding trauma everywhere now because trauma is, unfortunately, everywhere to be found, but healing starts by and with finding trauma where it is. Still, however, most commentators who speak about trauma today remain too afraid or too ashamed to fully acknowledge the depth of the trauma that is everywhere to be found, and so they tarry at the surface. Many, if not most, popular commentators focus their attention on the superficial Oedipal triangle: "Mommy, Daddy, & Me". They refuse to acknowledge the ways in which Oedipal dramas have been part and parcel of the advancement of imperialist patriarchies for five millennia and, more importantly for our time, they refuse to acknowledge the ways in which Oedipal dramas became part and parcel of the advancement of imperialist white-supremacist capitalist patriarchy over the past five centuries.

Gilles Deleuze and Felix Guattari made this same point fifty years ago now, when they published *Anti-Oedipus* in 1972. They pointed out that the Oedipal complexes of individual human beings diagnosed by way of Freudian psychoanalysis are part and parcel of the Imperial complexes of human societies diagnosed by way of an extra-Freudian psychoanalysis or "schizoanalysis". Then, going further, Deleuze and Guattari pointed out that there is no therapy that can effectively treat the individual's Oedipal complex without also treating a society's Imperial complex. To treat the individual's Oedipal complex alone, in the manner of a Freudian psychoanalyst, is to provide palliative care to the individual. Curative care, by contrast, must treat a society's Imperial complex concomitantly with the individual's Oedipal complex.

Putting the Pandemic in Context

Readers of these dispatches will note that I have refrained from writing about the event that has come to define our present moment more than any other: the pandemic spread of the novel coronavirus of 2019. Those of you who converse with me often will know that this event has haunted almost every dispatch that I have written, and you will know that I have not written about this event because, above all else, I felt that I couldn't write about the event without situating it in its wider context.

If I am able to speak out and say something meaningful about the pandemic now, here in this dispatch, it is only because I feel that I have properly "set the stage" for speaking out in a series of earlier dispatches. While I would like people to be able read the following commentary on the pandemic on its own, it is my hope that the commentary will be read alongside my previous dispatches, so that readers may better sense and understand how I and others who share my perspective have been experiencing and reckoning with the pandemic.

As I see it, there is no way to process what has happened over the past two years with respect to the present pandemic without having some sense and understanding of the manner in which the spread of disease was part and parcel of the colonization of the New World during the sixteenth and seventeenth centuries. For it was during the colonization of the New World that differential susceptibilities to disease became an integral part of imperial power formations: a means to filter and channel different populations apart from one another and to stratify them, establishing hierarchies of privilege founded in part upon differential susceptibilities to disease.

The colonizers of the New World were well aware of the fact that they brought diseases, smallpox in particular, to the New World and that these diseases decimated the indigenous populations of the New World. The records of the exploits of Portuguese and Spanish conquistadors during the sixteenth century indicate that they knew that plagues of smallpox, previously unheard of in the New World, were a common consequence of their contacts with the New World's indigenous peoples. This awareness, however, did not inspire the Portuguese and Spanish conquistadors to be careful when making contact with indigenous peoples. Much to the contrary, Portuguese and Spanish conquistadors recognizing this fact believed that the plagues that decimated indigenous peoples were blessings that enabled them to conquer, dominate, and exploit those peoples whom they came to consider cursed, lower races of humanity.

It is certainly not the case that the colonizers of the New World were unaware of the fact that being careful about making contact could reduce the spread of disease. During this very same period, the sixteenth and seventeenth centuries, when epidemics broke out in Europe the rich knew to flee to their country houses and to "social distance", and the poor knew that life in cramped quarters meant disease and death. A passage from the first volume of Fernand Braudel's *Civilization and Capitalism* is instructive on this very point:

At the first sign of the disease, the rich whenever possible took hurried flight to their country houses; no one thought of anything but himself: 'the plague making us cruel, as doggs, one to another' noted Samuel Pepys in August 1665. And Montaigne tells how he wandered in search of a roof when the epidemic reached his estate, 'serving six months miserably as a guide' to his 'distracted family, frightening their friends and themselves and causing horror wherever they tried to settle'. The poor remained alone, penned up in the contaminated town where the State fed them, isolated them, blockaded them and kept them under observation. Boccaccio's *Decameron* is a series of conversations and stories told in a villa near Florence at the time of the Black Death. Maitre Nicolas Versoris, lawyer in the Paris Parlement, left his lodgings in August 1523. But three days after he reached his pupils' country house at the 'Grange Bateliere', then outside Paris, his wife died of the disease — an exception that confirms the value of the customary precaution. The plague in Paris in that summer of 1523 once again struck at the poor. Versoris wrote in his *Livre de Raison*: 'death was principally directed towards the poor so that only a very few of the Paris porters, who used to run errands for a few pence and who had lived there in large numbers before the misfortune, were left. . . . As for the district of Petiz Champs , the whole area was cleared of poor people who previously lived there in large numbers.' One bourgeois from Toulouse placidly wrote in 1561: 'the aforesaid contagious disease only attacks poor people . . . let God in his mercy be satisfied with that. . . . The rich protect themselves against it.' J.P. Sartre was right when he wrote, 'The plague only exaggerates the relationship between the classes: it strikes at the poor and spares the rich.' In Savoy, when an epidemic was over, rich people, before returning to their carefully disinfected houses, would install a poor woman inside for a few weeks, as a sort of guinea pig, to test at risk of her life whether the danger had really departed.

Europeans at home knew to be careful not to crowd and come into contact with others when disease was running rampant. The conquistadors departing their disease ridden boats knew just as well, and they would have known what was afoot when the indigenous peoples they contacted were struck down by disease.

What made the situation in the Americas differ from that within Europe at the time was the fact that the New World populations-to-be-conquered were being decimated by a disease that was not decimating the conquering Old World European population to the same degree. Recognizing this, rather than fleeing from the diseased in order not to be infected themselves, the Portuguese and Spanish conquistadors with intentional carelessness pursued contact with indigenous peoples, knowing that this would aid them in their conquest. The Portuguese and Spanish conquistadors of the sixteenth and seventeenth centuries did not weaponize smallpox as intentionally as the British later would during the eighteenth century: we have no record of any conquistador writing, as a British officer once wrote, that smallpox ought to be deployed against Indigenous peoples as a means "to Extirpate this Execreble Race." Nevertheless, we have record enough of the fact that Portuguese and Spanish conquistadors were aware of the advantages that their lesser susceptibility to smallpox gave them and that they leveraged these advantages in order to establish themselves as the privileged ruling population in the lands they conquered.

Going further still, the indigenous populations of the New World were so susceptible to their conquerors' diseases that they could not properly serve their conquerors and provide them with the hard labor that was demanded to establish an economy based on the mining of silver and gold and plantation agriculture. It followed from this that the conquerors had to import laborers from the Old World who were less susceptible to the imported diseases but who were still easy enough to identify as belonging to a population "other" than that of the conquerors. And here we have the crucible from which imperialist white-supremacist capitalist patriarchy first emerged, with its characteristic racial hierarchy based on skin color.

Karl Marx wrote that "The discovery of gold and silver in America, the extirpation, enslavement and entombment in mines of the aboriginal population, the beginning of the conquest and looting of the East Indies, the turning of Africa into a warren for the commercial hunting of black-skins, signaled the rosy dawn of the era of capitalist production." Marx should have added to that list of horrors: "the plagues visited upon the aboriginal populations of the New World by violent and grasping European adventurers possessed of a careless disregard for life".

The lower susceptibility of the European colonizers to smallpox relative to that of the colonized peoples of the New World was a matter of natural historical accident, yes, but its dire consequences were the result of the European colonizers leveraging of this accident to the hilt in order to conquer, dominate, and exploit.

Fast forward to the present and reckon with the fact that the differential susceptibilities to the novel coronavirus of 2019 that characterize the world today are not a historical accident. Rather to the contrary, the differential susceptibilities to the novel coronavirus are more and more a matter of artifice resulting from inequitable distributions of (i) effective diagnostics, therapies, and vaccines (ii) the tools and the know-how to make effective diagnostics, therapies, and vaccines, and (iii) the resources needed to maintain sensible social distancing measures without wreaking havoc upon the social relations that make for fulfilling lives and livelihoods. These inequities are being actively maintained by the richer nations of the world — i.e., by the victors of colonization and their would-be successors — and these inequities are being leveraged by the richer nations in order to (i) further the neocolonial dependence of poorer nations on the charity and largesse of richer nations, and (ii) further restrict the global mobility of the peoples of the poorer nations. Some have, rightly, called this state of affairs a "viral apartheid" and called the victims of this state of affairs the "viral underclass"

In an essay attempting to criticize the global response to the pandemic, the Italian philosopher Giorgio Agamben wrote:

> What is striking [...] is [our] inability to examine [the measures that have been taken in response to the pandemic] outside of the immediate context in which they appear to operate. Rarely does anyone attempt to interpret these new structures, as any serious political analysis would demand, as signs and symptoms of a larger experiment in which a new paradigm for governing people and things is manifesting itself.

While I found that Agamben's criticisms betrayed ableist, classist, and Eurocentric biases, he is correct about our failure to put things in context. Not only must we grasp the fact that the global response to the pandemic was to develop arrangements for a regime of viral apartheid and to sacrifice a viral underclass, we must also ask ourselves why the global response was such. We must ask why the global response was not, as it might have been, a concerted three prong push to develop arrangements for (i) equitably distributing effective diagnostics, therapies, and vaccines, (ii) equitably distributing the tools and the know-how to make effective diagnostics, therapies, and vaccines, and (iii) equitably distributing the resources to needed to maintain sensible social distancing measures when pandemics arise so that people are not forced to choose between spreading disease and sacrificing social relations that make for a fulfilling life and livelihood.

Asking myself these questions, the first thing that I have become certain of is the fact that a core feature of imperialist white-supremacist capitalist patriarchy is a "necropolitics" that routinizes, normalizes, and optimizes the exposure of abject populations (non-whites, non-men, and non-capitalists) to a greater risk of injury, disease, and death. The second thing that I have become certain of is the fact that the viral apartheid that we are currently witnessing is part and parcel of the progressive refinement of a much broader global apartheid regime, concomitant with the militarized border regimes that are being constructed in anticipation of migration crises fueled by climate catastrophes and the un-remediated legacies of colonial domination and exploitation. It is worth quoting a recent article written by Max Granger in The Intercept to set the scene fully:

> According to estimates from the United Nations, there are more than 82 million people forcibly displaced by violence and persecution and over 280 million migrants worldwide (not counting the 780 million people displaced within their own countries). These numbers will continue to grow, as the climate crisis makes large parts of the planet uninhabitable, displacing an estimated 1.2 billion people by 2050. The main destinations for international migrants and asylum-seekers have long been the United States and Europe. The EU's response to the arrival of refugees from the former European colonies of Syria, Eritrea, Afghanistan, Iraq, and others has been a ruthless campaign of militarization and deterrence. It has included the construction of over 1,000 miles of walls and high-tech fencing, along with the rapid expansion of the European Border and Coast Guard Agency, or Frontex, whose budget has ballooned from 118 million euros in 2018 to a proposed 754 million euros in 2022.
>
> Like the United States, Europe increasingly outsources its border enforcement to other countries, through policies that seek to prevent migration and to detain and kill people before they even reach the southern shores of the Mediterranean. Once at sea, migrants face the likelihood of death: Since 2014, more than 45,000 people have died or disappeared while attempting the crossing. Many spend years in detention centers, clandestine prisons, and in conditions of forced labor before ever stepping foot on a boat. Meanwhile, the number of people who perish in the desert before even reaching the sea, or who die in captivity after being repelled by EU deterrence, remains largely unknown, since no government or organization is keeping track. The International Organization for Migration, an agency of the United Nations, estimates that deaths in the Sahara Desert are "at least double" those in the Mediterranean, but no one actually knows. These deaths, it bears repeating, are the result of policies created by the same governments now welcoming millions of Ukrainians without hesitation.

The perverse irony of this scene is that it involves a twisted process of psychological projection wherein and whereby the former colonizers, those who brutally conquered and spread disease amongst the peoples that they brutally conquered, are now actively bringing conditions into being that will enable them to cast those suffering and fleeing from the destructive legacies of colonization as violent, grasping, disease ridden invaders. In the midst of a planetary ecocide, the most outrageously brutal historical tragedy is replaying itself as the most outrageously brutal historical farce. We are witnessing a phase shift in which the Great Derangement turns in on itself and the repressed returns with a most horrific and twisted vengeance. Possessed of a bad conscience arising from the fact that they have yet to make artful reparations to the victims of colonization, the victors of colonization are now determined to replay the horrors of colonization so that they might misconstrue themselves as the ones suffering violent, grasping, disease ridden invaders and, worse still, so that they might misconstrue themselves as having the "right" to detain and kill "illegal" migrants and refugees in "self-defense".

The reality is so vile that many, if not most, are averting their gaze. Others are watching it all unfold with a steady gaze but absolving themselves from caring by rationalizing these events to be the inevitable result of humanity's innate aggression and death drive. This rationalization is a false one. As David Graeber puts it:

> It's not that as a species we're particularly aggressive. It's that we tend to respond to aggression very poorly. Our first instinct when we observe unprovoked aggression is either to pretend it isn't happening or, if that becomes impossible, to equate attacker and victim, placing both under a kind of contagion, which, it is hoped, can be prevented from spreading to everybody else. [...] The feeling of guilt caused by the suspicion that this is a fundamentally cowardly way to behave — since it is a fundamentally cowardly way to behave — opens up a complex play of projections, in which the bully is seen simultaneously as an unconquerable super-villain and a pitiable, insecure blowhard, while the victim becomes both an aggressor (a violator of whatever social conventions the bully has invoked or invented) and a pathetic coward unwilling to defend himself. [...] We equate aggressors and victims, [and] insist that everyone is equally guilty (notice how, whenever one hears a report of an atrocity, some will immediately start insisting that the victims must have committed atrocities too), and just hope that by doing so, the contagion will not spread.

Presently, the victors of colonization are being rationalized to appear simultaneously as unconquerable super-villains and pitiable, insecure blowhards; and the victims of colonization are being rationalized to appear as aggressors (violators of whatever social conventions the victors of colonization have invoked or invented) and pathetic cowards unwilling to defend themselves. Going further, it is important to recognize that both the victors and victims of colonization are themselves engaged in such rationalizations and that they are both often to be found reacting to such rationalizations. We may consider, for instance, those victims of colonization who become notorious global terrorists and violent traffickers of drugs and human beings: having rationalized themselves to be simultaneously both aggressors and cowards, they are reactively endeavoring to affirm their apparent aggression and to shed themselves of their apparent cowardice. Alternatively, we may consider those victors of colonization who, having rationalized themselves to be simultaneously both unconquerable super-villains and insecure blowhards, are now reactively endeavoring to appear as unconquerable super-heroes possessed of an irreproachable self-assurance, fighting global wars on drugs, terror, and human trafficking in the name of freedom, justice, and liberty. These two convergent reactions to rationalizing and rationalized histories of extreme violence are both serving only to further the progressive refinement of the global apartheid regime.

It is plain to me that there is no sensible way out of our present global apartheid regime and its sufferings unless the victors of colonization take responsibility for the legacies of colonization and make artful reparations to the victims of colonization. Ay, and there is no way to make sense of the viral apartheid that has emerged in response to the coronavirus pandemic without making sense of the fact that the victors of colonization are persisting in their refusal to take responsibility and make artful reparations to the victims of colonization. As climate catastrophes approach, the global response to the coronavirus pandemic seems poised to set the template for future global responses to fast unfolding catastrophes that threaten the health of the whole Earth and all of her peoples. Unless the victors of colonization and their would-be successors are induced to change their ways, we can only expect that new refinements to the global apartheid regime shall emerge with each and every crisis, up until the point at which the regime can no longer be refined further and it collapses in on itself to devastating effect.

This is why I believe that there is no project that is more urgent, more challenging, and more creative today than the project of encouraging and supporting the making of artful reparations — it is a project that will require remarkable works of storytelling, artistry, science, philosophy, and social activism. Ay, and I am writing this dispatch in the hopes that soberly observing our failure to respond gracefully to the pandemic will serve as a wake up call for those who have not yet realized that the project of making artful reparations will be the project of our times, no matter whether the project fails or succeeds.

THE NEW UNDERGROUND RAILROAD

Yesterday I dreamt
of the New Underground Railroad.

Its travelers seek
no destinations
only routes
from station to station —
all being
but a temporary refuge
for travelers grown weary,
needing rest and refreshment
for a meanwhile.

On a planet
otherwise barren,
the Railroad courses,
swelling and shrinking
with the seasons,
depositing cultural riches
where it runs
and over-runs itself,
like a river does
mud and silt.

All fertile
places and peoples
are now
to be found
along its lines
of flight.

THE THEORETI-CAL FRAME-WORK

Session 1: Processes of Becoming

Becoming precedes being. A being becomes what it is before it is what it is.

But there is also another sense in which becoming precedes being. We are beings in a world full of other beings, and every being in this world, ourselves included, may eventually cease to be. A being's ceasing to be, however, does not put an end to its becoming. Becoming doesn't stop where being starts, rather, becoming proceeds alongside being, from start to finish, and becoming continues to proceed after beings cease to be. In this way, becoming not only precedes being, it also exceeds and succeeds being. Whereas a being is a momentary product, a becoming is an enduring process.

I shall define three different kinds of processes of becoming in this session: phylogenetic processes, ontogenetic processes, and heterogenetic processes. There are, no doubt, other kinds of processes and, what's more, the three kinds of processes which I shall define in this session are only distinct from one another in theory, rather than in practice. That being said, however, theoretical distinctions can and should inform, transform, and enrich practical matters, and I invite you to judge the distinctions that follow accordingly.

Phylogenetic processes are processes of speciation, processes that group existing beings together to form species, classes, races, nations, tribes, personas and other populations with stable identities. Phylogenetic processes are processes through which species of beings come into being or, in other words, phylogenetic processes determine what kinds of beings have come into being. An example of a phylogenetic process: the process by which a number of individual life forms are grouped together to form a species, like ours, Homo sapiens, each individual life form becoming, through this process, a specimen of a species. Species do not pre-exist individuals, rather, species arise from the sampling of populations of beings. Phylogenetic processes are, thus, processes that sample populations of beings, turning individual beings into members of species of beings. Phylogenetic processes feed on ontogenetic processes—that is to say, in other words, phylogenetic processes produce species of beings by processing beings that have been produced by ontogenetic processes.

Ontogenetic processes are processes of individuation, processes whereby indeterminate potentials are actualized in determinate ways such that individual beings come into being. Ontogenetic processes determine why and how precisely an individual being comes into being. Take the process by which an individual life form develops, actualizing indeterminate potentials in a more or less determinate way. Ontogenetic processes feed on heterogenetic processes—that is to say, ontogenetic processes produce beings by processing potentials that have been produced by heterogenetic processes.

Heterogenetic processes are processes of potentiation, processes that produce indeterminate potentials. Heterogenetic processes (re-)generate the indeterminate substrate from whence beings comes into being or, in other words, heterogenetic processes are processes through which "pre-individual" potentials (i.e., potentials for 'beings likewise' and potentials for 'beings otherwise') come into being. Heterogenetic processes are auto-cannibalistic, feeding on themselves and processing the very same potentials that they produce as they produce further potentials. They are also an-archic: one cannot predict whether a heterogenetic process will produce a potential 'to be likewise' or a potential 'to be otherwise' and, what's more, there is no way to find out whether the product of a heterogenetic process, a succeeding potential 'to be likewise' or 'to be otherwise', was produced via the processing of a preceding potential 'to be likewise' or a preceding potential 'to be otherwise'.

For purposes of illustration, I will treat the three processes of becoming with respect to three different but interrelated "ecologies of existence". First, I will treat all three processes with respect to biogeochemical ecologies ; second, with respect to behavioral ecologies ; and third, with respect to cultural ecologies.

Biological Ecologies. It is easiest to treat the three processes of becoming with respect to biological ecologies because I have employed the language of the biological to describe the three processes of becoming. Phylogenetic processes are the processes of biological selection that create different varieties of life, ontogenetic processes are the processes of biological individuation that create individual life forms, and heterogenetic processes are the geo-physico-chemical processes that create potentials for life. Genes, the dividual units of life, are only ever indexes and indications of genetic processes.

Ethological Ecologies. What the genetic is for biological ecologies, the memetic is for ethological ecologies. If I had employed the language of the behavioral instead of that of biological,, I would have spoken of phylo-memetic processes, onto-memetic processes, and hetero-memetic processes. Phylo-memetic processes are the processes of behavioral selection that create different varieties of behavior; onto-memetic processes are the processes of behavioral individuation that create individual behaviors; and hetero-memetic processes are the biological and geo-physico-chemical processes that create potentials for behavior. Memes, the dividual units of behavior, are always simulacra and simulations as well as indexes and indications of memetic processes.

Ethnological Ecologies. What the genetic is for biological ecologies, and what the memetic is for ethological ecologies, the epistemic is for ethnological ecologies. It follows that, if I were to employ the language of the cultural rather than that of biologeochemical, I would speak of phylo-epistemic processes, onto-epistemic processes, and hetero-epistemic processes. Phylo-epistemic processes are the processes of cultural selection that create different varieties of custom; onto-epistemic processes are the processes of cultural individuation create individual customs; and hetero-epistemic processes are the behavioral, biological, and geo-physico-chemical processes that create potentials for custom. Epistemes, the dividual units of culture, are always symbols and representations as well as indexes and indications of epistemic processes. Epistemes may also be, but need not be, simulacra and simulations of epistemic processes: those epistemes that are simulacra and simulations are "analytic-and-aesthetic epistemes" or "synthetic epistemes"; those epistemes that are not simulacra and simulations are called "analytic epistemes".

Heterogenetic, ontogenetic, and phylogenetic processes of becoming, in conjunction and disjunction with one another, produce and populate flows of beings.

Conjunctions of heterogenetic and ontogenetic processes populate flows of beings with probable beings. If (i) heterogenetic processes create potentials 'to be likewise', and (ii) these potentials, 'to be likewise', are taken up by an ontogenetic process that individuates beings, then (iii) the ontogenetic process yields probable beings.

Disjunctions of heterogenetic and ontogenetic processes populate flows of beings with im-probable beings. If (i) heterogenetic processes create potentials 'to be otherwise', and (ii) these potentials, 'to be otherwise', are taken up by an ontogenetic process that individuates beings, then (iii) the ontogenetic process yields im-probable beings.

Conjunctions of ontogenetic and phylogenetic processes populate flows of beings with regularities. If (i) ontogenetic processes produce beings that are like one another, and (ii) their likeness is taken up by a phylogenetic process, relating like with like, then (iii) the phylogenetic process transforms "beings like others" into regular specimens of a species, "regularities" for short. Regularities are, by definition, probable beings, for a conjunction of heterogenetic and ontogenetic processes is a necessary condition for there to be a conjunction of ontogenetic and phylogenetic processes.

Disjunctions of ontogenetic and phylogenetic processes populate flows of beings with aberrations. If (i) ontogenetic processes produce beings that are unlike one another, and (ii) their unlikeness is taken up by a phylogenetic process, relating like with unlike, then (iii) the phylogenetic process transforms these "beings unlike others" into aberrant specimens of a species, "aberrations" for short. All improbable individuals are aberrations, but not all probable individuals are regularities: some probable individuals are also aberrations. In other words, an aberration may be a probable being or it may be an im-probable being.

Probable beings can yield aberrations, or probable aberrations, because a conjunction of heterogenetic and ontogenetic processes does not automatically yield to a conjunction of ontogenetic and phylogenetic processes: a conjunction of heterogenetic and ontogenetic processes is necessary but not sufficient for there to be a conjunction of ontogenetic and phylogenetic processes. A conjunction of heterogenetic and ontogenetic processes only yields individual beings that have a potential to be like one another. Subsequently, a conjunction of ontogenetic and phylogenetic processes is a successful actualization of a potential to be alike, and a disjunction of ontogenetic and phylogenetic processes is an unsuccessful actualization of a potential to be alike.

Probable aberrations are accidental aberrations, (co-)incidentally dis-similar beings. Although they do not share the likeness that constitutes the regularities produced by a given phylogenetic process, probable aberrations may share a likenesses with one another. In other words, two probable aberrations produced by a given phylogenetic process may share a likeness with one another apart from their being unlike the regularities produced by a given phylogenetic process. A probable aberration is only ever (co-)incidentally an aberration that deviates from a norm and, concomitantly, a regularity is only ever (co-)incidentally a regularity that conforms to a norm.

Im-probable aberrations are essential aberrations, essentially dis-similar beings. No two im-probable aberrations produced by a given phylogenetic process will ever share a likeness with one another apart from their being unlike all regularities and unlike all probable aberrations. In other words, every im-probable aberration is not only unlike the regularities produced by a given phylogenetic process but also unlike any and every other aberration produced by a given phylogenetic process. An im-probable aberration is always essentially (as opposed to (co-)incidentally) an aberration that deviates from the norm and, more profoundly still, an im-probable aberration is also always essentially (as opposed to [co-]incidentally) an outlier that deviates from other deviations. Probable aberrations, by contrast, can only ever (co-)incidentally (as opposed to essentially) be outliers that deviate from other deviations.

For purposes of illustration, I will treat regularities, probable aberrations, and improbable aberrations with respect to the three "ecologies of existence" identified in the last session.

Biological Ecologies. With respect to biological ecologies, we are dealing with flows of genes, the diversity of gene pools. In this context, "genetic replication" is the term for the conjunction of processes that yields regularities; "genetic recombination" is the term for the conjunction and disjunction of processes that yields probable aberrations; and "genetic mutation" is the term for the disjunction of processes that yields improbable aberrations.

Ethological Ecologies. With respect to ethological ecologies, we are dealing with flows of memes and the diversity of meme pools. In this context, "memetic replication" is the term for the conjunction of processes that yields regularities; "memetic recombination" is the term for the conjunction and disjunction of processes that yields probable aberrations; and "memetic mutation" is the term for the disjunction of processes that yields improbable aberrations.

Ethnological Ecologies. With respect to ethnological ecologies, we are dealing with flows of epistemes and the diversity of episteme pools: their regularities, probable aberrations, and improbable aberrations. In this context, "epistemic replication" is the term for the conjunction of processes that yields regularities; "epistemic recombination" is the term for the conjunction and disjunction of processes that yields probable aberrations; and "epistemic mutation" is the term for the disjunction of processes that yields improbable aberrations.

Session 3: *Organizations of Beings*

Organizations are "power formations" that restrict flows of beings. Organizations filter out different species and specimens of beings from the flows that pass through them, and they channel these different species and specimens of beings apart from one another. Organizations are composed of "paths of least resistance": a given organization admits and promotes a select species or specimen along a given path or channel by minimizing resistance to the select specimens/species along the given paths/channels. Organizations do not transcend the flows that they restrict. Rather, they are immanent to the flows of beings they restrict and they are created by beings that are a part of the flows of beings they restrict.

A *segregating organization* admits and promotes some species populating a given flow of beings and detains others and, thus, a segregating organization stratifies a given flow of beings. A segregating organization doesn't care whether a specimen is a regularity or an aberration with respect to its species: a specimen's admission and promotion by a segregating organization is determined by the species to which the specimen belongs. For example, a segregating organization that admits and promotes human beings over other beings will admit and promote any and every human being over any and every non-human being, no matter whether the human being is a regular specimen of humanity or an aberrant specimen.

A *standardizing organization* detains the aberrant specimens that it finds in a given flow of beings and, thus, inhibits variability within a given flow of beings. In other words, a standardizing organization concerns itself with making the characteristics of a given flow of beings conform to a norm, admitting and promoting regularities over aberrations. A standardizing organization assesses whether or not a specimen is a regularity or an aberration and, in doing so, it admits and promotes the regularity over the aberration. For example, an organization that standardizes a flow of human beings will admit and promote those human beings whom it has assessed to be regular specimens of humanity and will detain those human beings whom it has assessed to be aberrant specimens of humanity.

A *normalizing organization* determines the distribution of aberrations within a given flow of beings and, thus, normalizes a measure of variability within a flow of beings. In other words, a normalizing organization concerns itself with determining the prevalence of certain characteristics within a flow of beings, admitting and promoting deviations from the norm alongside regularities as long as they do not upset the normal distribution. Normalizing organizations will admit and promote aberrations alongside regularities within limits, assessing for and detaining only the outlying aberrations, the im-probable aberrations that are essentially outliers alongside the probable aberrations that are (co-)incidentally outliers. For example, an organization that normalizes a flow of human beings will promote those aberrant specimens of humanity who do not upset the normal distribution of the flow of human beings but it will detain those aberrant humans who, as outliers, upset the normal distribution.

An *optimizing organization* modulates the distribution of aberrations within a given flow of beings and, thus, optimizes a measure of variability within a flow of beings. In other words, an optimizing organization concerns itself with maximizing or minimizing the prevalence of certain characteristics within a flow of beings and, to this end, an optimizing organization needn't properly determine the prevalence of certain characteristics within a flow of beings. For an optimizing organization, outliers in general mustn't be detained, instead, only those outliers that would skew a distribution in a disadvantageous manner must be detained. Those outliers that would skew a distribution in an advantageous manner are, in fact, admitted and promoted by optimizing organizations. Optimizing organizations must always detain im-probable aberrations because one cannot predict the manner in which an im-probable aberration, an essential outlier, will skew a distribution of beings. By contrast, probable aberrations skew distributions in a predictable manner and, thus, an optimizing organization will only detain those probable aberrations that are likely to skew distributions in a predictably disadvantageous manner. For example, an organization that optimizes the flow of human beings will promote those outliers that predictably skew the distribution of the flow of human beings in an advantageous manner, but it will detain those outliers that skew the distribution of the flow of human beings in a predictably disadvantageous manner and those who do so in an unpredictable manner.

For purposes of illustration, I will treat organization with respect to the three "ecologies of existence" that we have identified in previous sessions.

Biological Ecologies. With respect to biological ecologies, organizations restrict genetic diversity: segregating organizations stratify different varieties of life; standardizing organizations create conformity within and amongst varieties of life; normalizing organizations normalize measures of variability within and amongst varieties of life; optimizing organizations optimize measures of variability within and amongst varieties of life.

Ethological Ecologies. With respect to ethological ecologies, organizations restrict memetic diversity: segregating organizations stratify different varieties of behaviors; standardizing organizations create conformity within and amongst different varieties of behaviors; normalizing organizations normalize measures of variability within and amongst different varieties of behaviors; optimizing organizations optimize measures of variability within and amongst different varieties of behaviors.

Ethnological Ecologies. With respect to ethnological ecologies, organizations restrict epistemic diversity: segregating organizations stratify different varieties of customs; standardizing organizations create conformity within and amongst different varieties of customs; normalizing organizations normalize measures of variability within and amongst different varieties of customs; optimizing organizations optimize measures of variability within and amongst different varieties of customs.

Session 4: Disorganizations of Beings

Disorganizations are "counterpowers" that liberate flows of beings.

Hybridizations. If a segregating organization concerns itself with stratifying the different species populating a flow of beings, to subvert a segregating organization is to de-stratify and re-integrate the different species populating a flow of beings.

One effects hybridizations (and subverts segregation) when one defers to specimens of species other than one's own.

Deviations. If a standardizing organization concerns itself with making a flow's characteristics conform to a norm, to subvert a standardizing organization is to allow a flow's characteristics to deviate from the norm.

One effects deviations (and subverts standardization) when one defers to aberrations.

Indeterminations. If a normalizing organization concerns itself with determining the probability distribution of a flow's characteristics, to subvert a normalizing organization is to make it impossible to determine the probability distribution of a flow's characteristics.

One effects indeterminations (and subverts normalization) when one goes beyond deferring to aberrations in general and one defers to outlying aberrations in particular.

Randomizations. If an optimizing organization concerns itself with modulating a given probability distribution so as to maximize or minimize the prevalence of certain characteristics in a flow, to subvert an optimizing organization is to randomize the prevalence of certain characteristics in a flow.

One effects randomizations (and subverts optimization) when one goes beyond deferring to outlying aberrations in general and one defers to improbable aberrations in particular.

For purposes of illustration, I will treat disorganization with respect to the three "ecologies of existence" identified in previous sessions.

Biological Ecologies. With respect to biological ecologies, disorganizations liberate genetic diversity: hybridizations subvert the segregation of varieties of life; deviations the standardization of varieties of life; indeterminations subvert the normalization of varieties of life; randomizations subvert the optimization of varieties of life.

Ethological Ecologies. With respect to ethological ecologies, disorganizations liberate memetic diversity: hybridizations subvert the segregation of varieties of behaviors; deviations the standardization of varieties of behaviors; indeterminations subvert the normalization of varieties of behaviors; randomizations subvert the optimization of varieties of behaviors.

Ethnological Ecologies. With respect to ethnological ecologies, disorganizations liberate epistemic diversity: hybridizations subvert the segregation of varieties of customs; deviations the standardization of varieties of customs; indeterminations subvert the normalization of varieties of customs; randomizations subvert the optimization of varieties of customs.

Session 5: Biopoetics and Necropolitics

A biopoetic organization is a life-creating organization. A biopoetic organization only exists to create living conditions for beings: it willingly dissolves itself and gracefully succumbs to dis-organization when it ceases to create living conditions for beings. For example, a biopoetic organization that creates food for human beings may detain a given animal and plant species for as long as doing so creates food for human beings, yes, but such a biopoetic organization willingly dissolves itself and gracefully succumbs to dis-organization if and when human beings are able to obtain food otherwise, without having to detain a given animal or plant species. More profoundly still, such an organization willingly dissolves itself and gracefully succumbs to dis-organization by continually breaking down, falling into disrepair, so as to either be abandoned if no longer needed or repaired if needed.

A necropolitical organization is a death-dealing organization. A necropolitical organization is gracelessly resolved against dis-organization, whether or not it creates living conditions for beings. For example, a necropolitical organization that once created food for human beings will detain a given animal or plant species even after it is no longer required to do so in order to create food for human beings. Indeed, such an organization will gracelessly resolve itself against disorganization whether or not human beings are able to obtain food without its assistance and, more profoundly still, such an organization will gracelessly resolve itself against dis-organization by working to prevent human beings from obtaining food without it, so that human beings must continue to maintain it. Indeed, such an organization is necropolitical because it would monopolize the provisioning of food for humans in order to assure its continued maintenance.

For purposes of illustration, I will treat biopoetic and necropolitical organizations with respect to the three "ecologies of existence" identified in the previous sessions.

Biological Ecologies. With respect to biological ecologies, the necropolitical organization is the full domestication of one variety of life by another that is gracelessly resolved against feralization and rewilding. The biopoetic organization, by contrast, is the partial domestication of one variety of life by another that willingly dissolves itself and gracefully succumbs to feralization and rewilding. Whereas the necropolitical organization precipitates and accelerates a decline in genetic diversity, the biopoetic organization temporarily slows a rise in genetic diversity.

Ethological Ecologies. With respect to ethological ecologies, the necropolitical organization is the full repression of one variety of behavior by another that is gracelessly resolved against the return of the repressed. The biopoetic organization, by contrast, is the partial repression of one variety of behavior by another that willingly dissolves itself and gracefully succumbs to the return of the repressed. Whereas the necropolitical organization precipitates and accelerates a decline in memetic diversity, the biopoetic organization temporarily slows a rise in memetic diversity.

Ethnological Ecologies. With respect to ethnological ecologies, the necropolitical organization is the full colonization of one variety of custom by another that is gracelessly resolved against decolonization and indigenization. The biopoetic organization, by contrast, is the partial colonization of one variety of custom by another that willingly dissolves itself and gracefully succumbs to decolonization and indigenization. Whereas the necropolitical organization precipitates and accelerates a decline in epistemic diversity, the biopoetic organization temporarily slows a rise in epistemic diversity.

Constructs organize beings according to their forms, according to their configurations: e.g., being a spherical particle or being a sawtooth wave.

A *heterogeny of forms* distributes one set of intervals along another set of intervals, constituting a space with the potential (i) to be measurable or (ii) to be immeasurable (i.e., otherwise than measurable).

A *ontogeny of forms* coordinates the constituents of a space. Or, in other words, an ontogeny of forms determines whether or not a space is measurable.

- An ontogeny of forms yields *probable forms* when it determines that a space is measurable.
- An ontogeny of forms yields *im-probable forms* when it determines that a space is immeasurable.

A *phylogeny of forms* relates two or more different spaces to one another on the basis of (dis-)similarities in their ontogenies, i.e., (dis-)similarities in manner in which the different spaces have been coordinated.

- *Particles* are forms that arise when a phylogeny of forms only includes regularities and includes no aberrations. That is to say, in other words, that particles arise when a phylogenetic process relates two or more different spaces that have only been coordinated in (co-)incidentally similar ways.
- *Waves* are forms that arise when a phylogeny of forms includes regularities and probable aberrations but includes no improbable aberrations. That is to say, in other words, that waves arise when a phylogenetic process relates two or more different spaces that have been coordinated in (co-)incidentally similar and (co-) incidentally dis-similar ways but not in essentially dis-similar ways.
- *Fields* are forms that arise when a phylogeny of forms includes regularities, probable aberrations, and improbable aberrations. That is to say, in other words, that fields arise when a phylogenetic process relates two or more different spaces that have been coordinated in (co-)incidentally similar, (co-)incidentally dis-similar, and essentially dis-similar ways.

A *construct* is an organization that admits beings according to their forms.

- A *standardizing construct* can only admit beings formed of particles.
- A *normalizing construct* and an *optimizing construct* can admit beings formed of waves alongside beings formed of particles.
- A *segregating construct* can admit beings formed of fields alongside beings formed of particles and waves, provided that the beings formed of fields are "well behaved" and not too noisy.
- A *constructive failure* is a dis-organization that occurs when beings formed of fields that have been denied for being noisy make so much noise that they compromise the constructs that deny them.
- *Biopoetic constructs* are gracefully dissolved by constructive failures.
- *Necropolitical constructs* are gracelessly resolved against constructive failures.

Mechanisms organize beings according to their transformations, according to changes in their form: e.g., being rotated, stretched, or twisted.

A *heterogeny of transformations* distributes a set of transformations along a set of intervals, constituting a space-time with the potential (i) to be measurable or (ii) to be immeasurable (i.e., otherwise than measurable).

An *ontogeny of transformations* coordinates the constituents of a space-time. Or, in other words, an ontogeny of transformations determines whether or not a space-time is measurable.
- An ontogeny of transformations yields *probable transformations* when it determines that a space-time is measurable.
- An ontogeny of transformations yields *im-probable transformations* when it determines that a space-time is immeasurable.

A *phylogeny of transformations* relates two or more different space-times to one another on the basis of (dis-)similarities in their ontogenies, i.e., (dis-)similarities in the manner in which the different space-times have been coordinated.
- *Displacements* are transformations that arise when a phylogeny of transformations only includes regularities and includes no aberrations. That is to say, in other words, that displacements arise when a phylogenetic process relates two or more different space-times that have only been coordinated in (co-)incidentally similar ways.
- *Deformations* are transformations that arise when a phylogeny of transformations includes regularities and probable aberrations but includes no improbable aberrations. That is to say, in other words, that deformations arise when a phylogenetic process relates two or more different space-times that have been coordinated in (co-)incidentally similar and (co-)incidentally dis-similar ways but not in essentially dis-similar ways.
- *Fluctuations* are transformations that arise when a phylogeny of transformations includes regularities, probable aberrations, and improbable aberrations.
  That is to say, in other words, fluctuations arise when a phylogenetic process relates two or more different space-times that have been coordinated in (co-)incidentally similar, (co-)incidentally dis-similar, and essentially dis-similar ways.

A *mechanism* is an organization that admits beings according to their transformations.

- A *standardizing mechanism* can only admit beings undergoing displacements.
- A *normalizing mechanism* and an *optimizing mechanism* can admit beings undergoing deformations alongside beings undergoing displacements.
- A *segregating mechanism* can admit beings undergoing fluctuations alongside beings undergoing deformations and displacements, provided that beings undergoing fluctuations are "well behaved" and not too noisy.
- A *mechanical failure* is a dis-organization that occurs when beings that have been denied because of their noisy fluctuations make so much noise that they compromise the mechanisms that deny them.
- *Biopoetic mechanisms* are gracefully dissolved by mechanical failures.
- *Necropolitical mechanisms* are gracelessly resolved against mechanical failures.

Systems organize beings according to their states, according to the variables that qualify changes in their forms: e.g., being of greater or lesser momentum or being of greater or lesser energy.

A *heterogeny of states* distributes a set of states along a set of transformations, constituting a state space with the potential (i) to be measurable or (ii) to be immeasurable (i.e., otherwise than measurable).

An *ontogeny of states* coordinates the constituents of a state space. Or in other words, an ontogeny of states determines whether or not a state space is measurable.
- An ontogeny of states yields *probable states* when it determines that a state space is measurable.
- An ontogeny of states yields *im-probable states* when it determines that a state space is immeasurable.

A *phylogeny of states* relates two or more different state spaces to one another on the basis of (dis-)similarities in their ontogenies, i.e., (dis-)similarities in the manner in which the different state spaces have been coordinated.
- *Stable states* arise when a phylogeny of states only includes regularities and includes no aberrations. That is to say, in other words, that stability arises when a phylogenetic process relates two or more different state spaces that have only been coordinated in (co-)incidentally similar ways.
- *Meta-stable states* arise when a phylogeny of states includes regularities and probable aberrations but includes no improbable aberrations. That is to say, in other words, that meta-stability arises when a phylogenetic process relates two or more different state spaces that have been coordinated in (co-)incidentally similar and (co-)incidentally dis-similar ways but not in essentially dis-similar ways.
- *Critical states* or when a phylogeny of states includes regularities, probable aberrations, and improbable aberrations. That is to say, in other words, that criticality arises when a phylogenetic process relates two or more different state spaces that have been coordinated in (co-)incidentally similar, (co-)incidentally dis-similar, and essentially dis-similar ways.

A *system* is an organization that admits beings according to their states.
- A *standardizing system* can only admit beings that are stable.
- A *normalizing system* and an optimizing system can admit beings that are meta-stable alongside beings that are stable.
- A *segregating system* can admit beings that are in crisis alongside beings that are meta-stable and stable, provided that beings in crisis are "well behaved" and not too noisy.
- A *systemic failure* is a dis-organization that occurs when beings that have been denied because of their noisy crises make so much noise that they compromise the systems that deny them.
- *Biopoetic systems* are gracefully dissolved by systemic failures.
- *Necropolitical systems* are gracelessly resolved against systemic failures.

Complexes organize beings according to their actions, according to the ways that their variables affect one another: e.g., the way in which a being's momentum affects and is affected by its energy.

A *heterogeny of actions* distributes one set of states along another set of states, constituting a function space with the potential (i) to be measurable or (ii) to be immeasurable (i.e., otherwise than measurable).

An *ontogeny of actions* coordinates the constituents of a function space. Or, in other words, an ontogeny of actions determines whether or not a function space is measurable.

·   An ontogeny of actions yields *probable actions* when it determines that a function space is measurable.
·   An ontogeny of actions yields *im-probable actions* when it determines that a function space is immeasurable.

A *phylogeny of actions* relates two or more different function spaces to one another on the basis of (dis-)similarities in their ontogenies, i.e., (dis-)similarities in the manner in which the different function spaces have been coordinated.

·   *Re-actions* (i.e., actions whereby dependent variables are determined by independent variables) arise when a phylogeny of actions only includes regularities and includes no aberrations. That is to say, in other words, that re-actions arise when a phylogenetic process relates two or more different function spaces that have only been coordinated in (co-)incidentally similar ways.
·   *Inter-actions* (i.e., actions whereby co-dependent variables "feedback" and co-determine one another) arise when a phylogeny of actions includes regularities and probable aberrations but includes no improbable aberrations. That is to say, in other words, that inter-actions arise when a phylogenetic process relates two or more different function spaces that have been coordinated in (co-)incidentally similar and (co-)incidentally dis-similar ways but not in essentially dis-similar ways.
·   *Intra-actions* (i.e., actions whereby variables complement each other in such a way that they cannot be determined simultaneously, one variable being indeterminate whenever another is determinate) arise when a phylogeny of actions includes regularities, probable aberrations, and improbable aberrations. That is to say, in other words, that intra-actions arise when a phylogenetic process relates two or more different function spaces that have been coordinated in (co-)incidentally similar, (co-)incidentally dis-similar, and essentially dis-similar ways.

A *complex* is an organization that admits beings according to their actions.

- A *standardizing complex* can only admit beings that are re-active.
- A *normalizing complex* and an *optimizing complex* can admit beings that are inter-active alongside beings that are re-active.
- A *segregating complex* can admit beings that are intra-active alongside beings that are inter-active and re-active, provided that intra-active beings are "well behaved" and not too noisy.
- A *complex failure* is a dis-organization that occurs when beings that have been denied because of their noisy intra-activity make so much noise that they compromise the complexes that deny them.
- *Biopoetic complexes* are gracefully dissolved by complex failures.
- *Necropolitical complexes* are gracelessly resolved against complex failures.